Budget Dining and Lodging in New England

"The many places to be found in this helpful guide prove that you don't have to give up good quality to get good value."
—*Camperways*

"The enthusiasm of these . . . scouts shines through their writing, and this makes the book interesting to armchair travelers."
—*Sunday Cape Cod Times*

"Anyone planning to travel in the New England states will find this a useful companion."
—*American Reference Books Annual,*
Libraries Unlimited, Inc.

Budget Dining and Lodging in New England

Third Edition

by Fran & Frank Sullivan

Illustrations by Kathy Michalove

A Voyager Book

The Globe Pequot Press

Old Saybrook, Connecticut

Library of Congress Cataloging-in-Publication Data

Sullivan, Fran.
    Budget dining and lodging in New England / by Fran & Frank Sullivan; illustrations by Kathy Michalove.—3rd ed.
        p.   cm.
    "A Voyager book."
    Includes index.
    ISBN 0-87106-190-2
        1. Restaurants, lunch rooms, etc.—New England—Guidebooks.
    2. Hotels, taverns, etc.—New England—Guidebooks. I. Sullivan, Frank.
    II. Title.
    TX907.3.N35S85 1992
    647.9475—dc20   92-6013
                                                                               CIP

Manufactured in the United States of America
Third Edition/Third Printing

We would like to dedicate this book
to our children—

Ellen, Matthew, and Julie

TABLE OF CONTENTS

TABLE OF CONTENTS

ACKNOWLEDGMENTS

We feel we made many special friends during this project. Hosts and owners listed in the book have been very helpful, and they often call us up to tell us about changes they have made or new items they have added to the menu. Some even send us family photographs and notes asking about the progress of the book. We value their sharing and advice.

We'd like to thank these people for recommending places to us: Diana and Jim Campbell, Bea Fitzgerald, Shirley and Phil Craig (Shirley has especially helped us with Martha's Vineyard, where she grew up and still spends each summer), Jan and Ron Lycette, Stephanie and Jim Cole, Cathy Mello, Marybeth Wells, Maureen Lavallee, Jay Moore, Jean Winslow, Bill Crocker, Jo Sullivan Streeter (Frank's sister in the Berkshires), Tom and Barbara Wyley, and John and Lisa Peterson.

Thanks to all who steered us in the right direction.

INTRODUCTION

Travel in New England is fascinating because there is so much diversity in the scenery and so many things to do. It's a unique part of the United States. The seacoast is probably the region's biggest drawing card in the summer months. People who enjoy white sandy beaches, swimming in the salt water, and relaxing in the sun flock from all over the country to New England's many coastal towns. In the winter months, the mountains of northern New England attract winter-sports enthusiasts from all over the world. The quaintness and charm of being snowbound in front of a roaring fire in a cozy lodge after a full day of skiing are unequaled anywhere. Of course, the rural charm of the area, and especially the brilliant fall foliage, are also important tourist attractions.

In New England, you can visit seventeenth-century houses, swim at the beach, fish in a river, enjoy delicious seafood—maybe even go to a Down East clambake, hike in the mountains, collect antiques, ski down a mountain or along wooded trails, hear the Boston Symphony at Tanglewood in the Berkshires, and participate in many other Yankee events.

But your New England travel need not cost a lot of money. This book will help you to drastically cut costs on meals and lodging, so you can have a quality vacation, see all the sights, and meet interesting people without going home broke. The recommendations you will find herein are the ones a good friend or relative might give you if you were coming to visit. You will travel in New England as if you were a native, and at the same time you will meet the unique people of this region.

Because Frank was a college professor, we have always had time to travel in the summer. We began traveling in Europe on a budget and found the European bed & breakfast lodgings great fun. When we returned home we explored New England for similar accommodations, and we looked for ways to travel as economically as we had done in Europe with the family. Gradually, we became quite Europeanized in our travel habits—less spoiled and more willing to settle for the shared bath, the simple room, and the bargain restaurant. Yet it always remained important to us that the lodging or restaurant have a friendly, cheerful, and caring atmosphere. Plus, we found we enjoyed ourselves more at small and simple places where we got to meet other guests, and we learned to delight in the camaraderie of bed & breakfasts and local diners. As a matter of fact, we became so enamored of bed & breakfasts that in 1985 we bought a lovely captain's house in York, Maine, and turned it into a B&B, the Wild Rose of York.

Thus, we have become budget-minded travelers who have learned how to get value for the money spent. We are writing this guide for people like ourselves who have economy in mind but need to get away and have the desire to see New England to the fullest. Of course, in writing the third edition of this book, we have added greatly to our original favorites. Our plan was to select areas already popular with visitors to New England, although we also added some areas that are equally delightful but not as well known.

We first looked for the lodgings in an area and then for the eating places one could use while staying there. Thus, in the listings lodgings and eating places tend to cluster around one locale in each town. Sometimes we've recommended restaurants that are somewhat isolated from the lodgings. We believe the traveler is willing to drive a few extra miles for a really outstanding meal.

We chose lodgings on the basis of ambience, quality, price, hospitality (or service), and decor. We decided they had to be places where we would want to stay, and they had to be clean, cheery, and comfortable, with hosts who make guests feel right at home. We looked for places that cost between $50 and $80 a night for two people and offered either a continental or full breakfast. This limit became difficult to work with in some areas, such as near New York City or in Boston, so we evaluated each lodging in terms of prices in the area and the availability of low-priced accommodations. We are confident that the establishments listed are some of the best bargains in each area.

To find restaurants, we talked with the local people about the relative merits of different restaurants and took copious notes as we found out what they thought were the best places to eat in town. Then we visited each restaurant ourselves. This meant sampling the food, talking to the staff, interviewing the owner, and generally evaluating the place in all details—even checking out the restrooms. Our general rule was that we would include a restaurant if it had good quality, acceptable quantity, and the right price. Our price guidelines were around $4 for full breakfast, about $4–$6 for lunch, and about $10 to $12 for dinner.

Everywhere we went we considered the morale of the employees. It was a good indicator of how satisfying a place would be. After a while we developed a pattern of selection, so that we could spot a good place right off. As one old Yankee advised us, "If it's a good place, you'll see lots of cars parked there." Places we usually excluded were franchise restaurants or lodgings, because we generally found them impersonal and plastic. In a few cases, however, we included a franchise motel because it was the only good bargain in an area.

We spent many hours on the road gathering information on new places, re-evaluating our old favorites, and talking with the local people of different towns. This aspect of writing the guide gave us the greatest pleasure. Meeting the enthusiastic restaurant owner who is also the chef, or the bed & breakfast couple who is starting a new business, was an exciting and fun part of the task. Also, meeting New Englanders who are proud of their towns and those towns' histories was a special delight. We'll always remember the Vermonter we met at Jad's in Brattleboro, Vermont. He made us envy him his good fortune in living in such a pleasant place.

We think you'll find that traveling on a budget gives you the opportunity for a more interesting and special vacation. We hope you enjoy New England!

WHAT DOES *BUDGET* MEAN?

In our interviews of establishment managers and our discussions of the book with readers, we discovered that to many people the word budget applied to a restaurant or lodging suggests that the place is of lesser quality. Regarding the places we recommend in this book, nothing could be further from the truth. We try to find the best value for your money. Whether it be a $50- or $150-a-night stay at a bed & breakfast or a $16 entree at a restaurant, we believe that what we list are the best bargains in that area. Establishments close to New York City charge higher prices than do their counterparts in northern New England, but in both areas we have listed the best values available. Some of our recommendations may even seem expensive for a book on budget travel. Don't be alarmed! Certain places, we feel, are worth a higher price. Remember, we select the best for its rates. *Budget Dining and Lodging in New England* helps you get the most for your travel dollar.

3

HOW THIS GUIDE IS ARRANGED

The chapters in this guide are arranged by state or subregion in this order: Connecticut, Rhode Island, Massachusetts, Cape Cod and the Islands, Vermont, New Hampshire, and Maine. Within each chapter is an introduction to the state; a state map and state index; a section on where to stay, arranged alphabetically by town; and a section on where to eat, arranged alphabetically by town.

The state map and state index will help you plan the itinerary for your next vacation. In addition, you can use them to help you locate places to eat, even if those places are not in the exact towns where you'll be lodging. At the back of the book is an index alphabetized by name of restaurant and lodging, so that you can find directions to a place even if you can't remember the town it's in.

Each complete listing gives the mailing address, street address, average prices, hours and days open, credit card information, owners' or managers' names, and driving directions. All information has been checked and rechecked to give you the most up-to-date facts. All prices quoted in this book, however, are subject to change due to economic conditions, change of structure or owner, or other unforeseen causes. Other facts, such as hours, may also change. It pays to call ahead! Those fruitless trips up a country road late in the day when you're tired can be avoided if you take the time to call first. A phone call also lets lodging owners know your time of arrival and that you are on your way so they can hold your room for you.

All prices are listed without taxes or gratuities, so you'll need to figure these in. The lodging and meals taxes in each state are as follows: Connecticut, 12 percent for lodging and 6 percent for meals; Rhode Island, 6 percent; Massachusetts, 9.7 percent; Vermont, 6 percent; New Hampshire, 7 percent; and Maine, 7 percent for lodging and 5 percent for meals.

Suggested gratuities are about 15 percent excluding tax, but you might inquire about these at each place. Some lodgings may have a service charge. Many places that do not accept credit cards will take personal checks; inquire ahead if this is important to you.

Although some lodgings may accept you on short notice, most of the lodgings prefer that you make reservations and send in one or two nights' deposit to hold the room. It is imperative that you contact very popular places even one or two months in advance, especially seacoast towns in the summer and popular ski areas such as Stowe, Vermont, or North Conway, New Hampshire, in the winter. Remember that the fall foliage season is the busiest for the New England tourist industry.

And as an added bonus: In case you have a problem getting into one of our listed restaurants or lodgings, we have included a number of "Also recommended" establishments for you to try. These are not substandard; we just didn't have time to visit them and check them out personally.

There is absolutely no charge for being listed in this book. If you have found lodgings or places to eat that you feel are especially good bargains and you would like to share them with others, please write us at our publisher, The Globe Pequot Press, 6 Business Park Drive, Old Saybrook, CT 06475. We will be happy to consider your recommendations for the next edition.

The prices and rates listed in this guidebook were confirmed at press time. We recommend, however, that you call establishments before traveling to obtain current information.

CONNECTICUT

Connecticut is a study in contrasts. The southern shore near New York City is cosmopolitan, fashionable, and very affluent. Connecticut has the highest per-capita income in the country mainly because of the suburban community that works in New York City.

The other side of Connecticut is the beautiful, rural northwestern part of the state and the eastern seashore farther up toward Rhode Island. Here you will find charming colonial villages and old whaling ports such as New London, Mystic, and Stonington on the seashore. You will experience New England hospitality at its finest, people who are exceptionally friendly, and a quality of life and a scenic beauty unsurpassed.

The beautiful Connecticut River, which divides the state, and the lands along its shores are a New England treasure. The history of the Connecticut River is the history of the region itself. The story of colonists starting on farms, banding together into villages, and establishing businesses and manufacturing enterprises was repeated throughout the river valleys and farmlands of New England all the way north to the Canadian border.

Of course, the story of a state or region is a story of its people, and Connecticut has many national heroes and celebrities whose homes are now open to the public. You should make it a point to visit them. But today you will find out about Connecticut people by staying at the bed & breakfast homes or small inns listed, visiting the craft shops and seaports, and eating at the special restaurants listed in this chapter.

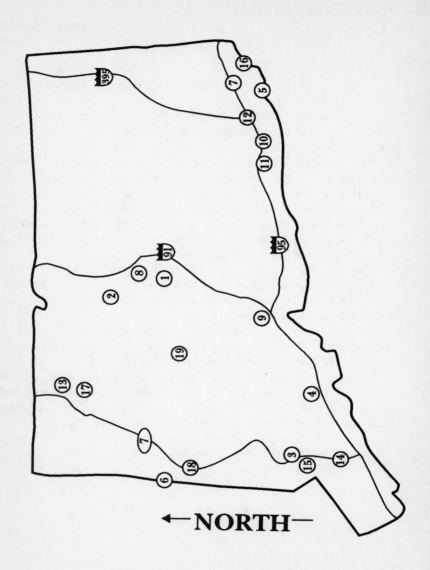

←NORTH—

CONNECTICUT

	🛏	🍴
1. Bristol	10	—
2. Canton	11	19
3. Danbury	—	19
4. Fairfield	—	20
5. Groton Long Point	11	—
6. Kent	12	—
7. Mystic	—	21
8. New Britain	—	22
9. New Haven	12	22
10. New London	—	24
11. Niantic	14	—
12. Noank	—	25
13. Norfolk	14	—
14. Norwalk	15	—
15. Ridgefield	15	26
16. Stonington	16	26
17. Torrington	—	27
18. Warren	17	—
19. Woodbury	17	—

WHERE TO STAY

CHIMNEY CREST MANOR
5 Founders Drive
Bristol, Connecticut 06010
(203) 582-4219

A trio of Catholic sisters staying at our own bed & breakfast said we had to include this place in our book. Right they were. This English Tudor mansion in the historic district has five beautiful suites, each with private bath. One suite is reserved for families with children. Some of the suites have fireplaces; some include sunny sitting rooms, breakfast nooks, and private kitchens. The amenities you find here are not to be found in most B&Bs. A full breakfast includes fruit salad, fresh breads, and an elegant entree served on fine china and crystal; a continental breakfast is made for late risers. All of the rooms have air conditioning and color television. There is even a private entrance for each suite, and free parking is provided. The hospitality of the hosts and the style and splendor of this home-away-from-home will be a special treat for the business traveler or tourist visiting this region of Connecticut.

Average rates: Double, $80–$95; single, $70–$85. Seniors 10 percent discount. 2-day minimum during foliage season. *Credit cards:* MasterCard and Visa. *Open:* Year-round, except Christmas. *Owners:* Dante and Cynthia Cimadamore. *Directions:* From I-84 eastbound, use exit 31 (West Street/Route 229). Go left and drive 5 miles. Follow signs for the Clock Museum. Go under the overpass and turn left (at blue "H" hospital sign) onto Woodland Street. Continue past the stop sign to the crest of the large hill. The manor is on the left, inside the wrought iron fence and brick pillars. *Children:* Yes. *Pets:* No. *Smoking:* Allowed in one suite.

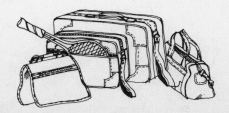

HILLSIDE MOTEL
Route 44
Canton, Connecticut 06019
(203) 693-4951

This was a good find for fair rates and quiet surroundings. This area tends to be higher priced than most, and the eleven clean rooms with pretty furniture, soft colors, and nature scenes on the walls are a real bargain. Each has a comfortable chair, air conditioning, and cable television, and there is complimentary coffee for guests in the office each morning. A deli and ice-cream shop is also on the premises. The owners are friendly and helpful, and we had a peaceful stay.

Average rates: Double and single, $38 plus tax. *Credit cards:* MasterCard, Visa, and American Express. *Open:* All year. *Owners:* Maurice and Joy Cho. *Directions:* From Route 8, go east on Route 202 for about 12 miles. Then where Route 44 joins it, backtrack to the west on Route 44 for about 1.5 miles. The motel is on the right. From Hartford, take Route 44 west for about 17 miles. *Children:* Yes. *Pets:* No. *Smoking:* Yes.

SHORE INNE
54 East Shore Avenue
Groton Long Point, Connecticut 06340
(203) 536-1180

The ocean across the street, the large lawn under a copper beech, and the bay window in the living room are the things we remember about this delightful little inn. The seven bedrooms are decorated in restful pink, blue, and rose comforters and sea blue carpeting. Five rooms have private baths; two have shared. Innkeepers Harold and Judith Hoyland maintain a warehouse of knowledge about the area's history, dining pleasures, special walks, and swimming places. They will make you feel right at home. You'll be able to sample delicious homemade baked goods at the complimentary breakfast. This inn is so restful and the area so pretty, you'll find it hard to leave. The Shore Inne is centrally located, so you can make day trips to Old Lyme, Essex, or Chester to the west, or go in the opposite direction to Mystic Seaport or Stonington.

Average rates: Double, $75–$85 in summer; $60–$70 off season. *Credit cards:* MasterCard and Visa. *Open:* April 1 to November. *Owners:* Harold and Judith Hoyland. *Directions:* Take exit 88 off I-95 and make a right on Route 117. At Route 1 turn left, go 100 yards, then turn right on Route 215, heading south toward the ocean. Continue past the Fisherman restaurant. Take the next left onto East Shore Road. The Shore Inne is about ½ mile down on the right. It's a white, wooden building with a copper beech in front. *Children:* Twelve and over. *Pets:* No. *Smoking:* No.

CONSTITUTION OAK FARM
Beardsley Road
Kent, Connecticut 06757
(203) 354-6495

This white Victorian farmhouse built in 1833 offers a quiet, rural setting for some serious unwinding only two hours (90 miles) from New York City. You can watch the cows, take walks, and photograph the scenery. With no sounds of radio or television to distract you, the sounds of the country provide a natural background. An expanded continental breakfast is provided, "everything but eggs and bacon." Four rooms are available: two upstairs with shared bath, two downstairs with private bath. There are good restaurants in the area. Swimming, boating, and fishing at Lake Waramaug nearby will provide summer activities for guests of the Deveuxs. A futon is available for children.

Average rates: Double, $55–$65. *Credit cards:* None; personal checks accepted. *Open:* Year-round. *Owner:* Debbie Deveux. *Directions:* Please call ahead, and the Deveuxs will give you directions. It's off Route 202 near Lake Waramaug. *Children:* Yes. *Pets:* No. *Smoking:* Yes.

ROYAL INN
1605 Whalley Avenue
New Haven, Connecticut 06515
(203) 389-9504

This very large, brick-front motel is just 4 miles from Yale University. The rooms are clean, pleasant, and nicely decorated.

Some rooms have two double beds, two chairs, a table, and a desk; others have a sitting area with a couch and one double bed. All have cable television and air conditioning and overlook a pretty little pond out front. Complimentary coffee is offered. An outside pool is open in the summer. Parking is free. The beauty of this reasonable place is its easy access to the Wilbur Cross Parkway and I-95. It's about a ninety-minute drive to New York City.

Average rates: Double, $39–$42; extra person in the room is $4. *Credit cards:* All major. *Open:* All year. *Owner:* Hasu Patel. *Directions:* From the Wilbur Cross Parkway take exit 59. The motel is right across from the end of the ramp. From I-95, take exit 45 and go north on Route 10 to Whalley Avenue, which is Route 63. Make a left and drive for a little more than 1 mile. You'll see the motel on the right. *Children:* Yes. *Pets:* Small ones. *Smoking:* Yes; few nonsmoking rooms available.

THREE JUDGES MOTEL
1560 Whalley Avenue
New Haven, Connecticut 06515
(203) 389-2161

This motel is a reasonable lodging right off the Wilbur Cross Parkway. It's neat and clean and has good restaurants nearby. The rooms are very large and include lounge areas with a table and chairs. The decor is plain with orange, brown, and white print quilts. The bathrooms are tiled and well lighted. Each room offers a color television and radio for entertainment. You enter from the rear parking lot, so there is no road noise from Whalley Avenue. The rooms are air-conditioned.

Average rates: Single, $35; double: One bed, $35; Two beds, $45. Senior citizen discount. *Credit cards:* All major. *Open:* Year-round. *Owner:* Mr. Jerrywala. *Directions:* Take exit 59 off the Wilbur Cross Parkway (Route 15). Take a right off the ramp, go 1 block (toward the city), and it's on your right. *Children:* Yes. *Pets:* No. *Smoking:* Yes.

13

MOTEL 6
269 Flanders Road
Niantic, Connecticut 06357
(203) 739-6991

Although we do not usually list chain motels, this one is too good to pass up. The prices are unbelievable, considering the new and modern condition of the rooms, the delightful outdoor swimming pool, and the cable television. They also have a coin-operated washer and dryer. Nonsmoking rooms are available. The charming rooms are air-conditioned and have desks for business travelers. You'll find the desk clerks very affable. You must book way ahead, as it's near the Naval and Coast Guard bases.

Average rates: Double, about $35; single, $29. Three people are $41, and four people are $47! *Credit cards:* All major. *Open:* Year-round. *Managers:* Judi and Frank Copson. *Directions:* On the Connecticut Turnpike, I-95, take exit 74, and you'll see the motel on the hill. *Children:* Yes. *Pets:* Yes. *Smoking:* Certain rooms.

MANOR HOUSE
Maple Avenue
Norfolk, Connecticut 06058
(203) 542-5690

This English Tudor/Bavarian mansion bed & breakfast won the Most Romantic Hideaway in Connecticut award in 1990. The rate is at our upper end, but the value is worth it. You can enjoy the area's beautiful country scenery and local attractions such as summer music festivals, theater, and lake swimming, as well as downhill skiing in the winter. There are nine rooms, some with canopy beds, balconies, and fireplaces. A full breakfast is served, complete with homemade muffins and breads and fresh fruit; you may choose an entree from among two or three dishes. Coffee, tea, and other beverages are available throughout the day. The gracious hosts show a special talent for selecting antiques that blend with the interior and its unique details. This B&B can serve as your base of operations for a long stay.

Average rates: Double $85–$150. *Credit cards:* MasterCard, Visa, and American Express. *Open:* Year-round. *Owners:* Diane and Hank Tremblay. *Directions:* From Route 8, exit onto Route 44. When you reach village, look for Maple Avenue and the Manor House sign. Pass ten or eleven houses on Maple, and the late Tudor building will come into view. *Children:* Twelve and over. *Pets:* No. *Smoking:* Restricted.

GOLDEN CREST MOTEL
596 Westport Avenue
Norwalk, Connecticut 06851
(203) 847-3833

Mr. Renzulli's cheerful grandson proudly showed us this complex of two buildings that his grandfather started to construct in 1969. In the main building, the rooms are medium-sized, neat, and attractive, and each has one double bed and a shower glassed-in on three sides. In the new building, the rooms are large and the furniture is new. There are two big beds, individual heating and air conditioning, a tub, and a shower. All rooms have television, radio, a telephone, and a refrigerator. There is a total of sixty-one units. One Renzulli daughter works here, too, and the family touch makes a difference.

Average rates: Double: one bed, $40; two beds, $48. *Credit cards:* Most major. *Open:* Year-round. *Owner:* Albert Renzulli. *Directions:* From the Merritt Parkway, take exit 41 to Route 33 to Route 1. Turn right and drive for a little over a mile. The motel is on the left. From I-95, take exit 16 to Route 1. Turn right, and the motel is about 2½ miles up on Route 1 (Westport Avenue). *Children:* Yes. *Pets:* No. *Smoking:* Yes.

RIDGEFIELD MOTOR INN
296 Ethan Allen Highway
Ridgefield, Connecticut 06877
(203) 438-3781

This handsome, brick-front motel, which caters mostly to business people, is a great place for folks to relax. Here you can visit

15

Wooster Mountain, Putnam Memorial State Park, or the lovely town of Ridgefield, where the Aldrich Contemporary Art Museum and Colonial Keeler Tavern are located. The motel has large rooms decorated with brightly colored bedcovers and carpets. Two soft chairs, a desk, color television, and air conditioning are provided in each room. Some rooms have refrigerators. Summer visitors can use the picnic tables on the back lawn. A restaurant is also on the premises, but we did not get a chance to try it.

Average rates: Double, $48–$55; single, $42–$48. *Credit cards:* All major. *Open:* Year-round. *Manager:* Alex Patel. *Directions:* Take exit 40 off the Wilbur Cross Parkway (Route 15), and go north about 10 miles. From I-84 take exit 3. Go south on Route 7 (also called Ethan Allen Highway) for about 5 miles. The motel is on the left. *Children:* Yes. *Pets:* No. *Smoking:* Yes.

FARNAN HOUSE
10 McGrath Court
Stonington, Connecticut 06378
(203) 535-0634

This family homestead is very neat and has been decorated with pretty personal touches by Mrs. Farnan. Her four rooms have four-posters, brass beds with George Washington spreads, and darling, puffed hanging lamps covered in calico prints. You can't help but enjoy her huge country kitchen with beams and knotty pine walls. The oversized fireplace with seating encircling it makes it easy to enjoy good conversation. You'll like her complimentary continental breakfast of orange juice, coffee, bagels, or sweet breads served on the red and white checked tablecloth. The old-fashioned Granny stove is still used for cooking and heating. The porch is great for lounging under the cool shade trees.

Average rates: Double, $65–$75; extra for a child in the room. *Credit cards:* None. *Open:* All year. *Owner:* Ann Farnan. *Directions:* Conveniently located in Stonington. Please get directions from the owner, as she wishes to have guests with reservations only. *Children:* Yes. *Pets:* No. *Smoking:* Restricted.

TURNING POINT FARM
Route 45
Warren, Connecticut 06754
(203) 868-7775

This bed & breakfast was written up in *Yankee* magazine. It is a charming 200-year-old colonial farm with a pond on ten acres of land. Three bedrooms converge on a common sitting room overlooking the pond. This was one of the first bed & breakfasts in Connecticut. Lyme Rock racetrack (where Paul Newman goes) and Tanglewood (an hour away) provide diversions. There are also museums and antique stores for the rainy days. A fantastic full breakfast is included in the room rate. Lake Waramaug is not too far should you wish to swim to work off the calories accumulated at the excellent restaurants in the area, or you can just vegetate on the screened porch.

Average rates: Double, $85. *Credit cards:* None; personal checks accepted. *Open:* Year-round. *Owner:* Evelyn Grossi. *Directions:* Go north on Route 7 to where Route 45 branches off. Go 2½ miles on Route 45 and you'll see a white colonial house with white barns and a sign in front that says TURNING POINT FARM. *Children:* Teenagers only. *Pets:* No. *Smoking:* No

CURTIS HOUSE
506 Main Street South
Woodbury, Connecticut 06798
(203) 263-2101

This historic 1754 inn dazzles guests with the colonial beauty of its guest rooms and dining area. The spacious rooms boast lovely sanded floors, oriental rugs, and dainty flower print wallpaper. Most have private baths, and one or two have canopied double beds! There are comfortable chairs and a desk in the rooms, and one large room features an extra room with a cot for a child. Guests have the use of the charming sitting room downstairs and its fireplace. Juice, coffee, and muffins are provided in the morning for a nominal charge. The famous Curtis House restaurant, which folks drive miles to visit, is another colonial fantasy with candles, dried flowers, and beautiful beams. Both lunch and din-

ner include soup, a potato, vegetable, salad, dessert, and coffee. Lunch, $7–$11; dinner, $11–$18, complete. The inn and restaurant are closed Mondays and Christmas.

Average rates: Double with private bath, $45–$70; double with shared bath, $30–$35; extra person is $10. *Credit cards:* MasterCard and Visa. *Open:* Year-round. *Owner:* Chester Hardisty. *Directions:* From Route 84, take exit 15 north. Go straight up Route 6 to the center of Woodbury; the inn is on your left. Route 6 in Woodbury is Main Street. *Children:* Yes. *Pets:* No. *Smoking:* yes.

Also recommended:

Another lovely old place to stay in the area is the **Yankee Pedlar Inn** in Torrington. Doubles are reasonable for this area, which tends to be more expensive than most. It is on 93 Main Street and the phone is (203) 489-9226.

And in Bantam Lake, on Route 209, is the **Lake Forest Bed & Breakfast.** This is a twenty-two-acre estate that once belonged to a president of the Pepsi Cola Company and is now the home of Dick Van Neese. He runs an award-winning art shop and Victorian antique store. There are six bedrooms in the house and two cottages with bedrooms. A double costs $50–$125, and a single is $50–$75. Continental breakfast is included. There are private trails, lots of outdoor activities, and swimming. The telephone number is (203) 567-8563.

WHERE TO EAT

MEL'S KITCHEN
Route 44
Canton, Connecticut 06019
(203) 693-1569

This is where the locals go for breakfast and lunch. The food warrants a visit. Breakfasts are reasonably priced and great tasting. Sandwiches are delicious, and the entrees—"plates"—are equally good. Both counter and booth service are provided.

Average prices: Breakfasts under $2.25 without meat; with meat and juice, under $5. Lunch: sandwiches and plates (clam, hamburger, ham, fish, and fried chicken), $4.50–$6. *Credit cards:* None. *Hours:* Weekdays, 5 A.M.–2 P.M.; Saturday, 6 A.M.–noon; Sunday, 7 A.M.–noon. *Owner:* Gemel Negaime. *Directions:* The restaurant is a few miles east of the intersection of routes 22 and 44 on the right in the Smokey Bear shopping complex.

THREE BROTHERS DINER
242 White Street
Danbury, Connecticut 06910
(203) 748-6008

We've recommended this diner in every edition, which gives you a clue as to its reliability. Its all-new modern-style building has a beautiful lavender interior decor. The diner has 150 seats, including ten at the counter, which means if you are alone you can get a meal without sitting all by yourself at a booth or table. This restaurant offers the usual diner bill of fare as well as Greek specialties. It also features items that are Diet Center–approved for those who are keen on healthy eating. We like their creativity. When we were there last they offered soft-shell crab, mussels marinara, chicken scampi, and monkfish with lemon wine sauce. Who would have expected those dishes in a diner? So you see you have something different and exciting here. The pastry kitchen maintains a display case in the dining room so you can end your meal on a sweet note. The menu defies description, but suffice it to say that if it is American, Italian, or Greek—or seafood—you'll find it here.

Average prices: Full breakfast averages around $4. Lunch and dinner: sandwiches, $1–$3; entrees $7–$12. *Credit cards:* MasterCard, Visa, American Express, and Diner's Club. *Hours:* Twenty-four hours a day, seven days a week. *Owners:* Nick and Tony Kallivrousis. *Directions:* Take exit 8 off I-84 and drive toward Danbury Center for about 2 miles on White Street. Look for the restaurant on the right; it is easy to miss.

SIDETRACKS RESTAURANT
2070 Post Road
Fairfield, Connecticut 06430
(203) 254-3606

You'll like the old railroad atmosphere here, with stop signs, cut glass, and other antiques about; and the old pictures of New York City and Fairfield. Recommended to us by a guest from Connecticut, who claimed they have the greatest French onion soup, this place also has great fresh seafood quiches, burgers, stir frys, Danish ribs, and swordfish. Soups, rolls, and desserts are homemade. You have a choice of tables or booths in a dining room decorated in mauve and natural wood, with a large field-stone fireplace to make you cozy. They do have high chairs and nonsmoking areas.

Average prices: Lunch and dinner entrees, $11–$14; sandwiches, $5–$7. *Credit cards:* All major. *Hours:* Monday to Friday, 11:30 A.M.–11 P.M.; Saturday, noon–11 P.M.; Sunday brunch, 11 A.M.–3 P.M. (you can order off the menu if you like) and then it's open till 10 P.M. *Manager:* David Head. *Directions:* From I-95 going east, take exit 21 and turn right; go to second stoplight, and turn right onto Post Road; go to the next stoplight, and SideTracks is on your right.

Also recommended:

If you're looking for good pizza in Hartford and don't mind "crowded and noisy," the **Keg Restaurant** on Sisson Avenue is your

20

place; call (203) 236-5423. The **Olympia Diner** on the Berlin Turnpike in Berlin is a favorite spot of the townfolks, especially for breakfast. It's just south of Hartford. Call (203) 666-9948.

BEE-BEE DAIRY RESTAURANT
33 West Main Street
Mystic, Connecticut 06355
(203) 536-4577

This very large, cheerful place was highly recommended by folks in Stonington. It is something like the Newport Creamery, clean with good service, excellent food, and prices geared to families. There are mostly booths and plenty of waitresses. You can watch the three cooks from the dining area. You get a soothing feeling of being cared for, and the decor is pleasing. All three meals are served here. At breakfast choose from omelets, waffles, pancakes, eggs any style, and the famous "Bee-Bee breakfast sandwich," muffins, and pastries. (Breakfast fare is served all day.) For lunch and dinner, there are many fish, chicken, and chopped beef dishes all served with a potato, vegetable or cole slaw, and bread or roll. They serve the usual sandwich fare, plus some wonderful ice-cream treats—their specialty. Choose from twenty-one flavors!

Average prices: Breakfast, $1–$3.40. Sandwiches, under $2 to under $5; dinner, $4–$7. They offer eight types of salad, some fruit, and children's sandwiches at lower prices. *Credit cards:* None. *Hours:* Every day all year, 6 A.M. to 10 P.M.; 6 A.M. to 11 P.M. in the summer. *Owner:* Peter Pappas. *Directions:* From I-95, take Route 27 south to West Main Street. Turn right, and you'll find the restaurant in a shopping center 2 blocks after the bridge on the left.

KITCHEN LITTLE
81½ Greenmanville Avenue
Mystic, Connecticut 06355
(203) 536-2122

This little white and blue building draws local fans like a lighthouse beacon. Once inside, usually after waiting in a short line,

21

you will find yourself in a miniature restaurant, with six stools at the counter and eight tables. The head cook serves up nacho cheese omelets, scrambled eggs, kielbasa with Swiss dill rye toast, and fresh strawberry-blueberry pancakes. With these delicacies, no wonder people line up in the doorway. You know the locals like this place because they keep their personalized coffee mugs hanging on hooks over the counter. Fancy egg dishes, such as spinach, mushroom, and cream cheese scrambled eggs with melted cheese and other unusual breakfast omelets are favorites. You'll love the atmosphere if you love people. No lunch served now. Another Kitchen Little with a more elaborate menu is located in Stonington.

Average prices: Breakfast: omelets, $4–$5; unusual scrambled egg dishes, $2–$3; add-ins like juice, bacon, sausage, or ham make a complete breakfast for $4–$5. A standard breakfast of eggs, bacon, juice, and coffee comes to about $4 plus change. *Credit cards:* None. *Hours:* Seven days a week from 6:30 A.M. to 1 P.M. *Owner:* Florence Brochu. *Directions:* Take exit 90 south off I-95. You will be traveling south on Route 27 (Greenmanville Avenue). Kitchen Little will be on the right.

MUIR'S FAMILY RESTAURANT
244 Allen Street
New Britain, Connecticut 06053
(203) 225-2243

This very popular restaurant caters to families and has a twin at 311 New Britain Avenue in Plainville. They specialize in steaks and seafood but offer a full menu with a wide variety of other entrees such as chicken and other meats. Your children get a menu of their own. You sit in booths, and the attractive wicker decor and soothing earthtones will add to your enjoyment of the excellent meals. The style is contemporary. Daily specials are featured at breakfast and lunch, and homemade chowder and two soups are offered every day. The seating capacity is about 158, and wine and beer are available. High chairs are provided for toddlers. Smoking is permitted in specific areas.

Average prices: Breakfast, $3–$4; lunch, $2–$4; dinner, $5 to about $8. *Credit cards:* None. *Hours:* 7 A.M. to 8 P.M., seven days a week.

Owner: Ken Tousignant. *Directions:* From I-84, take the Finnerman Road exit and turn right onto Farmington Avenue; continue on Farmington for 3 miles, then turn left onto Allen Street. The brick-front restaurant is on the left and down a few yards.

Also recommended:

In New Britain, you might like to try the **Miss Washington Diner** (telephone: (203) 224-3772) on West Main Street; or **Capitol Lunch** on Main Street (telephone: (203) 229-8237), which is very inexpensive and is famous for its excellent chili dogs. **East Side Restaurant** on Chestnut Street also has excellent food and is not inexpensive.

ATHENIAN DINER
1426 Whalley Avenue
New Haven, Connecticut 06515
(203) 397-1556

This very popular restaurant is a built-over diner. It is quite big and comfortable with red leather booths, dark wood, and hanging plants. The offerings are many and varied, with Greek food, Jewish dishes, Italian pasta, fresh seafood daily, Yankee pot roast, fried chicken, and goulash! Fran delighted in a large plate of lamb shish kebab on a bed of rice, with tomatoes, peppers, and onions—excellent flavor! Frank tried his old favorite, Yankee pot roast, and was tickled with every bite. Pies are made fresh daily in a bakery. Beer and wine are available. For a restaurant that now seats 140 people, the atmosphere is very intimate, relaxed, and jolly. Breakfast and sandwiches are very reasonably priced.

Average prices: Breakfast, $5; lunch and sandwiches, $2–$5. Dinners range from $4–$10, but most are under $8. *Credit cards:* Visa and MasterCard. *Hours:* Twenty-four hours a day, seven days a week. Closed only on Christmas Day. *Owner:* George Daoutis. *Directions:* From the Wilbur Cross Parkway, take exit 59. Go right on Whalley Avenue, and after about a ½ mile, it will be on your right.

Also recommended:

Try the **Elm City Diner** (telephone: (203) 624-0004) on the corner of Chapel and Howe streets. A little pricey, but it has an excellent Sunday brunch for $5–$6 in novel diner decor. Lunches and dinners are expensive, but lunch sandwiches are $3–$5. Noted for soups and salads. Jazz piano in the evening. Closed Mondays.

Gag's Jr. is a tiny but favorite spot on the corner of Chapel and Park streets. It's open 7 A.M. to 2 P.M. Monday through Saturday and closed Sundays. Here you can get eggs all day. Two eggs, coffee, juice, and toast are over $1 and change. You can also try the pancakes or French toast. For $1 more add sausage or bacon. The telephone number is (203) 624-1630.

The Bagel Connection, on Whalley Avenue next to the Athenian Diner, serves breakfast and lunch and is recommended to guests by the Royal Inn. The restaurant's telephone number is (203) 387-1455.

THE ROYAL DINER
280 Broad Street
New London, Connecticut 06320
(203) 443-3681

This very popular diner, run by a cheerful family, has won two awards for breakfast on the "P.M. Magazine." We tried the pot roast, and it was super! They also feature meatloaf, roast turkey, roast lamb (all roasted on the premises), lamb stew, and oyster stew. Fran had a very large yummy pastrami sandwich with pickles, chips, and the house favorite, Grapenut pudding. They make all their own soups and desserts. The diner has been in the same family since 1950. Frank voted for this diner as one of the top five in New England.

Average prices: Full breakfast, about $2–$4. Sandwiches, $2–$4. Dinners include soup, dessert, and coffee, and cost $10–$16, with lower-priced specials every day. *Credit cards:* None. *Hours:* Monday through Saturday, 5:30 A.M. to 8:45 P.M. Closed Sundays. *Owners:* Jim and Mary Ann Gibbons. *Directions:* From I–95, take the exit for Route 85, which is Broad Street. Follow it south; the diner is on the right after three stoplights.

ABBOTT'S
117 Pearl Street
Noank, Connecticut 06340
(203) 536-7719

Abbott's is a lobster-in-the-rough place located right by the water, with manicured lawns, picnic tables, and a view of sailboats at their moorings and distant islands beyond. You'll feel right in the mood for some fantastic seafood. We were impressed with the neatness of Abbott's. Everything was freshly painted for the beginning of the season when we were there. It is quite an unusual restaurant for its type. They even package their clambakes, so you can take them along. There is seating for four hundred, and they've been cooking up clams and lobsters here for forty years. There is plenty of seating indoors in case the weather becomes inclement. Only non-alcoholic beverages are served, although it is permissible to bring your own beer or wine. A favorite dish is the takeout "Clambake in a Canister"; ready to cook, it costs $12 per person.

Average prices: Lunch and dinner prices are the same. Clam chowder is just over $1; steamed clams and mussels are $5.75 and $4, respectively. Lobsters with cole slaw, chips, and drawn butter start at $12 and go up from there. Prices change with the market; they go down in summer. We would suggest the "opulent seafood rolls" if you're on a budget. Hot lobster rolls are $9. *Credit cards:* MasterCard and Visa. *Hours:* Daily from late April through Labor Day, noon to 9 P.M.; from Labor Day through Columbus Day, open only Friday, Saturday, and Sunday from noon to 7 P.M. *Owners:* Jerry and Ruth Mears. *Directions:* From Route 1, take Route 215 south to Noank. At the cemetery and stop sign, take a left on Mosher Street. Go right on Ward Street after the bridge, left on Main Street 1 block, then right on Pearl Street all the way to the end to Abbott's on the water.

Also recommended:

In Norwalk, in the Strawberry Hill Shopping Center, is the **Garden Cafe.** A favorite among the locals, it is roomy and has good soup and sandwiches and very reasonably priced meals.

Open 6:30 A.M. to 6 P.M. Monday through Friday and 8 A.M. to 2 P.M. Saturday and Sunday. It's at 406 Westport Avenue, next to the Grand Union Market.

FRANZESE'S
896 Ethan Allen Highway
Ridgefield, Connecticut 06877
(203) 438-9355

Plants and more plants, hanging and in flower pots, grace this trendy restaurant. It provides an excellent brunch on Sunday that probably will take care of your eating needs for one day. The dinner menu offers delectable entrees such as prime rib, veal Parmesan, veal Marsala, and other Italian specialties and fresh seafood at reasonable prices. The salad bar alone can provide a full meal, with fancy breads included. We like the choice of going light or heavy according to your appetite. There is a bar on the right as you enter. The service seems prompt and friendly. Dinner only, no lunches are served. The restaurant seats 125. A children's menu is available.

Average prices: Entrees, $9–$27; burgers, $4.50. *Credit cards:* All major. *Hours:* Monday through Saturday, 5–10 P.M.; Sunday brunch 11 A.M.–3 P.M.; dinner 4–9 P.M. *Owner:* Neil Franzese. *Directions:* From I-84 take exit 3. Go south on Route 7 for about 3 miles to the restaurant on your left. From the Wilbur Cross Parkway, take exit 40 north on Route 7 for 15 miles. Route 7 in Ridgefield is Ethan Allen Highway.

NOAH'S RESTAURANT
115 Water Street
Stonington, Connecticut 06378
(203) 535-3925

Noah's is a very good restaurant for the local people and should be given a visit while you're in the area. The young proprietors know most of the folks who eat here, and they occasionally pour extra coffee for their guests in order to greet them personally. The highlights were the super-fresh, crunchy, homemade bread, the fresh flowers on the pine tables, and the very helpful, pleasant waitresses. Our breakfast of homemade cinnamon rolls and fruit was scrumptious. We enjoyed a lunch of knockwurst and sauerkraut for Frank and a plate of delicate cheese and fruit for Fran. Choose from three sizes of cups of soup or chowder, quiche, fish platters, and good salads and sandwiches for lunch. All dinner entrees have good prices, from the pasta of the day, to cod Portuguese or pork chops, to filet mignon. Save room for delicious homemade desserts. Reservations for dinner are a must!

Average prices: Lunch $3–$6, dinner $8–$13. *Credit cards:* None. *Hours:* Breakfast, 7–11 A.M.; Sunday breakfast, 7–noon. Lunch, 11:15 A.M.–2:30 P.M. Dinner, 6–9 P.M. (reserve ahead!). Closed Mondays and month of February. *Owners:* John and Dorothy Papp, Stanley Schwartz. *Directions:* From I-95, take exit 91. Follow the signs to Stonington Borough, approximately 2½ miles. Cross over railroad tracks. Turn left at the Stonington Village sign. Be sure you go over the bridge into the village. You'll find yourself on Water Street. Noah's is 5 blocks farther on the left.

Also recommended:

In Stonington, **Skipper's Dock,** at 60 Water Street behind the Harborview Restaurant, has excellent seafood, and it's not as pricey as some other restaurants in the area. Check out the chalkboard menu in the bar at **Harborview** for some good deals. Another good one in the area is **Dodson's Boatyard Café.** Another **Kitchen Little,** like the one in Mystic (p. 21) but with a more elaborate menu, is also located here.

SCARPELLI'S FAMILY RESTAURANT
865 Migeon Avenue
Torrington, Connecticut 06790
(203) 482-6102

This restaurant is small and casual and caters to families. It has been owned by the Scarpelli family since 1936. They offer a large variety of sandwiches, grinders, and burgers. Their meal specialties are fried clams, fish, or scallops; broiled chops, steak, or chicken; and prime rib roast. They are also noted for their french fries.

Daily specials are offered, and you may have wine or beer with your dinner. You can get a fine breakfast here, too. There is ample parking on the property.

Average prices: Breakfast, $2–$5; lunch, $3–$7; dinner, $6–$12. *Credit cards:* All major. *Hours:* All year, seven days a week, 6 A.M.–9 P.M. *Owner:* Joe J. Scarpelli. *Directions:* It is on the north side of Route 4 in West Torrington, near the edge of town.

TWIN COLONY DINER AND RESTAURANT
417 East Elm Street
Torrington, Connecticut 06790
(203) 482-5346

This restaurant is owned by two brothers who owned the Colony Diner in another town for many years. They know the food business very well, and they know how to keep their customers happy. The decor is soothingly stunning with mauve seats and tables, hanging lights, and booths separated by Plexiglas windows for privacy. Floral posters and prints in steel frames adorn the walls, and the floor is simulated marble. The meals are served with soup and salad and are a super bargain. We tried the hot beef sandwich, which consisted of three large slices of medium-rare roast beef and delicious gravy. Terrific homemade heated bread and tossed salad were served with the meal. Frank tried the scrumptious roast chicken. There were about twenty different desserts to choose from. We tried the French horn and yummy crisp cherry and apple Danishes. All are baked on the premises. A full bar is available.

Average prices: Breakfast of bacon and eggs, $3–$4; waffles, $3–$4. Sandwiches run from under $2 to $4. Hot beef or turkey sandwich, a full dinner, is a remarkable $8! Roast turkey or roast lamb dinners are $11, roast prime rib is $10, and seafood dishes are $10–$15. *Credit cards:* MasterCard and Visa. *Hours:* Seven days a week, twenty-four hours a day. Closed only on Christmas. *Owners:* Gus and Lazarus Saltourides. *Directions:* Take exit 44 off Route 8. It is on the corner of East Elm and Elsie streets.

Also recommended:

These Connecticut restaurants were highly recommended to us by readers and by guests at our bed and breakfast. We haven't visited these establishments yet, but we hear they offer fine quality, fair prices, and, in many cases, special ambience. We hope to check them out soon.

- **Bloomfield Fish Market,** Tunxis Road, Bloomfield (north of Hartford). Excellent seafood, especially broiled salmon steaks and calamari.

- **Twain On The River,** East Hartford. Good for lunch and dinner.

- **The Gate House,** Avon.

- **Collin's Diner,** Canaan (near Norfolk).

- **Saybrook Fish House,** Old Saybrook (off Route 9).

- **Ski's Diner,** Torrington.

- **Wake Robin Inn,** Salisbury. More expensive.

- **Ragamont Inn,** Salisbury. One of the few German restaurants in New England.

- **Crakowia Restaurant,** Broad Street, New Britain. All-Polish menu.

- **Pepe's,** New Haven. Noted in *USA Today* as having the best pizza in the country.

- **Franco's,** Franklin Avenue, South Hartford.

- **Congress Rotisserie,** also Franklin Avenue, South Hartford. Fresh pasta, good specials.

- **Infantino's,** Franklin Avenue, South Hartford. Bring your own wine. Complete dinner for $15–$16. Huge portions.

- **Shiskabal House of Afghanistan,** Franklin Avenue, South Hartford. Only non-Italian restaurant on the street. Reasonable prices: lamb or beef dinners for $10–$12.

RHODE ISLAND

Rhode Islanders are proud of their state and rightly so. It thrives in the summer, when the many miles of waterways, inlets, and beaches make the state a natural vacationland. All year the people are civil, sophisticated, down-to-earth, caring, and enthusiastic about life. They know how to take care of themselves and will do their utmost to make their guests feel at home. You will soon catch their unguarded love of both nature and cultural activities. "Poor Little Rhode Island?" Not at all. "Smart Little Rhode Island!" is more like it. Whether you visit this state to try its fishing, boating, or swimming, or to enjoy the art fairs or antiques, you will be pleasantly surprised by the riches of Rhode Island.

If you look at a map of Rhode Island, you will see that Narragansett Bay splits the state partly from north to south, with Providence at the north end of the bay. Rhode Island is called the "Ocean State" because of this proximity to the sea. The early settlers, in fact, began their colony on an island in Narragansett Bay. The area of present-day Newport was discovered by the Italian explorer Verrazano in 1524, and in 1636 Providence became a haven for the religiously persecuted of the Massachusetts Bay Colony. Newport and Providence later became leading seaports in the early maritime trade.

Today Rhode Island is a marine playground for the people of the eastern United States, and Newport is a capital of the sailing world. Fishing, sailing, and beautiful seascapes are what a vacation by the country's most scenic warm-water beaches and harbors, in "Little Rhody," is all about.

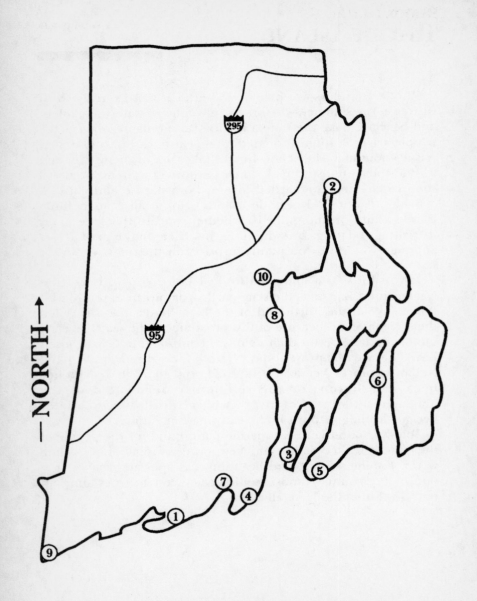

RHODE ISLAND

	🛏	🍴
1. Charlestown	34	—
2. East Providence	—	42
3. Jamestown	34	—
4. Narragansett	35	43
5. Newport	38	43
6. Portsmouth	—	45
7. Wakefield	—	45
8. Warwick	38	—
9. Westerly	39	46
10. Wickford	40	—

WHERE TO STAY

HATHAWAY'S
Route 1A, Box 731
Charlestown, Rhode Island 02813
(401) 364-6665

These immaculate cabins are probably the best buy of the area. They are roomy and have such amenities as air conditioning, television, and wall-to-wall carpeting. Located in a lovely, quiet spot with lawns and trees, near beaches, historic sites, and restaurants, Hathaway's is the perfect getaway for families. As guests, you receive beach passes to Charlestown beach, but you are also near Green Hill and East beaches. There are only seven cabins here, two of which are efficiencies, so you'll need to reserve space quite early in the season.

Average rates: Double occupancy price for two-room efficiency with stove and refrigerator, $330 per week, $50 per night; one-room cabin with full bath, $260 per week, $40 per night; one-room cabin with shower, $230 per week, $35 per night; $10 for extra person. *Credit cards:* MasterCard and Visa. *Open:* May 1 to October 15. *Owners:* The Cummings family. *Directions:* From Route 1, take the Cross Mills exit. Go south on Route 1A, and turn right at the end of the ramp. You'll see the big white farmhouse and cabins a few yards up on the left. *Children:* Yes. *Pets:* No. *Smoking:* Yes.

MARY W. MURPHY'S BED AND BREAKFAST
59 Walcott Avenue
Jamestown, Rhode Island 02835
(401) 423-1338

This is a beautiful two-story, twenty-five-year-old colonial bed & breakfast in one of the prettiest areas in New England. Farms line one side of the road leading into Jamestown, and the other side harbors a fascinating seascape with Block Island auto ferries, sailboats, and fishing trawlers making their way up and down

Narragansett Bay. This has been a popular house ever since Mary returned from England and decided she would use her extra bedrooms for tourists, now that her daughters are away from home. She really likes the companionship and sharing stories with her guests. There are three rooms available: one with a double bed, another with a queen-sized bed, and an extra-large room with two twin beds. Many antiques grace the eggshell-colored walls. The second floor, where the rooms are located, has a shared, tiled bath, which is kept very neat. All rooms share baths. Mary has recently built a new deck for sunning.

The complimentary full breakfast includes fruit or juice, eggs cooked in any style, bacon or sausage, Rhode Island johnnycake, cereal, and coffee, tea, or milk. It is served from about 8 to 9 A.M. No pets are allowed. Cribs and cots cost extra.

Average rates: Double, $50–$60; single, $45; 6 percent sales tax and 4 percent room tax. *Credit cards:* None. *Open:* May through September. *Owner:* Mary W. Murphy. *Directions:* In Narragansett, on Route 1A, turn east on Route 138 for the Jamestown bridge. Instead of going over the Newport bridge, bear right on Route 138 to Jamestown. The street becomes Walcott after you pass Narragansett Avenue on the left at the town wharf. Mary's B&B is ⅛ mile on the left past the town wharf and police station at the top of the hill. *Children:* Yes. *Pets:* No. *Smoking:* Yes.

ILVERTHORPE COTTAGE
41 Robinson Street
Narragansett, Rhode Island 02882
(401) 789-2392

Among the shady trees sits this 1885 Victorian house, built as a wedding present for Edgar Watt's wife, Jessie. The experienced and gracious hosts will make your stay here a pleasant one. Full breakfast with fresh fruits and homemade baked breads and muffins is served inside or on the sunny porch at separate tables, buffet style. There are four flower-filled bedrooms with fluffy pillows and restful colors. Both private and shared baths are available. The decor is Victorian, with antique dresses hanging in the hall, antique furniture all about, and bric-a-brac around the ground-floor fireplaces. Cots and cribs are also available.

Average rates: Double, $60–$70; single, $55–$65. *Credit cards:* None; personal checks accepted. *Open:* May through November. *Owners:* Chris and John Webb. *Directions:* Take Narragansett exit off Route 1. Turn left on Route 108 (Kingstown Road) at the rotary. One mile down, turn right at the traffic light onto Robinson Street. Number 41 is a gray Victorian, close to the road, on the right. *Children:* Yes. *Pets:* No. *Smoking:* On porch only.

MON REAVE
41 Gibson Avenue
Narragansett, Rhode Island 02882
(401) 783-2846

This National Register Victorian bed & breakfast is a consistent winner. Jim and Eva Doran will make you feel right at home and always entertained with pleasant conversation. Their home is tastefully decorated with elegant antiques, paintings and prints, and fresh flowers. The atmosphere is European. The sunporch with its view of a small fountain lends enchantment. Eva's culinary skills will amaze you—especially her presentations at breakfast. She is fluent in Italian and French, so European travelers may receive special guidance. The artist Florence Brevoort Kane lived here; she created many of the sculptures in Narragansett. The house is set on Gibson, a broad avenue that originally led to the polo field. Rooms are rented as suites to accommodate families. The third floor has two bedrooms, one with twin beds and one with a double bed, and one bath. The second floor has a similar arrangement. On the front porch are white wicker chairs and a swing. You might also like to lounge in the living room and look at the coffee-table-sized art books or take in some television in the drawing room. Bicycles are available.

Average rates: Double or twin, $55. *Credit cards:* None; personal checks accepted. *Open:* Year-round. *Owners:* Eva and Jim Doran. *Directions:* Take I-95 south to Route 4. Route 4 becomes Route 1. Take Route 1 south to Narragansett exit. Go 1 mile to stop light. Turn left on South Pier Road and proceed to the stop sign. Turn right onto Gibson. The B&B is two or three houses down on the right, at the corner of Westmoreland and Gibson. *Children:* Yes. *Pets:* No. *Smoking:* Restricted.

PLEASANT COTTAGE
104 Robinson Street
Narragansett, Rhode Island 02882
(401) 783-6895

This quaint cottage and year-round home looks small from the outside but spacious and cozy inside. Two rooms, one twin and one double with private or shared baths, are neat as a pin and beautifully decorated in bright colonial colors. A veranda with an umbrella table for relaxing with cool drinks is on the side of the dining room. Terry and Fred Sepp are pleasant hosts who used to live in Pleasantville, New York, but fell in love with Narragansett and decided to run a B&B here. They serve a full breakfast. An enclosed shower is outside for rinsing after a day at the beach. This B&B is in a quiet setting at the end of the street.

Average rates: $45–$55. *Credit cards:* None. *Open:* Year-round. *Owners:* Terry and Fred Sepp. *Directions:* On Route 1 from Boston, take the Narragansett exit. At the rotary, get onto Kingstown Road. Drive approximately 1½ miles to Robinson Street, and turn right. Proceed 3 blocks; it's the last house on the left. *Children:* Ten and over. *Pets:* No. *Smoking:* Restricted.

RICHARDS BED AND BREAKFAST
144 Gibson Avenue
Narragansett, Rhode Island 02882
(401) 789-7746

This three-storied, gabled 1885 stone home (nominated for the National Register of Historic Places) of a prominent Rhode Islander has been fashioned into a beautiful bed & breakfast by the Richards family, who had another B&B before this. The rooms are large and spacious. Elegance is the word here. Two of the rooms have canopy beds, while a third has an antique sleigh bed. This B&B offers private and shared baths, working fireplaces in some rooms, and a library to browse in. The real beauty here is that you find yourself in an English manor house with ivy-covered walls, being spoiled by the hosts, Nancy and Steve. They also serve a delicious gourmet breakfast; their strudels, roulades, and blintzes are terrific. All this at reasonable rates.

Average rates: Double, $55–$75. *Credit cards:* None; personal checks accepted. *Open:* Year-round. *Owners:* Nancy and Steven Richards. *Directions:* Come off I-95 to Narragansett via exit 92; follow Route 2 to Route 78 and Rhode Island beaches, Route 1. Then take the Narragansett exit to South Pier Road and go right. Take the second right at stop sign and the second left to Gibson. *Children:* Twelve and up. *Pets:* No. *Smoking:* Outdoors only.

CLOVER HILL GUEST HOUSE
32 Cranston Avenue
Newport, Rhode Island 02840
(401) 847-7094

This 1891 Victorian is off the beaten path and is reasonably priced by Newport standards. The rooms are neat and cozy. The downstairs has decorative wooden paneling, and a dining room fireplace and mantel that remind us of *Life With Father* days. There is one double and one twin guest room, both with shared bath. Television is available in one room. The wharf area with shops, restaurants, and a marina is easily accessible.

Average rates: In season, $80; off season, $70. *Credit cards:* None. *Open:* Year-round. *Owners:* June and Audrey Gallen. *Directions:* From Route 138, traveling east, take second exit after Newport bridge. Turn left up hill at light. At Broadway, where there are gas stations at each corner, turn right. Take the third left after Newport Hospital. About 200 yards up Cranston on the left, you'll see a brown house with a high hedge. *Children:* Yes. *Pets:* No. Cat and dog in residence. *Smoking:* No.

THE SUSSE CHALET INN
36 Jefferson Boulevard
Warwick, Rhode Island 02888
(401) 941-6600

This motel boasts friendly, courteous service. Its rooms are as neat as a pin and are thoughtfully laid out for the traveler's needs.

Each guest room has a bathroom with a shower, as well as a washstand outside the bathroom so that one person can wash up while the other is showering or taking a bath. A color television, telephone, table, two easy chairs, an overhead lamp, and wall-to-wall carpet make you feel comfortable. Why not, you have everything you need! There's even a pool for the youngsters at the end of the first-floor corridor. A washer and dryer are also available if you have been on the road for a while and want to "revitalize" your wardrobe or get the kids into something clean.

Average rates: Single, $44.70; double, $49.70; triple, $52.70. Children under five free. *Credit cards:* MasterCard, Visa, and American Express. *Open:* Year-round. *Managers:* Larry and Elaine Craig. *Directions:* Take exit 15 off I-95. Turn left at the stop sign onto Jefferson Boulevard. The Susse Chalet is at the top of the hill on the left. *Children:* Yes. *Pets:* No. *Smoking:* Smoking rooms available; nonsmoking rooms on third floor.

BLUE STAR MOTOR INN
110 Post Road
Westerly, Rhode Island 02891
(401) 596-2891; (800) 543-8429

This motel is located right on Route 1, convenient to Mystic Seaport and the great beaches of Rhode Island. Its star attraction is a pretty, oval pool. The rooms are of different sizes, the standard ones being small, clean, and adequate. The large rooms have two double beds. All rooms have a color television. The best bargains are the larger family rooms, as children twelve and under stay for free. In July and August, complimentary coffee is offered. For a stay of five days or more you can get weekday rates. In the summer, a minimum two-day stay is required on weekends. Inquire for summer specials.

Average rates: Mid-June to Labor Day: double, $65 weekdays, $75–$90 weekends. Off season: $43 weekdays, $53 weekends; $10 extra person. *Credit Cards:* MasterCard, Visa, American Express, and Discover. *Open:* All year. *Owners:* Jerry and Connie Martell. The manager is Esther Wait. *Directions:* From I-95 north, take exit 92. Go right on Route 2 and drive 1 mile, left on Route 78 and go to the light, and left again on Route 1. The motel is ¾ mile farther on the left. *Children:* Yes. *Pets:* No. *Smoking:* Yes.

THE JOHN UPDIKE HOUSE
19 Pleasant Street
Wickford, Rhode Island 02852
(401) 294-4905

This beautiful colonial bed & breakfast built in 1745 has two rooms with access to a lovely, large deck that overlooks beautiful Wickford Harbor and Narragansett Bay. You get a private living room, semi-private bath, continental breakfast with fresh fruit and baked goods, and, best of all, you can walk to your own private beach in the back yard! You will find Wickford quaint and picturesque, a good place to tarry a while, and a painter's paradise. The Sabos will make sure you enjoy your stay in this lovely New England village.

Average rates: $75–$85; private kitchen is available at extra charge, and you can reserve both rooms as a suite. *Credit cards:* None; personal checks accepted. *Open:* Year-round. *Owners:* Mary Anne and William Sabo. *Directions:* Going south on I-95, exit onto Route 403. There is a sign posted to North Kingston, Davisville. Go south on U.S. Route 1, and follow Route 1A through Wickford to Main Street. At the last left on Main, turn left onto Pleasant Street. It's the second house on the right, a two-story off-white house with a hip roof and gable with a white fence. *Children:* Yes. *Pets:* No. *Smoking:* Restricted.

THE MORAN'S
130 West Main Street
Wickford, Rhode Island 02852
(401) 294-3497

This is a cozy two-story home with two rooms, one twin-bedded, the other a double, both sharing a bath. The decor is a mixture of early American and Victorian. There is a picnic table in the back yard for summer meals. Shops are within walking distance. A full breakfast including scrambled eggs and more will get you off to a good start. There is off-street parking. You will love this place because of its charm and its location in the scenic historic district—a good place to sample Yankee hospitality. Ed and Grace Moran recommend **Jeremiah's** in North Kingstown for a reasonable meal.

Average rates: Double or twin, $60; breakfast included. *Credit cards:* None; personal checks for deposit only. *Open:* All year. *Owners:* Ed and Grace Moran. *Directions:* Follow directions for the John Updike House into Wickford, from the traffic light at the junction of routes 1 and 1A. It's ⅛ mile farther on the right. *Children:* Eleven and older. *Pets:* No. *Smoking:* Yes, but restricted.

WHERE TO EAT

GREGG'S
1940 Pawtucket Avenue
East Providence, Rhode Island 02914
(401) 438-5700

Pies, Black Forest cakes, and strawberries piled high with whipped cream greet you when you enter Gregg's. This restaurant even mesmerizes you with a rotating pastry case five shelves high. Oh, temptation! If you get by the calorie traps, then you're in for a good meal. There is a great variety of salads, dinner favorites, club sandwiches, New York–style deli sandwiches (Reubens, melts, carved roast beef, and turkey). We had the meatloaf special, the baked haddock, and the fettucine Alfredo when we were there. The meatloaf was tasty with liver mixed through it, and it was served with a generous portion of real mashed potatoes and gravy. You can also order macaroni or spaghetti. You get a large, freshly tossed garden salad and a choice of five or six dressings. You may also have a dish of half-sour deli pickles. One interesting feature is that they serve a breakfast menu from noon to closing at 1 A.M. You can also take out anything on the menu including whole pies and cakes, from the takeout shop.

There is another Gregg's in Warwick, Rhode Island, at 1390 Post Road. To reach it, take exit 14 off I-95 and bear left on Route 37. Circle onto Pawtucket Avenue, and Gregg's is on the left after you pass under the overpass. The telephone number is (401) 467-5908. Another Gregg's is located at 1303 North Main Street in Providence; the telephone number there is (401) 831-5900.

Average prices: For lunch, sandwiches of all types and sizes range up to $5. Italian specialties average around $6. Dinner entrees run up to $11, with most items under $8. Pastry desserts, such as slices of homemade pie and cake, are just over $1 a slice. (All contain natural ingredients.) *Credit cards:* MasterCard, Visa, and American Express. *Hours:* Open year-round every day, 11:30 A.M. to 1 A.M. Closed Thanksgiving and Christmas. *Owner:* Ted Fuller. *Directions:* Going west on I-195, take Route 114 north. Turn right on Route 44 and follow it until you come to the junction with Pawtucket

Avenue. Gregg's is at the northeast corner of this intersection. It's surrounded by two shopping centers.

SPAIN RESTAURANT
1 Beach Road
Narragansett, Rhode Island 02882
(401) 783-9770

This popular restaurant has a circular dining room with a view of the bay. Handsome, young Spanish and Portuguese men in black pants and white shirts scurry about to provide that hovering European service. Paella was served with lots of mussels, shrimp, and scallops in saffron rice topped with half a lobster. Hard-crusted bread, soft on the inside, made our meals memorable. Portions are huge. Meats and poultry dishes are done in Spanish style. An extensive selection of wines is offered. Blue tablecloths and white napkins complement the seaside environment. Strolling minstrels entertained with Spanish songs the night we were there.

Average prices: Lunch, $7–$12; dinner $10–$17. *Credit cards:* All major. *Hours:* Lunch, noon–3 P.M.; dinner, noon–10 P.M.; Friday and Saturday, open until 11 P.M. *Owners:* Felix Rodriguez and Jose Gomes. *Directions:* Take Kingstown Road into Narragansett. Restaurant is in back of Village Inn (hotel), a gray building after the Texaco station, on the left. Free parking on ocean side of inn.

THE MARINA PUB
Goat Island
Newport, Rhode Island 02840
(401) 846-2675

This is where the sailors and yachtsmen hang out when they want some serious grub on the beach. You can wet your whistle at the copper-covered bar or relax at a table. It's informal. Lunch items include a variety of sandwiches, salads, and grills. The dinner menu offers baked and fried fish and shellfish, seafood casserole, steak, and chicken. Large omelets and egg dishes are available for brunch.

Average prices: Lunch, $6–$7; dinner, $7–$15. *Credit cards:* MasterCard, Visa, and American Express. *Hours:* Every day, 11:30 A.M.–10:30 P.M. *Owner:* Greg Gamon. *Directions:* Follow signs to Goat Island. Go over causeway bridge. Turn left at Doubletree Hotel. Look for the building with "U.S. Yacht Racing Union" on it. The pub is on the ground floor of the building's west end.

NEWPORT CREAMERY
46 Long Wharf Mall
Newport, Rhode Island 02840
(401) 849-8469

Thanks to this restaurant, families can visit the expensive town of Newport. A very pleasant place inside, it has dozens of reasonable dishes to choose from, including sandwiches, seafood platters, salads, and breakfasts. Ice cream is their star attraction. It is served in all the imagined styles and is extra creamy and good! Menus for kiddies and dieters are available too. We liked the clam chowder and had terrific coffee here.

There is another Newport Creamery at 181 Bellevue Avenue in Newport, and also one in Warwick, with the same prices.

Average prices: Sandwiches, mostly $2–$5. Fish dinner is $5; fried clams are $5. Sundaes served on Sunday have a special price. *Credit cards:* None. *Hours:* In season, every day, 7 A.M. to 11 P.M.; off season, every day 7 A.M. to 9:30 P.M. *Manager:* Joe Baccaro. *Directions:* From Route 138, take the exit for downtown Newport. Follow that street, then take the second right, go around the bend, and make a left at the second light into Long Wharf parking area. Parking is free; your ticket will be validated at the restaurant.

REIDY'S FAMILY RESTAURANT
3351 East Main Road
Portsmouth, Rhode Island 02871
(401) 683-9802

Reidy's, established in 1971, is on the way to Newport before you hit the big prices. A yellow front with black lettering marks the spot, and you can tell by a crowd of local license plates that this is where the locals eat. We had breakfast here one morning. They offer heaping portions of whatever kind of breakfast you want, including chourico, corned beef hash with dropped eggs (Frank's favorite), S.O.S., or whatever your heart desires. Families make chitchat about local happenings and willingly give you directions to the locations of events in the Newport area. You can also get seafood here and the usual—and unusual—plates, chowders, and sandwiches. Baked goods, especially muffins, are a specialty. Some of the waitresses have worked here nine to twelve years or more. That says something about a well-run restaurant!

Average prices: Breakfasts from $2 to $4 with omelets the most expensive. Lunches and dinners of soups and stews (beef or kale) cost under $3 for a large bowl. Turkey with dressing, French meat pie, steak sandwich, and American chop suey are all around $5. Fried or baked haddock is $5, and fried clams and shrimp are $5 and $6, respectively. *Credit cards:* None. *Hours:* Monday, Tuesday, and Wednesday, 6 A.M. to 2 P.M.; Thursday and Friday, 6 A.M. to 7 P.M.; Saturday 6 A.M. to 4 P.M.; Sunday, 6 A.M. to 12:30 P.M. *Owners:* Steve and Dora Reidy. *Directions:* Take Route 24 south from Fall River. Turn off onto Route 138. Drive about 1½ miles, and Reidy's is on your left at the top of the hill.

108 HOUSE RESTAURANT
515 Kingston Road
Wakefield, Rhode Island 02879
(401) 783-0008

This family restaurant, dressed in brass and copper, has fine casual dining. The cooks put on a good show for the diners at their open-hearth grill right in the dining room. Choose from fifty items and check out the Blackboard Specials every day. They serve a wide range of dishes to accommodate all types of eaters, from the soup and salad eater to the large-steak lovers. The Baked Stuffed Lobster has the highest price on the menu, and burgers have the lowest. Breakfast, lunch, and dinner are served every day.

Average prices: Most dinners cost between $12 and $17 (for example, baked scallops, fried clams, and open tenderloin steak); burgers are about $3. *Credit cards:* Visa and MasterCard. *Hours:* All year, seven days a week. Weekdays and Sundays, 7 A.M.–10 P.M.; Friday and Saturday, 7 A.M.–11 P.M. *Owners:* Jack and Denise Sirrano. *Head Chef:* Pat Brown. *Directions:* From Route 1, take the Wakefield exit; go north 1 mile. The restaurant is on the right on Route 108 in downtown Wakefield.

FORTUNA'S
140 Franklin Plaza
Westerly, Rhode Island 02891
(401) 596-1883

This is one of the most fantastic Italian delicatessen-restaurants we have ever eaten in. Though small in size, it offers ample tables for dining. There is cafeteria-style dining on one side of the display cases, while the other side of the serving counter has cold cuts, salads, and the retail part of the business. The Roman sculptures, set high on the walls, add to the Italian spirit of the place.

But the food is where Fortuna's excels. They have a rich array of pastas with an equally long list of "add ons." Veal and eggplant parmigiana, sausages, meatballs, and more fill the menu. Heroes (we call them subs) are served hot or cold in twelve-inch, over-stuffed portions. Breakfast specials are also available for ridiculously low prices. The Friday night special is shrimp and scallops or shrimp scampi over spaghetti. Try this place—you won't believe the prices. For the teenagers or young people with insatiable appetites, there is always plenty to eat. Takeouts are available. Breakfast is served until 11:30 A.M.

Average prices: Breakfast, $1 to $4. Lunch: hot dishes (lunch-size), under $4; super size, $5; salad, $2; soup, under $2. *Credit cards:* None. *Hours:* In season: Monday to Thursday, 8 A.M.–8 P.M.;

Friday and Saturday, 7 A.M.–9 P.M.; Sunday, 7 A.M.–6 P.M.; off season: 8 A.M.–8 P.M.; Sunday, 8 A.M.–5 P.M. *Owners:* Paul and Patti Stannard. *Manager:* Mary Dugan. *Directions:* Take Connecticut exit 92 (off I-95) south toward Westerly. Then go left on Route 78, which circles Westerly, for 4 to 5 miles. Turn right on Route 1. The Franklin Plaza shopping center is about ¾ of a mile on your right. Fortuna's is at the back of the array of shops parallel to Route 1.

Also recommended:

Both these restaurants in North Kingston (Wickford is a hamlet in this town) are worth a visit: **The Carriage Inn,** at (401) 294-2727, and the **Red Rooster,** at (401) 295-8804. The latter has a good selection of wines. Both serve moderately priced entrees.

MASSACHUSETTS

Massachusetts offers not only rich historical settings of early American life, but also varied recreation provided by its ocean beaches and extensive coastline, cultural centers, and the Berkshire mountains. The state has been able to preserve its countryside and traditions in the face of a highly successful high-tech industry. Visitors to Massachusetts feel they are living in two worlds—the present and the past—blended in a special way of life.

Boston is an exciting city to visit because of its mix of the old and new, but it is an expensive city to stay in. If you want to be immersed in the city, it pays to seek out the inexpensive tourist and bed & breakfast homes that we have listed. The alternative is to stay in the suburbs and travel into the city by train. You won't want your car in Boston because of the many one-way streets. There's very little in the way of inexpensive parking, so it is advisable to leave your car parked outside of town and take the MBTA (the transit authority train) into Boston.

If you stay in Brookline, you'll be near the MBTA green line, which is a direct route into the city. Or you can stay farther out in Lexington or Bedford and drive to the Riverside Station on Route 128, the major highway that rings Boston, and take the MBTA into the city. It's about a twenty-five-minute ride. Staying in these towns affords you the opportunity to explore them— their houses and history—on the days when you don't want to be in Boston. Cambridge is another possibility. The MBTA red line takes you quickly into Boston, and you can see the Harvard Square area while you are in Cambridge.

Another town to stay in while visiting the area is Salem. This town is very historic and offers lots to see, as well as good restaurants and accommodations—an excellent choice for a base for launching visits to Boston. The Boston and Maine Railroad carries passengers to North Station in Boston for a moderate cost. This links up with the MBTA that takes you to all parts of the city.

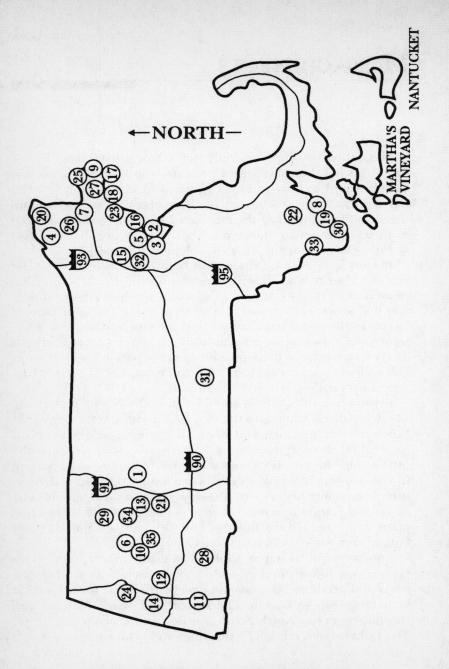

NANTUCKET

MARTHA'S
VINEYARD

←—NORTH—→

MASSACHUSETTS

	🛏	🍴
1. Amherst	—	79
2. Boston	54	80
3. Brookline	57	—
4. Byfield	57	—
5. Cambridge	58	83
6. Cummington	59	—
7. Essex	60	84
8. Fairhaven	—	85
9. Gloucester	—	86
10. Goshen	—	88
11. Great Barrington	61	—
12. Lee	—	88
13. Leeds	—	89
14. Lenox	62	—
15. Lexington	63	90
16. Lynn	—	91
17. Manchester	64	—
18. Marblehead	64	92
19. New Bedford	—	92
20. Newburyport	65	93
21. Northampton	67	—
22. North Dartmouth	68	—
23. Peabody	—	97
24. Pittsfield	68	98
25. Rockport	69	99
26. Rowley	—	101
27. Salem	72	102
28 Sandisfield	75	—
29. Shelburne Falls	—	105
30. South Dartmouth	—	106
31. Sturbridge	76	107
32. Waltham	—	110
33. Westport	—	111
34. Williamsburg	77	—
35. Worthington	77	—

An alternative for North Shore locations is to park your car at the Riverside Station in Revere, near the Wonderland Dog Racing Track, and take the MBTA blue line into the city. This takes less time than taking the B&M from Salem.

Salem is a city of fascination and beauty. Tales of witches and their evil spells hang about the city, but, above all, as you visit the antique wooden homes and old streets with patches of cobblestone, you'll get a real sense of what the colony was like 350 years ago. Other towns along the North Shore are equally interesting. Newburyport boasts superb captain's homes on High Street, and the town's interesting waterfront has a personality all its own. A whole section of State Street and Water Street has been renovated to reveal the beauty and elegance of Newburyport's colonial and federalist past.

Gloucester and Rockport, sister cities on the tip of Cape Ann, are somewhat isolated from the rest of the North Shore and are very different from each other in character. Rockport is more tourist-oriented, with shops, antiques, art galleries, quaint little streets, and harbor scenery. Gloucester is its working counterpart, with fishing fleets and Gorton's Fish Factory stealing the show. It has many pleasant sites to visit, and the Annisquam River offers many lovely boating scenes you'll want to paint or photograph.

To the south are Plymouth, known for Plymouth Rock and Plimouth Plantation, and New Bedford. New Bedford's situation at the mouth of the Acushnet River and on protected Buzzards Bay has contributed to its having the largest fishing fleet on the East Coast today. It has always been a fishing community and once was the whaling center of the world; today fishing brings the city over $80 million a year! New Bedford's entire downtown area has been handsomely renovated and deserves a visit. The Dartmouth-area towns also provide inexpensive places to stay.

In just about the center of the state, you'll find the beautiful town of Sturbridge, widely famous for its re-created Old Sturbridge Village. Sturbridge is lovely in its own right and offers much to see and do. And to the west are the small towns of the Berkshires, one of the prettiest areas of New England, with old country charm and many towns not yet discovered by tourists. Highlights of this part of the state include Lenox, summer home of the famous Boston Symphony Orchestra, nearby Lee, where the Jacob's Pillow dance festival is held each year, and West Stockbridge, the home of Norman Rockwell.

WHERE TO STAY

THE EMMA JAMES HOUSE
47 Ocean Street
Boston, Massachusetts 02124
(617) 288-8867; 282-5350

This lovely 1894 Victorian is situated on Ashmont Hill in Dorchester. It belonged to a very rich leather merchant and has been restored to its earlier splendor. The woodwork and stained glass in the large entry hall and ascending staircase are impressive. The six rooms are large. Two have private baths, four share baths. A spacious parlor, cozy oak-paneled sitting room with a television, sunny dining room, and adjacent kitchen are available for your relaxation and enjoyment. Sit on the porch to read the paper or enjoy a second cup of coffee. A substantial "help yourself" breakfast is provided. The kitchen is available to guests for light meals and snacks. This B&B serves as an excellent base of operations for getting to sights in Boston, including the JFK Library and Bayside Exposition Center. The red line of the MBTA is a few minutes' walk and it whisks you quickly downtown.

Average rates: Double, $50–$70; single, $40–$60. *Credit cards:* None. *Open:* All year. *Owners:* Vicki Rugo and Moo Bishop. *Directions:* Call ahead for reservations and you will be sent the directions. *Children:* Yes, all ages. *Pets:* No. *Smoking:* Yes, but restricted.

FLORENCE FRANCES
458 Park Drive
Boston, Massachusetts 02215
(617) 267-2458

Florence Frances has a beautiful 120-year-old brick house with rooms like pages out of *House Beautiful* or *Better Homes and Gardens*. Miss Frances is a warm and friendly lady and an interior decorator who makes you feel right at home. There is the Spanish room in red and black, the Carousel room in red and white, and the Gold Stripe room with a Windsor desk and a fireplace. One double and three singles are available. There is a radio or television in each room. All have shared baths. Guests may relax in the sumptuous living room with gorgeous carved fireplaces and an antique crystal chandelier. A beautiful basement kitchen in green and white with hanging plants is available to guests for light meals. No pets or small children are allowed because of the antiques. Parking is available behind the house at no charge.

The house is across from the MBTA Riverside D train stop and near the MBTA Cleveland Circle stop. Also, you are within walking distance of Fenway Park where the Boston Red Sox baseball team plays its home games. Don't be amazed to find a surprise on your pillow from Miss Frances when you turn in after a busy day of sightseeing.

Average rates: Double, $60; single, $50. Owner prefers a reservation with a check for one night as a deposit. *Credit cards:* None. *Open:* Year-round. *Owner:* Florence Frances. *Directions:* From Kenmore Square, take Beacon Street to Park Drive (church on left). Go left, and the house is on the right near the end of the block. *Children:* No. *Pets:* No. *Smoking:* Yes.

NORTHEAST HALL RESIDENCE
204 Bay State Road
Boston, Massachusetts 02215
(617) 267-3042

Northeast Hall Residence is not a dorm but a private guest home with ten rooms. It's very nice and cozy with an attractive parlor-living room with a television where guests can relax in front of the fireplace. There is a shared bath on every level and a sink in each room. A tea tray is set on a table in each room, so you can make your own continental breakfast. Parking is available in the rear for two cars. This is a good lodging place for students.

Average rates: Double, $30; single, $20; room with three single beds, $35. *Credit cards:* None. *Open:* Summer only. *Owner:* Mrs. Caroline Muzichuk. (Mrs. Muzichuk has a hearing loss; you must speak loudly when you call.) *Directions:* From Kenmore Square, go west on Commonwealth Avenue about 2 blocks to Sherbourne

Road (just past the Texaco station). Turn right and go to Bay State Road. The Northeast Hall Residence is 2 blocks up on the left. *Children:* Yes. *Pets:* No. *Smoking:* Yes.

"23 CUMBERLAND STREET" BED AND BREAKFAST
23 Cumberland Street
Boston, Massachusetts 02115
(617) 267-5973

This brick-and-brownstone in the center of Boston is a fun place to stay in large part because of the humorous hosts, the Burnses. Bill Burns told us that his decor was "antiques and late attic" and that the old portraits on the wall are all relatives, not from a secondhand shop. All three rooms in this Victorian house have walk-in closets. One room has a double, a twin bed, and a charming sitting area in the bow front. Another room, in the back, has air conditioning. These two rooms share a bath and are decorated in oranges and dark reds. Downstairs with a private entrance is the Patio Room with a Murphy bed (it folds up into the wall), rattan furniture, a Spanish-style patio, and an herb garden. This room has a private bath, cable television, and kitchenette. "Creative continental" breakfasts are served with fresh ground restaurant coffee and sherry. Hard candy is placed in all the guest rooms.

Average rates: $70, $75, and $80 for two people. *Credit cards:* None. *Open:* All year. *Owners:* Nancy and Bill Burns. *Directions:* This house is on a dead-end street off St. Botolph's and not far from Symphony Hall. We suggest you call for directions or ask for a copy of their very precise directions from the north, south, and west and from the airport. *Children:* Yes. *Pets:* No. *Smoking:* No.

Note: For Boston visits, see also the Brookline and Cambridge lodgings. They are just as handy, since you can travel very easily to any part of Boston by MBTA from these cities.

BEACON STREET GUEST HOUSE
1047 Beacon Street
Brookline, Massachusetts 02146
(617) 232-0292

Beacon Street Guest House is close to Boston on the green line. There are fourteen attractively decorated rooms, eleven with private baths. One of the twin-bedded rooms is a spacious front room containing an intricately hand-carved fireplace and desk—tastefully decorated. (Fireplaces cannot be used.) Coffee, tea, fruit juice, and pastries are served. Parking is not available. In the basement is a kitchen for guests. In another room are a washer and dryer (coin-operated) and an ironing board. Across the street, the Busy Bee opens at 6:00 A.M. for breakfast.

Average rates: Double: $55–$65 in season; $45–$55 in winter. *Credit cards:* All major. *Open:* All year. *Owner:* Harold Parritz. *Manager:* Sandra Johnson. *Directions:* From Kenmore Square, take Beacon Street to Brookline. *Children:* Yes. *Pets:* Yes, with deposit. *Smoking:* Yes.

Also recommended:

The **Beacon Plaza** at 1459 Beacon Street in Brookline is a neat house with spacious rooms (forty of them). They are quite inexpensive, most with private bath and television. Call Mrs. Pappas at (617) 232-6550.

RAMBLING ROSE BED AND BREAKFAST AND ANTIQUES
4 Forest Street
Byfield, Massachusetts 01922
(508) 462-9143; (508) 463-0067

This charming 1826 colonial home is located in the heart of Olde Byfield Centre, site of the old Red Top Snuff Mill, and just one minute from I-95 and forty minutes north of Boston. Nestled in a wonderful country setting, bordered by a brook and willow trees, from this B&B you can walk to the village store, library, or post office or to the intriguing Snuff Mill with its stream and waterfall. The house, behind a rose-covered white picket fence, invites you to step back in time and admire the antiques, braided rugs, collections of cobalt and cranberry glass, art, and Marcia's photography. Each room has been tastefully decorated by Jean, who clearly has a flair for interior design.

A full breakfast is served in the elegant dining room with a fireplace or the large deck overlooking the perennial gardens in the back yard. The rose living room is a quiet place to enjoy the fireplace, relax, read, do puzzles, or play games. Ideal for summer or winter activities, this is a perfect place to rest on your way to Maine or New Hampshire and it is only minutes from the beaches of Plum Island and historic Newburyport. Antique lovers can start right in the hosts' Antique Barn and meander to countless shops in all directions.

Average rates: Double, $60 plus tax; single, $50. *Credit Cards:* None. *Open:* All year. *Owners:* Marcia Burnham and Jean Vrettos. *Directions:* From I-95, take exit 55. Follow Central Street to Byfield center, then go left on Main Street and right on Forest Street. The house is second on right, with a white picket fence. *Children:* Over 6. *Pets:* No. *Smoking:* No.

A CAMBRIDGE HOUSE, BED AND BREAKFAST
2218 Massachusetts Avenue
Cambridge, Massachusetts 02140
(617) 491-6300; (800) 232-9989

We visited this house at Christmastime when it looked especially beautiful, but this 1892 restored colonial is a feast for the eyes at any time. Elegantly flowered walls are draped with matching material around doorways, and the marvelous carved fireplaces are a delight. Classical music is played softly in the double living rooms. A cared-for feeling pervades, with coffee and cookies served all day and a large staff prepared to help you with directions. The rooms are exquisitely furnished. You'll find canopy beds with European down duvets and many mirrors. Each room has a vanity. Some rooms have private and some have shared baths; one bath has a sunken tub. Some folks return here for sumptuous breakfasts of fresh-squeezed orange juice, fresh fruit, and asparagus omelet or eggs Benedict. Located in the Porter Square area, this B&B is near a bus stop; and you can walk to the subway in two and a half minutes. Free off-street parking is provided. This is a perfect place to stay while visiting Boston, as well as Cambridge. These rates might seem high but you get your money's worth in elegance.

Average rates: Double: May to December, $80–$185; off-season, $69–$135. *Credit cards:* MasterCard, Visa, and American Express. *Open:* All year. *Owners:* Ellen Riley and Tony Femmino. *Manager:* Joyce Kerrigan. *Directions:* From Route 95 (128), take Route 2 toward Boston for about 8 miles; go left on Route 16 and drive for about ¾ mile; then go right on Massachusetts Avenue and proceed about a mile. The house, a yellow colonial with green trim, is on the right just past a Catholic church. *Children:* Over six. *Pets:* Seeing Eye dogs only. *Smoking:* Restricted.

CUMWORTH FARM BED AND BREAKFAST
R.R. 1, Box 110
Cummington, Massachusetts 01026
(413) 634-5529

Cumworth Farm is a grand place for families! This working mountain farm has a sugar house and a red barn in the back with sheep. When we arrived, the hosts, Ed and Mary, were across the street with their children, sawing wood for the maple-sugar stove. We were warmly welcomed into their big farm kitchen to chat over fresh coffee. The six bedrooms all share baths, and guests are welcome to use the living room and family room. We chose the room with the antique sleighbed and slept under blankets made from the wool of the hosts' own sheep! Two rooms use fireplaces and wood stoves for heat—quite rustic.

This lovely two-hundred-year-old colonial farmhouse, a vision of Currier & Ives, will charm you. Children are welcome and anyone can help with farm chores. In the summer, you can fish in the brook and swim in the hole at the Creamery on Route 9. You can also pick your own blueberries and raspberries in season. Our visit was in winter. We had the most inspired cross-country ski tour of our lives just behind the farm the next morning, over hill and dale and unplowed roads, and along a river. It was beautiful! The farm is open to guests all year except Christmas.

Average rates: Double, $50; extra cot in room, $10. Full breakfast can include homemade breads and muffins; eggs; and slab bacon, ham, or sausage. Or try pancakes with homemade maple syrup! *Credit cards:* None. *Open:* All year. *Owners:* Ed and Mary McColgan. *Directions:* Take Route 9 to Cummington, turn onto Route 112, and head south for 3.4 miles. You'll see a white farmhouse on the right with a sugar house beside it. *Children:* Yes. *Pets:* No. *Smoking:* No.

THE GEORGE FULLER HOUSE
148 Main Street
Essex, Massachusetts 01929
(508) 768-7766

This is a gray 1830 Federalist house with white trim in historic Essex, a colonial shipbuilding center between Ipswich and Gloucester. Six lovely rooms, decorated with period antiques and equipped with private bath, television, and phone, let you relax in this quiet but scenic village. You can choose the brass bed or canopy bed dressed in soft colors like mauve and white or sand and light blue, and wake up to a hearty full breakfast in the morning. Set aside time to explore the more than fifty antique shops in the area. The inn is AAA-approved.

Average rates: Double, $70–$100 ($10 less from November to May). *Credit cards:* All major. *Open:* All year. *Owners:* Cindi and Bob Cameron. *Directions:* Take I–95 north to exit 45, and follow Route 128 to Gloucester. Take exit 15 (School Street, Manchester and Essex). Go left at the stop sign and proceed to the end of the road at Route 133. Turn left. Three houses past the Gulf station on the right is the Fuller House. *Children:* Yes. *Pets:* No. *Smoking:* Restricted.

ELLING'S GUEST HOUSE
250 Maple Avenue (Route 23)
R.D. 3, Box 6
Great Barrington, Massachusetts 01230
(413) 528-4103

This very large rambling 1740s home overlooks fifty acres of cornfields against a backdrop of purple mountains. It's a great place to enjoy birds, flowers, and the company of very interesting people, some from other countries. You can chat with others over the complimentary breakfast buffet, which includes fruit, hot muffins or biscuits, jam, and all the coffee you want while sitting on the porch, in the dining room, or in the guest parlor by the fireplace. The rooms are large and decorated with period antiques. You can try a swing on the long rope in the front yard, play badminton or horseshoes in the field, or swim in the river nearby. Jo and Ray have run this house for sixteen years, and they say that June through October is their high season, so you should reserve way ahead.

Average rates: From June through October and on holidays: double with shared bath, $70; double with private bath, $85. November through May: double with shared bath, $55; double with private bath, $65. Extra person in room is $10. Two-night minimum stay in July, August, on holidays, and during fall foliage season. *Credit cards:* None. *Open:* All year. *Owners:* Ray and Jo Elling. *Directions:* From New York City, take the Taconic State Parkway north to Route 23 east. From Boston, take the Massachusetts Turnpike to exit 2 in Lee. Take Route 102 south to Route 7 south to Great Barrington. Maple Avenue is about a mile from the town center. *Children:* Over twelve. *Pets:* No. *Smoking:* Restricted.

LITTLEJOHN MANOR
1 Newsboy Monument Lane
Great Barrington, Massachusetts 01230
(413) 528-2882

This delightful bed & breakfast provides an excellent bucolic setting within range of many tourist attractions in the Tanglewood region, including numerous summer-stock theaters. There are four rooms, one with a king-sized bed, couch, and working fireplace. A full gourmet English breakfast is served with extras such as broiled tomatoes, mushrooms, homemade muffins, and homemade preserves. The beautiful grounds with their south lawn garden and surrounding mountains are idyllic. Two rooms share a bath, but all the guest rooms are handsomely decorated.

Average rates: $60–$80 per couple with breakfast. Off-season and weekday rates are less. *Credit cards:* None. *Open:* All year. *Owners:* Herb Littlejohn, Jr. and Paul A. Dufour. *Directions:* Take Route 23 south out of Great Barrington. Directly behind the Newsboy monument on the left you'll see the building, which is off-white with red trim. (Elling's is farther down on the right.) *Children:* No. *Pets:* No. *Smoking:* Yes, except in the dining room.

BROOK FARM INN
15 Hawthorne Street
Lenox, Massachusetts 01240
(413) 637-3013

Brook Farm Inn was named by a descendant of Emerson after the writer's Utopian community. It is a lovely Victorian home. The new owners, the Jacobs, have a 1,000-volume collection of poetry and other good literature, and they encourage guests to borrow the books and mail them back when through. The two common rooms, with fireplaces, are elegant, and afternoon tea with scones is served in the library. A full breakfast of fresh-squeezed orange juice, homemade granola, yogurt, fresh fruits, homemade muffins, sticky buns, bagels, cream cheese, and jams and jellies is served with coffee (regular or decaffeinated) or tea. Third-floor rooms are air-conditioned. Tanglewood is very near. You may enjoy the heated pool in summer.

Average rates: Double, $55–$155. *Credit cards:* MasterCard and Visa. *Open:* All year except Monday, Tuesday, and Wednesday from November 1 to May 1. *Owners:* Bob and Betty Jacob. *Directions:* From the Massachusetts Pike take exit 2 to Route 20W and then Route 7N. Proceed to the TO LENOX CENTER sign. Turn left, continue to the monument, and turn left again. At the bottom of the hill turn right, and Brook Farm is 100 yards to the left. *Children:* Over twelve. *Pets:* No. *Smoking:* No.

BATTLE GREEN MOTOR INN
1720 Massachusetts Avenue
Lexington, Massachusetts 02173
(617) 862-6100 (in Lexington); (800) 322-1066 (in rest of Massachusetts); (800) 343-0235 (outside Massachusetts)

Battle Green Motor Inn is a large motel buried amidst the smart shops of downtown Lexington. The rooms are neatly decorated and recently remodeled, and there's a heated underground garage and a pool in an interior courtyard. Doughnuts and coffee are available in the lobby at no charge. If you want to see the Lexington Green, where the Revolutionary War began, or to visit nearby Concord and the "Rude Bridge," this is a strategic lodging place. The Pewter Pot Restaurant, which specializes in muffins and coffee, is next door; Mario's is across the street; and Goodies, a gourmet takeout, is a few doors down Massachusetts Avenue. The special features include laundry facilities. This inn is AAA-recommended. Efficiencies are also available.

Average rates: Double, $59–$64; a small amount extra for children, cots, and cribs. *Credit cards:* MasterCard, Visa, American Express, Diner's Club, and Discover. *Open:* All year. *Owner:* Michael Hanafin. *Directions:* From Route 128, take exit 31A south to Lexington center. It is 500 yards past the Lexington green on the right. *Children:* Yes. *Pets:* Yes. *Smoking:* Yes.

Also recommended:

The **Wayside Inn** in Sudbury will interest folks as a place to stay. Although rebuilt, it retains all of its colonial charm, and it's great fun knowing that Longfellow, a U.S. president, and other famous men stayed there over one hundred years ago. A gift shop and lovely restaurant are there, too. The food is priced moderately high, but they've managed to keep room prices at a reasonable level. This establishment deserves a visit whether you stay or not. It's on the old stagecoach Route 20, very much in the country. The telephone number is (617) 443-8846.

THE OLD CORNER INN
2 Harbor Street
Manchester, Massachusetts 01944
(508) 526-4996

The Old Corner Inn is a good suggestion for people who want to see Gloucester and Rockport but would like to stay in a community with fewer tourists. This elegant Victorian manse, built in 1865, was for thirty years the Danish summer embassy at the turn of the century when Manchester was a diplomatic community. You step right into the attractive living room decorated in dark reds and blues, with fine European lace curtains. In the winter, you may enjoy a drink around the fireplace while lounging on the baroque velvet couch. The rooms are pleasant, with soft, flowered wallpaper and carpeting of muted colors. They have private baths. Just 2 blocks up Harbor Street to the left is Tuck's Point, offering a beach, sailing, fishing, picnicking, and best of all, a view of the quiet inner harbor. In the summer, the inn provides daily rides to Singing Beach, one of the prettiest beaches along this coast of fine sand that hums as you walk in it. In the summer only, a complimentary continental breakfast of coffee and rolls is served at the inn.

Average rates: Double, $50–$95. *Credit cards:* All major. *Open:* All year. *Owner:* David Bush. *Directions:* From Route 128, take the Pine Street exit to where it ends, and turn right on Central Street (Route 127). The inn is about a mile farther on the left. *Children:* Yes. *Pets:* No. *Smoking:* Yes.

THE GOLDEN COD
26 Pond Street
Marblehead, Massachusetts 01945
(617) 631-1846

A delightful B&B with two rooms awaits you in the quaint "old town" section where colonial houses are crowded along narrow streets. A quiet room is available for letter-writing or reading. Your hosts will direct you to the harbor to see the sailboat races or to nearby galleries, shops, and beaches. Each room has a private bath. An excellent full breakfast is served.

Average rates: Double, $65. *Credit cards:* None. *Open:* All year. *Owners:* Jean and Rufus Titus. *Directions:* From Salem, take Route 114 (Pleasant Street) into town. When you reach Mugford Street, turn left. Continue 3 blocks, then turn right on Pond. Three blocks farther on the left is The Golden Cod. *Children:* Yes. *Pets:* No. *Smoking:* No.

PLEASANT MANOR
264 Pleasant Street
Marblehead, Massachusetts 01945
(617) 631-5843

Pleasant Manor is a big, white Victorian house just a few miles from Salem State College and the Coach House Inn. Built by leather industrialists in 1872, it has a gorgeous, carved wooden door, marble fireplaces, and fine antiques. Guests may relax by the sitting room's large fireplace, or, as a special bonus, use the Phelans' private tennis courts! Devereaux Beach is within walking distance. An extended continental breakfast is served. The rooms, all named for famous people, have coffee makers in them. Mrs. Phelan is very proud that Amelia Earhart once slept here. A bus to Boston stops right across the street.

Average rates: Double, $65–$75; all have private baths. Extra cot or person is $10. *Credit cards:* None. *Open:* April 1 to December 1. *Owners:* Dick and Takami Phelan. *Directions:* From Salem, stay on Routes 1A and 114, and go to the left of Salem State College. This becomes Pleasant Street in Marblehead. The inn is about 1½ miles from the college, set back on the right side. *Children:* Yes. *Pets:* No. *Smoking:* Yes.

ESSEX STREET INN
7 Essex Street
Newburyport, Massachusetts 01950
(508) 465-3148

Essex Street Inn, just a block off State Street in the town's center, is a handsome, renovated building with double front doors. We list this inn for its lower-priced rooms, which are almost as pretty as the high-priced ones. One guest room has brass beds and a couch, some have huge, antique oak beds with fancy carving, and all have delightful handmade quilts. Some rooms are under the eaves, and all have color television, private baths, and air conditioning. Some have whirlpool baths. There is even an apartment with full kitchen, living room, fireplaces, whirlpool bath, and cable television. Continental breakfast is served.

Average rates: Most rooms, $65–$90; apartment, $145. Prices are the same in summer and winter. Extra cot in room, $10; a crib is also available. *Credit cards:* All major. *Open:* All year. *Owners:* The Pearson family. *Manager:* Lori Hay. *Directions:* From I-95, take the exit to Route 113 to Newburyport. You'll be on High Street. Go left on Fruit Street, and your fourth left is Essex Street. The inn will be on your right. *Children:* Yes. *Pets:* Yes. *Smoking:* Yes.

MORRILL PLACE INN
209 High Street
Newburyport, Massachusetts 01950
(508) 462-2808

This inn is hosted by an expert on innkeeping. There are eleven rooms available. This elegant 1806 mansion has a formal drawing room with a piano and a library with a marble fireplace. The complimentary continental breakfast is served in a conservatory at the rear, except in winter, when it is served in the Victorian dining room. The canopy beds and antique decor give the visitor a taste of New England charm during the Victorian period even though the house itself is federalist. Some bedrooms have fireplaces; one has delicate stenciling; another is decorated in a glorious shade of pink, and another in Laura Ashley style. A special feature is afternoon tea. Both private and shared baths are available.

Average rates: Double, $60–$75, tax included. Children twelve and over, $10; additional adults, $20. *Credit Cards:* Visa and MasterCard. *Open:* All year. *Owner:* Rose Ann Hunter. *Directions:* From I-95, take Route 113 toward Newburyport (east); this is High Street. Travel about 2.4 miles down High Street from the I-95/113 intersection, and you will see a large, three-story, white building on your right—Morrill Place Inn. *Children:* Yes. *Pets:* Yes. *Smoking:* No.

THE KNOLL BED & BREAKFAST
230 North Main Street
Northampton (Florence), Massachusetts 01060
(413) 584-8164

This magnificent English Tudor-style home is a wonderful find in the Northampton area. The rooms are large and nicely decorated with antiques and pretty bedcovers; all share a large, attractive bath. The Leskos share their spacious living room and fireplace with their guests, and they are quite charming to talk to. They spoke of having guests from many different countries. The grounds are a marvel. Set back off Route 9, there are seventeen acres of farmland and woods to wander through. Just a three-minute walk away is Look Park, with tennis courts, a picnic area, and a swimming pool open to the public in summer. The home is within 3 to 15 miles of four colleges, and historic Deerfield is only 12 miles away. Mr. Lesko likes to cook, and he offers a choice of dishes for the full breakfast, which is included in the room rate.

Average rates: Double, $45; single, $40; all seasons. *Credit cards:* None. *Open:* All year. *Owners:* Lee and Ed Lesko. *Directions:* From I-91, take exit 18; turn left onto Route 5 to Northampton. One mile up at the lights in Northampton center turn left onto Route 9 (Main Street). Continue for 3½ miles to the second set of lights, go through lights and continue for another ¾ mile. The Knoll is on the left, set back with a circular driveway. *Children:* Twelve and over. *Pets:* No. *Smoking:* No.

Also recommended:

The **Inn at Northampton** is another find in this area. Inquire about their "Weekday Wonder Break"—Sunday through Thursday for a total of $77 per couple. A scrumptious breakfast is included, and you can order anything on the menu. A pool, putting green, and tennis courts are also on the premises—a real deal. Call (800) 582-2929. The inn is located at the junction of I-91 and Route 5.

THE CAPRI MOTEL
Route 6 (741 State Road)
North Dartmouth, Massachusetts 02740
(508) 997-7877

The Capri Motel is about the most reasonably priced place to stay in the New Bedford area. All of its ninety-five units fill up, however, so you do need to call ahead. The rooms are large, nicely decorated, with big private baths and televisions. Coffee and toast or doughnuts are served in a sunny breakfast room and are included in the price. The Capri Motel is open all year. Its large pool is open in the summer. The motel is AAA-approved.

Average rates: Double, $36–$44 Sunday through Thursday; $39–$47 Friday, Saturday, and holidays. These are in-season prices. Off-season, rooms cost about $4 to $7 less. The motel offers cash discount coupons for return trips and to senior citizens. *Credit cards:* All major. *Open:* All year. *Owners:* Melvin and Bea Davis. *Directions:* Take Route 24 to Route 195; turn right toward Route 6 at Reed Road; then turn left onto Route 6. The Capri is a short way down on the left on Route 6. *Children:* Yes. *Pets:* Yes. *Smoking:* Yes.

AMERICAN HOUSE
306 South Street
Pittsfield, Massachusetts 01201
(413) 442-0503

American House is a beautifully decorated 1898 Victorian bed & breakfast, very accessible to downtown stores, but in a pleasant neighborhood. Braided rugs, freshly varnished pine floors, and its decorations give it a truly cozy environment. You'll have your pick of antique brass twins or an inlaid design bed with a quilt. One room has a private bath. There is a deck in the back. The sitting room with a television and fireplace is available in cooler months. The wide, cool porch is perfect for lounging in the summer. Full breakfast, served in a glassed-in breakfast room, is included. The house specialty is homemade cinnamon-bread French toast.

Average rates: In season, $60–$85; off season, $50–$75; extra child, $15. *Credit cards:* None. *Open:* All year. *Owner:* Ernest Wolff. *Directions:* From Pittsfield center, take Routes 7 and 20 south. About ½ mile from the center on the right, you'll see the white house beside the Catholic church. *Children:* Yes. *Pets:* No. *Smoking:* Restricted.

Also recommended:

Dave and Judy Loomis have a wonderful old-fashioned home on Simonds Road in Williamstown, called **River Bend Farm,** that you should look into. The quaint colonial rooms cost $60 for a double and a continental breakfast with homemade breads is included in the price. This B&B is open from April to Thanksgiving. Call (413) 458-3121.

BEACH KNOLL INN
30 Beach Street
Rockport, Massachusetts 01966
(508) 546-6939

Beach Knoll Inn is directly across from the water on Beach Street and has delightful views. The old section, built in 1740, has oriental rugs on wide board floors, bright floral wallpaper, and antique beds. The newer section has wall-to-wall carpeting and both antique and modern furniture. This fascinating house has secret stairways and once had a tunnel leading to the water for safety from privateers. All rooms have a color television and private entrance. Some are suites of three rooms with a kitchenette. No breakfast is served here, but Jack's Place and The Coffee Shop are nearby.

The Goldens own another house called **The Second Settler House,** which is remodeled and has televisions and similarly priced doubles in season.

Average rates: Double, $57–$83; apartment, $75–$97. *Credit cards:* None. *Open:* All year. *Owners:* Terry and Diane Golden. *Directions:* Drive north on Route 128 over the Annisquam River, through two rotaries, to the light at Route 127. Turn left and drive 4 miles to where the road forks in four directions. Go left on Railroad Avenue, take the first right onto King Street, go to the end, and turn left onto Beach Street. The inn is 1 block up on the left. *Children:* Yes. *Pets:* No. *Smoking:* Yes.

LINDEN TREE INN
26 King Street
Rockport, Massachusetts 01966
(508) 546-2494

The rooms in Linden Tree Inn are decorated with delicate floral prints, some have color television, and some have private decks. Some rooms are air-conditioned. Every room has a private bath. There are several common rooms for guests to enjoy, including a large living room and a sun porch. Antiques fill the inn, and you'll be delighted with Mrs. Olson's sour cream chocolate chip coffee cake or rhubarb bread in the morning (included in the room fee). Look for their three friendly cats. Climb into the cupola on top of the house for a super view of Rockport. The Annex, with a separate entrance, is great for a family or two couples.

Average rates: Double in season, $75–$80; single, $55; efficiency (four units in the Annex), $88. *Credit cards:* MasterCard and Visa. *Open:* April to mid-November. *Owners:* Penny and Larry Olson. *Directions:* Take Route 128 to its end, then go left on Route 127 to its end. At four corners, go left onto Railroad Avenue. The first right is King Street. Go right. The inn is about 50 yards down on the left. *Children:* Yes. *Pets:* No. *Smoking:* Yes, except in dining room.

OLD FARM INN
291 Granite Street
Rockport, Massachusetts 01966
(508) 546-3237

Old Farm Inn in Pigeon Cove is on four beautiful acres with barns and horses. The inn has three inviting guest rooms, all filled with colonial furniture; two have fireplaces. The grounds have charming old elm and birch trees, and you may relax outside in the chairs or at the picnic tables. Relaxation is a high priority here, as the innkeepers have put reading lamps and comfortable chairs in each room. There is one sitting room upstairs shared by two of the rooms. There are four more rooms in the Barn Guest House next door, where each room has a television, private bath, and a queen- or king-sized bed. These rooms are somewhat higher priced.

The large complimentary continental breakfast includes cereals, fruit, bread, and coffee. It is just a short walk to the famous Halibut Point where rocks meet the moody sea. You can birdwatch in the woods on the way down. There is a wonderful living room with a fireplace, and a good supply of games is kept on hand.

Average rates: Double, $65–$88 mid-season; lower prices off-season. *Credit cards:* MasterCard and Visa. *Open:* Early spring to December. *Owners:* Susan and Bill Balzarini. *Directions:* Take Route 127 north out of Rockport center to Pigeon Cove. Go about 3 miles, and you'll see the inn on a bend on the right. *Children:* Yes. *Pets:* No. *Smoking:* At owners' discretion.

ROCKY SHORES INN AND COTTAGES
Eden Road
Rockport, Massachusetts 01966
(508) 546-2823

Rocky Shores Inn and Cottages is a large, dignified inn overlooking the ocean, with spectacular grounds and gardens. The gracious innkeepers, who come from Germany, have done everything to make guests feel comfortable and welcome. The long living room has many windows facing the sea and is tastefully decorated and enticing with its books and fireplace. A perfect place to relax in the summer is the porch, as long as the building and shaded from the sun. The rooms are snug and attractive with antique beds and flowered wallpapers. At night you'll have a rare view of twin lighthouses. An extended continental breakfast buffet is served and included in the price! Children under eleven cannot stay in the inn but are welcome in the housekeeping cottages.

Average rates: Double in season, $79–$97; double off-season, $55–$83; deduct $3 for singles; add $10 for child over ten or extra adult. *Credit cards:* MasterCard, Visa, and American Express. *Open:*

71

Early April to late October. *Owners:* Gunter and Renate Kostka. *Directions:* Go to the end of Route 128 and turn left onto Route 127 to Rockport center. Go south on Route 127A, which becomes South Street, about 1½ miles to Eden Road on your left. Drive almost to the end (about ½ mile), and the inn is on a hill on the right. *Children:* Yes. All ages in cottages; over ten in inn. *Pets:* No. *Smoking:* Yes, except one room.

SEVEN SOUTH STREET
7 South Street
Rockport, Massachusetts 01966
(508) 546-6708

Seven South Street is a big, handsome colonial house with a pool and lovely gardens. Of the five large bright rooms, two have fireplaces. There are two huge decks for sunning. The complimentary continental breakfast is good: white, wheat, or oatmeal toast; English muffins; baked bran muffins with cream cheese—all you can eat! Great beamed ceilings add to the coziness of this house.

Average rates: Double with shared bath, $55–$65; with private bath, $65–$75. *Credit cards:* None. *Open:* February to November. *Owner:* Aileen Lamson. *Directions:* Go to the end of Route 128 and turn left onto Route 127. Drive into Rockport center. At the end of Broadway Street, go right. This street turns into South Street, and the inn is on the left. *Children:* No. *Pets:* No. *Smoking:* Yes.

THE COACH HOUSE INN
284 Lafayette Street
Salem, Massachusetts 01970
(508) 744-4092; (800) 688-8689

The Coach House Inn is an elegant Victorian mansion with twelve rooms built by Captain Augustus Emmerton. Colonial antiques, wicker, and floral prints make this home a delightful place to stay. Some of the rooms have window seats. Breakfast is continental. The location of the Coach House is very handy, as buses to downtown stop nearby about twice an hour. You may also take a bus to Lynn or Boston in the other direction. Catch a train in downtown Salem for a quicker route to Boston. No charge at this inn for children up to eighteen!

Average rates: Double with shared bath, $59–$64; double with private bath on the second and third floors, $70–$84; suites, $86–$135. All doubles cost $10 less after November 1. A small amount is charged for an extra adult or cot in room. *Credit cards:* MasterCard, Visa, and American Express. *Open:* All year. *Owner:* Patricia Kessler. *Directions:* From Salem center, take Route 114 east. It becomes Lafayette Street, and the house is about a mile up on the right. From Boston, take Route 1A north to Lafayette Street. The house is 3 blocks from Salem State College on the left. *Children:* Yes. *Pets:* No. *Smoking:* Yes.

THE HOTEL LAFAYETTE
116 Lafayette Street
Salem, Massachusetts 01970
(508) 745-5503

The Hotel Lafayette is a family-owned, very clean, and pleasant hotel near the hub of activity in Salem. The rooms are carpeted and paneled in different woods. All have television and fancy private baths. A coin-operated laundry is handy. This place is ideal for many types of travelers and businesspeople because it's right on a bus line and only minutes from the train station. The fifty-five rooms have twenty-four-hour supervision by one of the owner's sons or friends.

Average rates: Double with shared bath, $40; double with private bath, $50; single, $40; extra person, $5. Children under twelve stay for free! *Credit cards:* None. *Open:* All year. *Owner:* Adele McKinnon. *Directions:* Take Route 114 to Salem. Take Washington Street ("circular road") to Derby Street. Turn right on Lafayette. Drive south 1½ blocks; the hotel is on the right. *Children:* Yes. *Pets:* No. *Smoking:* Yes.

THE STEPHEN DANIELS HOUSE
1 Daniels Street
Salem, Massachusetts 01970
(508) 744-5709

The Stephen Daniels House has been standing since 1667 and was built by a sea captain. It retains much of its old flavor, with low ceilings, authentic antique high-back chairs, pewter, and baskets of herbs. The two-sided, walk-in fireplace serves two rooms: one a large dining room where Mrs. Gill holds wedding or dinner parties, and the other a small, cozy reading room. The five guest rooms have four-poster and canopy beds, and split-level rooms are charming. There is a lovely garden with a stone patio where guests can have refreshments. Kay Gill has run this tourist home for twenty-one years and can recall entertaining Eve Arden, Brian Ahern, and recently, Bill Shatner from *Star Trek*.

Average rates: Double with private bath, $80–$90; three people in adjoining rooms, $85–$95; four or five people in adjoining rooms, $160. *Credit cards:* American Express. *Open:* All year. *Owner:* Mrs. Kay Gill. *Directions:* From Salem center, take Washington Street to Church Street to Brown Street, which ends up on a common (park). Go 1 block south on Congress Street and 3 blocks east on Essex Street (Hawthorne Hotel is on the corner). The house is right on the corner of Daniels and Essex streets. If you approach from Derby Street, it is only 2 blocks north of Pickering Wharf. *Children:* Yes. *Pets:* Yes. *Smoking:* Yes.

THE SUZANNAH FLINT HOUSE
98 Essex Street
Salem, Massachusetts 01970
(508) 744-5281

The Suzannah Flint House is a small, charming eighteenth-century home in the shadow of the Hawthorne Inn. It has four very cozy guest rooms, each with a fireplace and furnished with lovely antiques. There are also four common rooms for guests to mingle or read in, and a sweet, quiet guest room on the third floor has a secret stairway to the second floor. All guest rooms have private baths. This is one of two inns we have located in

Salem that serve complimentary breakfast. That scrumptious breakfast includes homemade breads, muffins, fresh fruit, and coffee. This B&B has an excellent location near museums, shopping, Derby Street, Pickering Wharf, and many historical sites. Group and weekly rates are available.

Average rates: In season, $79 per room; off season, $69 per room. *Credit cards:* MasterCard and Visa. *Open:* All year. *Owner:* The Jones Company. *Directions:* From Salem center, take Washington Street to Church Street to Brown Street, which ends up on a common (park). Go 1 block south on Congress Street and 3 blocks east on Essex Street (Hawthorne Hotel is on the corner). The inn is directly behind the Hawthorne Hotel. *Children:* Yes. *Pets:* Yes. *Smoking:* Yes.

DAFFERS MOUNTAIN INN
Route 57, Box 37
Sandisfield, Massachusetts 01255
(413) 258-4453

Daffers Mountain Inn is in the remote mountain town of Sandisfield, about 17 miles southeast of Great Barrington. Bill Daffer, a retired New York cafe owner, operates this homey seven-room inn in the Swiss style: lots of hospitality and plenty of food and drink. He makes you feel right at home with his storytelling. In fact many skiers come down in their pajamas to sit around the fire, play cards or cribbage, or just to chat. The decor is plain but clean, and there are plenty of extra blankets, towels, and bars of soap. Each room has a television and shares a bath. Butternut Basin Ski Area is twenty minutes away, and there's cross-country skiing in the State Forest. In summer you can swim at York Lake in Sandisfield State Forest. The inn has a bar that is open year-round but closed on Tuesdays. Dinners are available at extra cost but big breakfasts are included in room rates.

Average rates: Double in the summer, $40; in the winter, $35 per person. Skier's special, $18 a night. *Credit cards:* MasterCard and Visa. *Open:* All year. *Owners:* Bill and Jean Daffer. *Directions:* Turn off Route 7 just north of Great Barrington onto Route 23. Go east a short way to Route 57; then go east on Route 57 to New

Marlboro where the road turns east. Stay on Route 57 for 5 to 7 more miles and you will see Daffer's on the left. *Children:* Yes. *Pets:* No. *Smoking:* Yes.

GREEN ACRES MOTEL
Route 131, P.O. Box 153
Sturbridge, Massachusetts 01566
(508) 347-3496; (508) 347-3402

Green Acres Motel, off Route 131, just past Rom's Restaurant, is another family-owned, very clean, and reasonably priced motel that really caters to families. The twelve big rooms all have pretty, bright quilts, television, and private baths. The motel is set on a little less than six acres, with a picnic area, pool, basketball hoop, and volleyball and badminton nets. The double rooms are decorated in knotty pine and have two double beds. Families are encouraged to stay, and children thirteen and under stay free! The motel lies 1¼ miles from Sturbridge Village.

Average rates: Double, $52–$58; small amount extra for children over thirteen and cribs. *Credit cards:* MasterCard, Visa, American Express, and Discover. *Open:* All year except January. *Owners:* Mina and Vijay Chah. *Directions:* Take Route 131 off Route 20. Go past the Publick House, and slow down at Rom's Restaurant. Turn onto Shepard Road. The motel is on the right. *Children:* Yes. *Pets:* No. *Smoking:* Yes.

STURBRIDGE HERITAGE MOTEL
Route 20 West, P.O. Box 243
Sturbridge, Massachusetts 01566
(508) 347-3943

Sturbridge Heritage Motel is small, a mile away from Old Sturbridge Village, and tended carefully by its owners. The eight rooms are pretty, very clean, and good-sized, and are supervised at all times by the family. Each room has a television and a private bath.

Average rates: Double from July 1 to October 30, $48–$54; single,

$39–$44. Off-season rates are somewhat lower; in the winter, they drop to $36 for a double and $31 for a single. *Credit cards:* MasterCard and Visa. *Open:* All year. *Owner:* Nancy Gresenz. *Directions:* Take Route 20 to the center of town. The motel is on the left, across from the Whistling Swan Restaurant. You must drive around behind some buildings, but you'll see the sign. *Children:* Yes. *Pets:* Small pets only. *Smoking:* Yes.

SYLVESTER'S B&B
9 South Street
Williamsburg, Massachusetts 01096
(413) 268-7283

This lovely 1878 Victorian house, surrounded by tall trees and gardens, is a great place to stay while visiting Amherst or Northampton. We stayed in a charming flowered room with twin beds. Another flowered room with twin beds has a sweet doll collection, and the third room has a queen-sized bed. All rooms share a large bath. There is a separate living room with a fireplace and television for guests. The hosts serve a wonderful full breakfast of juice, fruit, coffee, tea, and eggs or pancakes and bacon, plus the most sensational sweet rolls from the nearby Country Store. Williamsburg is a fun place to visit in itself; there are great gift shops, the General Store, a craft supply shop, and even a blacksmith. The Christmas Inn right on Main Street serves from a full menu with quite reasonable prices; it is quaint and fancy inside and out.

Average rates: Double, $45; single, $40. *Credit cards:* None. *Open:* April 1 to December 1. *Owners:* Carl and Lottie Sylvester. *Directions:* Take Route 9 to the center of Williamsburg. Just before the General Store, go left on South Street. The large white house is the third on the left. *Children:* Over twelve. *Pets:* No. *Smoking:* Restricted.

THE HILL GALLERY
Cole Street (HC 65, Box 96)
Worthington (Cummington), Massachusetts 01098
(413) 238-5914

This is a mountain "palace" that serves Walter and Ellen Korzec as home, bed & breakfast, art gallery, and artist's studio. You will love the natural setting in the woods—it's about as high up as you can get in the Berkshires. This bed & breakfast offers the traveler a modern, beautifully decorated home with three levels and a deck. Walter is a professor of art at Westfield State College. Owing to the creatively designed use of windows and glass, natural light illuminates his paintings and prints. Ellen matches with artistry in the kitchen: gourmet breakfasts of homemade croissants, eggs Benedict, and hearty country bill of fare. A beautiful pool is available in the warmer months. You might make this a choice for a longer stay because it's so beautiful and there is so much old-fashioned New England countryside to see on the backroads. The two doubles have private baths and bunk accommodations for children. Cross-country skiing is available nearby.

Average rates: Double, $60; single, $50; cottage rates on request. *Credit cards:* None. *Open:* All year. *Owners:* Ellen and Walter Korzec. *Directions:* From Route 9 in West Cummington, exit onto Route 143. Go south. The inn is in 4 miles on the left. *Children:* Yes, if well behaved and supervised. *Pets:* No. *Smoking:* No.

WHERE TO EAT

JUDIE'S RESTAURANT
51 North Pleasant Street
Amherst, Massachusetts 01002
(413) 253-3491

Judie is so enthusiastic about her restaurant and her new ideas for it ("petite meals," combinations, and substitutions) that we could see why people stand in line, day after day, to eat at her restaurant. Her energy, creativity, and upbeat attitude are reflected in her cheerful waitresses and the superb combinations of delicacies offered. The Broiled Chicken Breast with Marsala, a hot sandwich on French bread ordered by Fran, was delectable. It had sautéed zucchini, mushrooms, onions, and tomatoes in a sherry-flavored sauce. Frank tried the Half Salad-lite Greek, with Judie's famous poppyseed dressing, and a cup of seafood bisque—very tasty! With it he got an oversized popover with yummy apple butter. Unusual offerings include dishes such as curried chicken salad with cranberry, banana, artichoke, coconut, and peanuts—all glazed with curried sour cream. Half of the dinners come in both "petite" and "full" sizes, a good idea for dieters and people with small appetites. The hot sandwiches are definitely a full meal. Choose from a number of award-winning desserts: Cold Peach Fuzzy Navel Pie, Chambourd Layer Cake, or Truffle Fudge Cake. Judie is truly a "food inventor"!

Average price: Lunch: over $3 to $7, many in $5 range. Dinner: $6 to $14.50; varied pastas, $10. *Credit cards:* All major. *Hours:* All year, seven days a week, 11:30 A.M. to 11 P.M. *Owner:* Judy Teraspulsky. *Directions:* From Route 91, take Route 9 to Amherst center; turn left at lights at Amherst College, go through next light. The restaurant is on the left across from the fire station.

Also recommended:

If you fancy Chinese food, there are three great Chinese restaurants in the Pioneer Valley. The first one is **Hunan Gourmet** at 261 King Street in Northampton, convenient for Smith College visitors and students. Another is **Amherst Chinese Food,** 60 Main

Street, Amherst. The former has more class; the latter saves the cash. Another favorite of Jo Streeter, Frank's sister, is the **Panda Gardens,** 34 Pleasant Street, Northampton, which is a fine place for overdosing on Chinese delights. Jo's top award, however, goes to Hunan Gourmet.

DURGIN PARK
340 Faneuil Hall Marketplace (North Market Street)
Boston, Massachusetts 02109
(617) 227-2038

Durgin Park, at Quincy Market, was established in 1826 and is famous for its large servings of good old New England dishes such as beef short ribs, prime rib, lobster, fish, roast duckling, Indian pudding, apple pie, and strawberry shortcake. The atmosphere is publike: checkered tablecloths, bustling waitresses, and plenty of folks to laugh with at your long table that seats ten. Take a moment to read the list of famous people throughout history who have eaten here.

Average prices: Dinner, $4–$25 (most items, $8–$10). Lunches until 2:30 P.M. are low priced. *Credit cards:* None. *Hours:* Monday through Saturday, 11:30 A.M.–11 P.M.; Sunday, noon–9 P.M. Open all year except Christmas and Thanksgiving. *Owner:* Martin Kelley. *Directions:* Take the Southshore Expressway to Quincy Market, which is the center building in the Faneuil Hall Marketplace. Durgin Park is in the North Market Building.

IMPERIAL TEA HOUSE
70 Beach Street
Boston, Massachusetts 02111
(617) 426-8439

Imperial Tea House is one of the best Chinese restaurants in Chinatown but it has reasonable prices. It was selected by *Boston Magazine* as having the best dim sum in town. Dim sum is an array of Chinese specialties that can be eaten early in the day. The menu lists thirty selections that are served from a cart, and you are charged per serving. This is Cantonese-style cooking at its best.

The quality of all the entrees is excellent, and portions are generous. Be adventurous and try something different. The manager recommends the spicy shrimp and the clams in black bean sauce. The upstairs dining room is beautifully decorated with a paneled ceiling and is above the noise and bustle of the street. They have a full liquor license.

Average prices: Lunch specials, $4 to $5; dinner, many items in the $8 to under $15 range; dim sum items are under $2. *Credit cards:* All major. *Hours:* Every day, 9 A.M. to 2 A.M. *Manager:* Key Wong. *Directions:* Exit off Southeast Expressway going south at South Station, but continue straight through the lights to Beach Street on the right. The Tea House is on the corner.

JACOB WIRTH CO. RESTAURANT
31-37 Stuart Street
Boston, Massachusetts 02116
(617) 338-8586

Jacob Wirth Co. Restaurant is a Boston landmark that dates back to 1868. The atmosphere is Victorian with dark paneling and well-worn floors (recently the sawdust was removed from the floors). Waitresses dress in black pants and white shirts with black ties. The food is German-American. There's plenty of draft beer to wash down the platters of knockwurst, bratwurst, sauerbraten, noodles, red cabbage, and sauerkraut. The blackboard specials on the day we visited were crabmeat plate, sardine plate, and fried sole. The favorite dish is sauerbraten. Every day there are two lunch specials in addition to the blackboard items. These range from stew, roast turkey, salisbury steak, and short ribs to chili—all inexpensive and served with a potato and vegetable. As you sip your seidel of special dark draft beer, you can think yourself back in gaslight days. Posters of famous ball players, such as Cy Young and Jimmy Foxx, adorn the walls in the bar to complete the mood.

Average prices: Lunch: sandwiches, $4 to $5; specials, $4 to $7. Dinner runs about $10–$14. Fried scrod is $9; sauerbraten and Jake's sampler of German goodies are $9. Children's menu. *Credit cards:* All major. *Hours:* Every day. Lunch, 11 A.M. to 4 P.M.;

dinner, 4 to 10 P.M.; Sunday brunch, 11 A.M. to 2 P.M. *Owner:* Kevin Fitzgerald. *Directions:* Turn off Southeast Expressway onto Stuart Street. The restaurant is about 3 blocks up on the right. Since parking is difficult, park south of Stuart and walk to the restaurant.

NO NAME RESTAURANT
15½ Fish Pier
Boston, Massachusetts 02210
(617) 338-7539; 423-2705

No Name Restaurant is the place for the freshest seafood in Boston. There are no refrigerators, so the fish has to be brought in as needed to be cooked for the many devoted diners. It is conveniently located on the Boston Fish Pier where trucks are being loaded with seafood to be transported to the interior of the country. Nick Contos's father came over from Greece seventy years ago and started this landmark, and the family has been cooking seafood in the same style ever since. When they deep fry, they use only cracker meal—no batter. Try the scallops—excellent. The fried oysters and shrimp are also delicious. If it swims in New England waters, it's on the menu. Don't overorder as portions are large; vegetables, cole slaw, and large rolls are served with the seafood. This place sells about 300 pounds of seafood a day. It has expanded with the renovation of the fish pier, and new upstairs dining has doubled their capacity, but plan to wait in line on Fridays during tourist season. Wine and beer are served.

Average prices: Dinners are about $5 to $10; lobster costs more. *Credit cards:* None. *Hours:* Monday through Saturday, 11:30 A.M.–10 P.M.; Sunday, 11 A.M.–9 P.M. *Owner:* Nick Contos. *Directions:* Exit on Southeast Expressway at South Station. Take Congress Street south to Sleeper, and go north to Northern. Go south to the Fish Pier. You'll see the green wood porch. Don't park in front of the loading platforms.

Also recommended:

To know what really terrific oyster stew is, you must try the **Union Oyster House** on 41 Union Street, not far from Faneuil Hall. The telephone number is (617) 227-2750. It's open Sunday through Thursday from 11 A.M. to 9:30 P.M. and on Friday and Saturday from 11 A.M. to 10 P.M. Benjamin Franklin ate his oysters here. **Tangiers Cafe** at 37 Bowdoin Street on Beacon Hill in Boston offers inexpensive Middle Eastern cuisine. Its hours are Monday through Friday, 11 A.M. to 11 P.M. and Saturday, 5 P.M. to midnight. Call (617) 367-0273. Also, **The Blue Wave** on 142 Berkeley Street is making big waves with Boston diners. Call (617) 424-6711.

Another good eatery is the **Bluestone Bistro** way out on Commonwealth Avenue in Brighton—1799, to be exact. The pastas, great pizzas, barbecue, and salads are very popular with students. The telephone number is (617) 254-8309. Frank's niece, Irene Richard, endorses it enthusiastically!

ACROPOLIS RESTAURANT
1680 Massachusetts Avenue
Cambridge, Massachusetts 02138
(617) 492-0900

Acropolis Restaurant is in Cambridge across the Charles River and north on Massachusetts Avenue. It is an old family favorite that never disappoints. It's worth the drive. The Greek waiters with napkins on their arms give an old-world atmosphere. The food is scrumptious. Greek specialties, fresh seafood, and broiled entrees are always tasty. Salads and omelets are available during lunch hours, and generous sandwiches too. Diet items are also available for weight-watchers. Try some of their Greek wines for a treat. American dishes are served, too. All come with salad, rice pilaf, or a potato.

We recommend having your big meal at noon when the prices are considerably lower than in the evening. This is a trick we learned while traveling in England. It takes a while to adjust to a dinner-at-noon routine, but it will save you money.

Average prices: Lunch, under $4 to under $7 for full meals. Dinner, under $7 for spinach pie to under $14 for combination shish kebab (chicken, lamb, and sirloin). From Sunday to Thursday there is a special for two: a wide choice of entrees with soup, salad, rice, vegetable, and beverage plus a half-carafe of wine for about $19. *Credit cards:* All major. *Hours:* Sunday through Thursday,

11:45 A.M. to 10 P.M.; Friday and Saturday, open until 11 P.M. *Owner:* Harry N. Kitis. *Directions:* From Harvard Square in Cambridge, go north on Massachusetts Avenue. The restaurant is 1 mile farther on the left.

Also recommended:

We have many young student guests from Cambridge, and they like to recommend their favorite eating places; here are a few. The **Little Osaka,** Concord Avenue, Cambridge, has a sushi bar with full meals for $9. It's near Fresh Pond Circle. **Grendel's** on JFK Avenue is an old favorite with great salads; the **Black Forest Cafe** on Massachusetts Avenue near the Acropolis has a great variety. Visit **The Coffee Connection** inside the Arcade on JFK not far from Harvard Square; and for good Tex-Mex try the **Border Cafe** on Church Street. We had an excellent and tasty meal at a Spanish place, **Iruña's,** on JFK, not far out of Harvard Square on the left. It's across from the parking barn. **Red Bones** in Somerville at the corner of Chester and Elm streets serves up great barbecue items and Southern hospitality.

JERRY PELONZI'S HEARTHSIDE
Route 133
Essex, Massachusetts 01929
(508) 768-6002

The Hearthside is a favorite of ours in the town of Essex. In a lovely, warm old farmhouse, this restaurant offers terrific meals. Some of their delicacies are baked stuffed codfish; 40-ounce prime rib; seafood Audrey with crab, shrimp, and haddock; boneless chicken breast; baked stuffed haddock or sole. A special that Fran loves is a Greek salad that's quite large. The meals above are served with cheese, crackers, rolls, a potato, vegetable, or salad. Ask to sit in the loft, from which you can look down on the lower floor and watch all the magical shadows cast by the myriad of perforated tin lanterns. For this very popular place, you'll need reservations most of the time, unless you arrive very early.

Average prices: Lunch and dinner, over $7 to $17. Greek salads, $5. *Credit cards:* MasterCard and Visa. *Hours:* 11:30 A.M. to 10 P.M., every day. *Owner:* Jerry Pelonzi. *Directions:* From Route 128, take Route 133 (exit 14) toward Essex. You'll find the restaurant 2½ miles down on the left. This road is also called Eastern Avenue.

Also recommended:

Another fine Essex restaurant almost at the end of Route 133, on the right, is **Lewis' Oyster House.** They have excellent lunch specials, Monday through Thursday, 11:30 A.M. to 9 P.M., and Friday and Saturday until 6 P.M. Native scrod, haddock, and sole dishes are reasonably priced. Some very nice specialties are petit filet mignon with mushroom sauce and tenderloin of beef Wellington. It is open every day from 11:30 A.M. to 9 P.M. It opens at noon on Sunday and closes at 10 P.M. Friday and Saturday. Telephone (508) 768-6551.

Nearby in Ipswich, **The Henrich House** is tops for quality, good prices, and ambience. It has four pages of specials. It is located at 24-26 Hammett Street. Telephone (508) 356-7006.

THE PHOENIX RESTAURANT
140 Huttleston Avenue
Fairhaven, Massachusetts 02719
(508) 996-1441

The Phoenix Restaurant is the place to be when it comes time for breakfast. You won't believe this place. The breakfasts are massive, freshly cooked, and quickly served. You can sit at the counter if you're in a hurry, or you can take one of the tables for four. We usually order a scrambled egg dish with linguica, home fries, toast, and a "bottomless" cup of coffee. A great buy! We also love the blueberry pancakes, which, according to the locals, are the best around. If you like a thick slab of ham, you can watch Paul, the head chef and owner, cut a ham steak off an upright baked ham and throw it on the grill with sizzling eggs, sausage, bacon, and other goodies. If you do not want a full breakfast, try one of the freshly baked cheese rolls, which are a specialty of this region of southern Massachusetts. Portuguese and Greek specials are also offered. There is usually a full house of eager eaters here.

Average prices: Full breakfast, $5. Lunch, about $5. *Credit cards:* None. *Hours:* Monday through Wednesday, 5:30 A.M.–11 P.M.; Thursday, 5:30 A.M.–2 A.M.; Friday and Saturday, 6 A.M.–2 A.M.; Sunday, 6 A.M.–11 P.M. *Owner:* Paul Tassopoulos. *Directions:* Take the Fairhaven Bridge east through Fairhaven along Route 6. The Phoenix is about 1½ miles farther on the left across from Benny's.

CHARLIE'S PLACE
83 Bass Avenue
Gloucester, Massachusetts 01930
(508) 283-0303

Charlie's Place has a cheerful, diner-like atmosphere and is bustling most of the time with townspeople. The walls are papered with blue and white ships, and the upstairs dining room, open only in summer, is more spacious, with white walls, brick-colored drapes, and captain's chairs. It is open year-round. Dinner entrees are served with cole slaw, fries, and rolls.

Average prices: Breakfast: eggs, toast, homefries, and meat for $3 to $4; French toast with sausage or bacon is under $3. Lunch: clam chowder in a bowl, $3; clam roll, under $7; other sandwiches were $2–$4 when we visited. Dinners run from over $5 to under $11 (fish and chips under $6; fried clams about $9, and scallops under $7—these are terrific prices!). Children's specials run $2 to $3. *Credit cards:* None. *Hours:* Every day, 7 A.M. to 8 P.M. *Owner:* Charlie Teiran. *Directions:* Take Route 128 to the end. Go through the light and take the next left. The restaurant is about 2 blocks down on the right.

THE GLASS SAILBOAT
3 Duncan Street
Gloucester, MA 01930
(508) 283-7818

This natural food store, which also sells lovely clothes made in India, has a delightful takeout or eat-in health food restaurant in the back. They bake their own bread and feature a different one each day. Two of Fran's favorites are five-grain and onion oatmeal. When you select your own tasty vegetable chowder or lentil-vegetable soup, you always get a crispy roll made of the day's bread. They have wonderful spinach quiches, vegetarian pizzas, and yummy sandwiches, and you can choose a pesto pasta salad or tossed salad served with their homemade yogurt dressing. So many choices—and all so healthy! Fran even enjoys the unusual carob-flavored soy milk, although they offer many more common drinks, including good fruit drinks. Meals are eaten in their black-and-white art deco checkered lunch room.

Average prices: Lunch, $3–$5; muffins, cookies, and drinks available outside of lunch hours. *Credit cards:* None. *Hours:* 8 A.M. to 2 P.M. (store is open until 6 P.M.). *Owner:* Mac Bell. *Directions:* Take Route 128 to the end. Go right into Gloucester; then turn right onto Main (one-way). Duncan Street (also one-way) is on the left. The store/restaurant is on the immediate right.

Also recommended:

Cameron's, across from the A&P, at 206 Main Street (508-281-1331), is becoming a favorite of the townspeople of Gloucester. Another place along the water, near the statue of the Fisherman, is an excellent, reasonable Portuguese restaurant called **The Boulevard Ocean View Restaurant.** It is at 25 Western Avenue; call (508) 281-2949. We visited a happy little place at the beginning of Main Street called **Halibut Point.** It has very inexpensive yet delicious food, and the pubby atmosphere gives you a warm feeling.

Near Gloucester are several restaurants in Manchester. Try **Seven Central,** on the main street, for atmosphere and some good specials. For excellent Mexican fare, take Route 127 to the Magnolia sign. Turn right into Magnolia to the **Edgewater Restaurant** on Lexington Avenue. It's open for dinner only. **The Patio,** on the same street, is also good and has some budget-minded specials. Lunch and dinner are served daily. Telephone (508) 525-3230.

COUNTRY CORNERS RESTAURANT
Route 9, Box 40
Goshen, Massachusetts 01032
(413) 268-7313

Country Corners Restaurant, a charming blue building with large picture windows in the front, has some tremendous buys. Pancakes and omelets are featured for breakfast. There is a counter and a large friendly room with interesting people eating there. Homemade pies are their specialty, and the whole menu comes highly recommended by a number of folks who know good food when they taste it. Try their creative homemade soups such as broccoli or turkey-vegetable.

Average prices: Breakfast, $4 and up; lunch, $2–$5; dinners, $4–$11. *Credit cards:* None. *Hours:* 6 A.M.–9 P.M. (in winter closes 7 P.M.). *Owner:* George Still. *Directions:* Take Route 9 west to the tiny town of Goshen. The restaurant is on the right.

Also recommended:

A few miles west of Goshen, in the southern part of Cummington, the **Old Creamery Store** on Route 9 serves excellent sandwiches, salads, and desserts. The owner is Ronald Berenson. Telephone (413) 634-5560.

JOE'S DINER
63 Center Street
Lee, Massachusetts 01238
(413) 243-9756

Joe's Diner looks like a small luncheonette, but looks are deceiving. This restaurant causes truckers to leave the Massachusetts Turnpike to have a sumptuous meal at any time of the day. The prices, quality, and quantity make this our four-star pick for the best Berkshire bargain in dining. They say if you have a roast beef dinner at Joe's, it must be Monday. That's the special on that day. Every day has a special: Tuesday is meatloaf, Wednesday is roast pork, and so on.

Twelve stools at the counter and four vinyl tables is all Joe has space for, so get there early during Tanglewood season if you don't want to stand in line. There is a full menu for breakfast, lunch, and dinner. All dinners are served with a vegetable, a potato, and bread. The specials are on cardboard signs hung over the counter. Joe and his many sons provide for the hungry in many ways; read the articles on the walls before you leave.

Average prices: Full breakfast (bacon and eggs), about $3. Lunch, $3–$5. Dinner, about $5–$7. Roast beef, ravioli, and a large club steak sandwich are specials. On Fridays they feature sole, fish and chips, and swordfish. *Credit cards:* None. *Hours:* Monday through Friday, 6 A.M. to midnight; Saturday, 6 A.M. to 6:30 P.M.; closed Sunday. *Owner:* Joseph F. Sorrentino, Jr. *Directions:* Drive south on Route 20. After crossing the bridge near the center of town in Lee, Joe's is on the left, next to a laundromat. This street is also called Center Street.

LOOK RESTAURANT
410 North Main Street (Route 9)
Leeds, Massachusetts 01053
(413) 584-9850

This was a real find we made while visiting Frank's mother at a nursing home in the Leeds area. This restaurant features homemade bread, which makes their sandwiches special. They serve homemade pies, too. When we were there, swordfish and baked sole cost under $7—a real bargain. Homemade soups and chowders are what attracted Frank. This is a good place to eat when visiting Look Park. No-smoking tables are available. Counter seating provides a dinerlike but quiet atmosphere.

Average prices: Breakfast, $4; lunch sandwiches, $2–$3; dinner, under $8. *Credit cards:* None. *Hours:* Monday through Saturday, 6 A.M. to 8 P.M.; Sunday, 7 A.M. to 8 P.M. *Owner:* Allen Sylvester. *Directions:* Head west out of Northampton on Route 9. The restaurant is on the left, across from the VA Medical Center just past Look Park.

Also recommended:

In Lawrence, check out this city's favorite—**The Cedar Crest Restaurant** at 187 Broadway. A large dinerlike restaurant is combined with a more formal dining area. Telephone (508) 685-5722.

MARIO'S
1733 Massachusetts Avenue
Lexington, Massachusetts 02173
(617) 861-1182

Mario's is a popular Italian, family restaurant and was very busy when we were there. Lots of families were munching away on Mario's famous pizzas (nineteen selections, in small and large sizes). We enjoyed the lasagna and ravioli, very tasty. There are also entrees of breaded veal cutlets, spaghetti, baked ziti, shells, and the other popular Italian dishes. Sub sandwiches are also available. Those who do not mind hustle and bustle will get their fill of good pasta and sauces at reasonable prices. Almost every item is available for takeout.

Average prices: Lunch specials from Monday to Wednesday (11 to 3) are about $5. A good bargain any time is spaghetti and meatballs with garden salad. Dinners are $6. Small cheese pizza was under $4. Children's menu items are $3. A half-gallon of spaghetti with meatballs and bread can be taken out for about $9. *Credit cards:* None. *Hours:* Sunday to Thursday, 11 A.M. to 10 P.M.; Friday and Saturday, 11 A.M. to 10:30 P.M. *Owner:* Mark Miminos. *Directions:* From Route 128, take exit 44 south to Lexington Center. Pass the Lexington Green on your left. Mario's is about ¼ mile past the green on the left amidst the fancy shops and stores.

PORTHOLE RESTAURANT AND PUB
98 Lynnway
Lynn, Massachusetts 01902
(617) 595-7733

Porthole Restaurant and Pub is our four-star selection for quality, quantity, and price in New England! This restaurant is charmed with buzzing sociability. The huge area into which you enter, with its central bar and hanging glasses, is something to behold—and always crowded. They take no reservations, so your best bet on weekends is to get there early (although we've never encountered longer than a half-hour wait). Half the dining room has a publike decor and half is in English Tudor. It's a very busy space with good service! The Porthole's best bargain is the baked stuffed haddock with scallop stuffing, fries, and salad. Tuesday to Saturday an Irish band plays for your entertainment and dancing pleasure. On Sunday and Monday there is music of the 1950s. You can make a night of it for a reasonable price at this place—one of our all-time favorites.

Average prices: Lunch, $4–$10; dinner, about $2–$3 higher. Scrod (haddock), seafood supreme with lobster, shrimp, scallops, Claire's Swedish meatloaf, twin lobsters (in season), chicken cordon bleu, baked stuffed lobster, and prime rib are featured. *Credit cards:* MasterCard, Visa, Diner's Club, and American Express. *Hours:* Sunday and Monday, 11:30 A.M. to 9 P.M.; stays open until 2 A.M. Wednesday through Sunday for drinks and entertainment. *Owners:* Jay and Robert Gaudet. *Directions:* From Salem, take Route 1A through Swampscott and into Lynn, and head toward Nahant. Make a U-turn at Market Street, and go back north 1 block. The restaurant is on the water side.

Also recommended:

Monte's Restaurant, at 141 Eastern Avenue, in Lynn, run by Frank McAskill, offers a great veal parmigiano and other Italian specialties inexpensively. Call (617) 599-0478.

DILL'S RESTAURANT
141 Pleasant Street
Marblehead, Massachusetts 01945
(617) 631-9820

Dill's Restaurant in Marblehead is a favorite for seafood. It is inconspicuous from the street with no windows and a red front, but inside there is a pub-like warmth inspired by red colors and a boating theme. The drinks are generous and the seafood is cooked to perfection. We've never been disappointed by the clam chowder or the haddock. You can sit in booths by the fireplace as you enter, or go the lounge, which is more open. This is a place that is liked so well by a friend that he keeps a running tab and pays by the month. Lobster is cooked ten ways. Blackboard specials are available daily, and there is a children's menu. Italian dishes and sandwiches are also served at lunch. Specials during the week are priced low.

Average prices: Lunch specials (11:30 A.M. to 4 P.M.) range from $3 to $6; many dishes cost under $6. A real treat is a cup of chowder, fish sandwich (large), and onion rings for about $4.50. Baked or fried haddock is under $6. The dinner menu lists dishes ranging from shrimp casserole for over $8 to a combination seafood plate for about $10. *Credit cards:* MasterCard and Visa. *Hours:* All year, Sunday through Thursday, 11:30 A.M. to 9 P.M.; Friday and Saturday, 11:30 A.M. to 10 P.M. *Owner:* Larry Gallagher. *Directions:* Take Route 114, which winds around through Peabody and Salem, into Marblehead. You'll see Dill's on the left as you enter town (before the theater).

DAVY'S LOCKER
1480 East Rodney French Boulevard
New Bedford, Massachusetts 02744
(508) 992-7359

Davy's Locker is the best place to get seafood at a reasonable price in New Bedford. It is right on the water just beyond the dike that protects the inner New Bedford harbor. In fact you can see trawlers and scallopers laden with their morning catches sailing by as you sit at your table. The meals are served by attentive waitresses. Fresh pumpernickel and rye breads give variety. Try the delicious clam chowder, thick and creamy with lots of clams. We tried the broiled scrod, baked stuffed scrod with Creole sauce, and the baked haddock Mornay, which featured a white wine sauce with mushrooms. All were excellent but the Mornay was the show-stopper. These were all reasonably priced and included a potato, vegetable, or cole slaw. Lunch prices are good from 11 A.M. to 4 P.M. every day except holidays. The decor is pleasant with nautical wall pieces. The sign at the cashier states that the "captain" will perform marriages upon request. We are not sure how that ties in with paying your bill!

Average prices: Lunch, $4 to $8; bowl of clam or fish chowder a bargain at $2; New Bedford scrod and broiled seafood for $7. The dinner range is $6 to $13; lots of items are in the $8 to $10 category, including steak and chicken. *Credit cards:* American Express, Discover, MasterCard, Visa, and Diner's Club. *Hours:* Every day, 11 A.M. to 11 P.M.; cocktails under 1 A.M. *Owner:* Marvin Dolinsky. *Directions:* From Route 195, turn south onto Route 18 (exit 15), and take a left on Cove Road. This bends around to the right becoming East Rodney French Boulevard. Davy's is on the left (sea side).

FOWLE'S RESTAURANT
17 State Street
Newburyport, Massachusetts 01950
(508) 465-0141

This unusual place, situated in a Federalist building in the downtown historic district, is the "pulse" of Newburyport. All the town's businesspeople meet here for lunch. It's homey and magical, all in one. The first thing that strikes you as you step in the door is the authentic 1930s soda fountain counter with a solid marble top and a fascinating country scene depicted in the wall behind the bar, all done in inlaid woods. The heart that keeps the pulse of the place going is the superb home cooking. They are proud of their creative and healthful soups and sandwiches: homemade chicken and beef soup; bacon, avocado, and grilled vegetable sandwich with melted cheese; and turkey or ham with sprouts and melted cheese. The blueberry pie, with designs on the crust, is absolutely delectable! Morning glory and pineapple coconut are our favorite muffins. A past owner called Fowle's a "living theater" because so many fun people interact there—many of the staff members are writers, artists, and poets.

Average prices: Breakfast, $2 to $4.50 (omelets). Fancy lunch sandwiches, $2 to $4. At dinner, a daily special such as hearty beef stew with bread, lasagna, chicken pot pie, or lemon chicken with bread and salad is between $3 and $4. *Credit cards:* None. *Hours:* All year, every day. Monday through Friday, 6 A.M. to 6 P.M.; Saturday, 7 A.M. to 6 P.M.; no warm food after 4 P.M., Monday–Saturday; Sunday for breakfast only 7 A.M. to 12:30 P.M. *Owners:* J. Frase-White and C. Stuart. *Directions:* From I-95, take Route 113 into Newburyport. Go right at High Street and left on Green Street. Go down to the end and either park in the three-hour free public parking lot or go right on to Water Street and right again on State Street, which is the business center in town. The restaurant is 2 blocks up on the left.

THE MALL
Corner of Green and High Street
Newburyport, MA 01950
(508) 465-5506

This family restaurant has a mixed menu offering dishes from broasted chicken to pizza, as well as barbecued and blackened items and Mexican fare. There's something for everybody. A bar and lounge is on the lower level. They pride themselves on their Yankee grill marinade derived from an Olympic recipe—the 1984 Culinary Olympics in Frankfurt, Germany. The decor is a knotty pine, and seating is arranged in divided booths. A great place for a light lunch or supper.

Average prices: Breakfast, $2 to $6. Lunch and dinner: sandwiches, $3 to $7; hot dishes or specialties, $6 to $14. *Credit cards:* MasterCard, Visa, and American Express. *Hours:* 8 A.M. to 11 P.M. *Owners:* Darlene and Bob Vanderbulck. *Directions:* Take Route 133 from I-95 into Newburyport. This is High Street. After you pass over Route 1, watch for Green Street on left. The Mall is on the corner.

MICHAEL'S HARBORSIDE
Tournament Wharf
Newburyport, Massachusetts 01950
(508) 462-7785

Michael's Harborside, located right on the wharf, has two open-air decks and is a great place to eat while watching fishermen unload their catch. Inside you can dine by candlelight among driftwood and "salty" decor. Of course, fish is their specialty, but you can get a hamburger or broiled chicken fingers, which will delight the kids. The bargains include broiled scrod or baked stuffed haddock. Even better bargains are fried haddock and fried clams! Other specials are fresh fruit with cottage cheese and delicious fish sandwiches. A jolly pub is upstairs.

Average prices: Lunch, $5 to $10; dinner, $7 to $13; *Credit cards:* MasterCard, Visa, and American Express. *Hours:* All year, every day 11:30 A.M. to 10 P.M. Winter hours may vary. *Owner:* Michael Roy. *Directions:* Take the Newburyport exit off I-95, then go east to Route 1. Go down the street (to the north) as if entering Route 1, but at the bottom of the hill go straight into the Harborside driveway to your right. (It is just to the right of the entry to Route 1.)

MIDDLE STREET FOODS
25 Middle Street
Newburyport, Massachusetts 01950
(508) 465-8333

This cafe has an aura of brightness and cheer about it, with colorful food prints and many long windows that let in the light. Long, skinny loaves of bread stick jauntily out of ceramic jars, and there's always a splashy bouquet of pink or orange flowers on the counter. Margaret ran a place similar to this in Nantucket, and her wonderful soups, tasty sandwiches and picnics, rich desserts, and cheeses reflect her confidence in pleasing the public. Her French breads, croissants, and Danish pastries are superb, as are her choices of pasta salads or spinach and cheese sandwiches enclosed in crisp, flaky dough. Even her varieties of coffee are a delight. Try the patio in back in summer. The cafe is within walking distance of all the great shops on State Street and many historic sights as well.

Average prices: Breakfast, $2–$5; lunch, $2.75–$6; dinners to go, $4–$7. *Credit cards:* None. *Hours:* Monday through Friday, 7 A.M. to 7 P.M.; Saturday and Sunday, 8 A.M. to 6 P.M. *Owner:* Margaret Degive. *Directions:* Take the Newburyport exit from Route 95 and bear right off ramp. Take a left at sign for downtown; then turn right at blinking light and bear right at fork. The second left is Middle Street. The cafe is a block down on the left. It is a specialty food store also.

SPORTSMEN'S LODGE
Plum Island Turnpike
Newburyport, Massachusetts 01950
(508) 465-9013

Sportmen's Lodge has consistently offered great food for many years, and we are proud to recommend it in this edition for the first time. We have heard about their prime rib and steaks from many friends and locals. They also have good seafood and other delicacies. Their specials include fried fish for $5 on Mondays and a turkey dinner for $7 on Thursdays. On Wednesdays kids eat for free, and on Sunday senior citizens get a 20 percent discount. The back windows of the large dining room look out on the Merrimack River. Nonsmoking tables are available.

Average prices: Dinner, $8–$14; sandwiches, $3–$10; children's plates available. *Credit cards:* MasterCard and Visa. *Hours:* Saturday and Sunday, noon–9 P.M.; Monday through Friday, 4–9 P.M. Open year-round. *Owner:* Troy Dagres. *Directions:* Take Route 113 toward Plum Island. This route cuts across Route 1 in Newburyport and becomes Water Street along the waterfront. Sportmen's is on left before the bridge to Plum Island, and is across from a small airfield.

Also recommended:

The Grog at 13 Middle Street is a funky but cozy and popular place with a bar. It offers various tasty items such as Cajun steak, swordfish, grilled chicken, and Mexican delights. Open every day from 11:30 A.M. to 11 P.M. Telephone: (508) 465-8008.

For good dining outside of town, follow Route 1A south about

10 to 15 miles to Ipswich. Go through the center and continue on 1A to the **Millstone Restaurant** on your left (just before the entrance to Route 133). They have a great variety of entrees in the low-budget range. Their specialty is homebaked dark and white breads—and desserts. They have excellent fish and clam plates, the atmosphere is jovial and warm, and you can enjoy a cocktail while you wait. You can reserve, and remember, New Englanders are not late diners. The restaurant closes at about 8 P.M. (9 P.M. on the weekend) and is closed on Tuesday. For reservations call (508) 356-2772. The owners are David and Roselyn Doane.

Also down Route 1A, in the center of Hamilton, is a very cozy place called **Hunters Inn.** It has good prices, fine food, and a special atmosphere. It is quite small, so be sure and reserve. You'll find it on 26 Bay Road, just after Railroad Avenue on the right. Telephone: (508) 468-2573.

NEW BROTHERS RESTAURANT DELI
11 Main Street
Peabody, Massachusetts 01960
(508) 532-1202

This is an excellent cafeteria-style restaurant with Greek and American specialties. There are two other restaurants with the same menu and same popularity but run by different owners, one in Salem and the other in Beverly. Our family frequents the Peabody and Beverly locations the most. The lamb dishes are excellent, but the roast chicken is a perennial favorite. The Greek salads come with a slice of roast beef or a scoop of tuna and make a heart-healthy and filling lunch. Every day has its specials. Breakfast is served all day.

Average prices: Breakfast, about $3. Lunch and dinner, $4–$9 (steak and prime rib). *Credit cards:* None. *Hours:* Monday through Saturday, 6 A.M. to 9 P.M.; Sunday, 6 A.M. to 1 P.M. *Owners:* Ted Kougianos and Kary Andrinopoulos. *Directions:* Exit off Route 128 and drive south on Lowell Street in Peabody. Continue to Peabody center, where Lowell becomes Main Street. The restaurant is 100 yards past the Peabody center intersection, on the right.

DAKOTA RESTAURANT
1035 South Street
Pittsfield, Massachusetts 01201
(413) 499-7900

This Berkshire roadside restaurant with its knotty pine walls, fieldstone fireplace, hand-hewn beams, and unhurried lifestyle puts you in mind of a hunting lodge in the West. It has very reasonable prices: sirloin steaks from $9 to $11; chicken teriyaki, fresh salmon, or shrimp from $9 to $13 (all cooked over Texas mesquite wood). All prices include salad bar, rice or potato, and homebaked whole-grain bread. Nightly specials may include grilled lime chicken, crab legs, or fresh mesquite-broiled fish. Even the prime rib and fresh swordfish are quite reasonable. After dinner you can savor a specialty coffee with a scrumptious dessert like Mud Pie or Nuns of New Skete Cheesecake or premium ice cream. You may also purchase ground sirloin and sirloin tips to take home.

Average prices: Dinners, under $7 to about $16, many in the $9 to $11 range. *Credit cards:* MasterCard, Visa, American Express, and Diner's Club. *Hours:* Sunday through Thursday, 5–10 P.M.; Friday and Saturday, 5–11 P.M. Open year-round. *Owner:* Tony Perry. *Directions:* From Pittsfield, go south on Route 7 (only three minutes). The restaurant is on the Lenox line, on the left.

THE HIGHLAND RESTAURANT
100 Fenn Street
Pittsfield, Massachusetts 01201
(413) 442-2457

The Highland Restaurant in Pittsfield is famous for its Italian dishes. Prices are outrageously reasonable for such dishes as chicken with spaghetti and salad, manicotti with salad and a roll, veal cutlet with spaghetti and salad, corned beef and cabbage (only on Thursday), hamburgers, and open steak sandwich with fries and salad. The one high-priced item is filet mignon. The feeling is homey and lighthearted, and the portions are ample! Daily specials are available on weekdays.

Average prices: Italian dishes, $3 to $7; steaks and chops, $7 to $10. Sandwiches, over $1 to $6 (open steak). *Credit cards:* None. *Hours:* All year, Tuesday through Sunday, 11 A.M. to 10 P.M.; closed Monday. *Owners:* Rudolph Sondrini and Leon Arace. *Directions:* From Park Square in Pittsfield, go north on North Street. Fenn Street is the next right. The restaurant is on the right in the middle of the block.

JIMMY'S STONEBRIDGE RESTAURANT
114 West Housatonic Street
Pittsfield, Massachusetts 01201
(413) 499-1288

Jimmy's is a fun place to eat that is popular with local people. It features homemade Italian dinners, pasta, and pizza. There is even an Italian Pu-pu platter. Jimmy's has a pleasant dining room and a separate bar and lounge. Lots of waitresses bustle about. Blackboard specials are available every day. Add soups and a garden salad, and you have an inexpensive meal. Takeout is available on all dinners. A variety of sandwiches and half sandwiches is available. All dinners come with a potato or spaghetti, salad, and bread.

Average prices: Lunch sandwiches, about $4; 16-inch pizzas, $6–$10; spaghetti, $6; prime rib, $13. *Credit cards:* MasterCard and Visa. *Hours:* Monday through Thursday, 11:30 A.M.–10 P.M.; Friday and Saturday, 11:30 A.M.–midnight; Sunday, 1–10 P.M. *Owners:* Joe Breault and Frank Penna. *Directions:* From Pittsfield center, go west on Housatonic Street (Route 20) for ½ mile. The restaurant is on the right.

DEPOT COFFEE SHOP
Whistlestop Mall
Railroad Avenue
Rockport, Massachusetts 01966
(508) 546-6284

Depot Coffee Shop has wonderful food at very decent prices. For breakfast, try a homemade muffin, coffee roll, or Danish and coffee, or a larger breakfast. At lunch the sandwiches are excellent. Homemade chowders are a specialty, and their beef stew is very popular. Dinners such as fried chicken, fried haddock or sole, seafood casserole, and roast pork are all served with French fries and cole slaw. This is a terrific find in an area of high prices.

Average prices: Lunch or dinner, $3 to $5! Fried chicken is under $4; most other meals are $4. Breakfast is under $2 to under $3; sandwiches are $1 to $2. *Credit cards:* None. *Hours:* Monday through Saturday, 6 A.M.–4 P.M.; Sunday, 8 A.M.–noon (breakfast only). Open all year. *Owners:* Joan and Stan Danckwicz, Jr. *Directions:* Take Route 127 into Rockport. At the four corners, instead of taking a right on Broadway, turn left onto Railroad Avenue. Turn left into the Whistlestop Mall, and you'll see the Coffee Shop on your right.

ELLEN'S HARBORSIDE
1 T-Wharf
Rockport, Massachusetts 01966
(508) 546-2512

This restaurant, near Motif #1 (famous harbor view), is restful with its little side room overlooking the harbor. Run by the same family for years, there are still three generations working here. We've come here for years since it was quite small, and now it is bigger and better. We still enjoy the fabulous prices and excellent food. Frank likes the chowder and fresh fish, which is their specialty along with sirloin tips. Fran always has the shrimp or the clams. All dinners are served with a potato, vegetable or salad, and rolls. Clam rolls, pit-barbecued ribs and chicken, homemade Grapenut bread, and rhubarb puddings are favorites. They take no reservations and the place is very popular, so get there early on summer nights.

Average prices: Lunch, $2 to $5; dinner, over $4 to $10. All types of fish run from $5 to $6; clams, $7; shrimp, $8; steak and prime rib, $10. *Credit cards:* MasterCard and Visa. *Hours:* May 1 to November 1, every day, 5:30 A.M. to 9 P.M. Closed in winter. *Owner:* Jim Balzarini. *Directions:* Take Route 127 to Rockport. As

100

you enter town on Broadway, cross Mount Pleasant Street, and you'll be on T-Wharf. Ellen's is on the right.

Also recommended:

This was recommended by Penny Olson of Linden Tree Inn. Try the charming little **Portside Chowder House** on the left as you go down Bearskin Neck; they keep a fire going in winter, and you can look out at the water. It's a place we could sit in all afternoon. Owned by Linda and Larry Church, it suits a budget pocketbook.

THE AGAWAM DINER
Route 1
Rowley, Massachusetts 01969
(508) 948-7780

The Agawam Diner is a friendly favorite of ours. Owned by the same family for fifty years, it is still successful and famous for its homemade cream and fruit pies, baked on the premises. The warm, homey atmosphere draws in satisfied customers time and time again. Try their stews and "blue plate specials," such as hot turkey sandwich and pork cutlets. Fried clams and fried shrimp are good and reasonably priced. Fran's favorite feature of this diner is that breakfasts are offered all day—order eggs, pancakes, or French toast, and sausage. Desserts are very low priced.

Average prices: Lunch or dinner, $3 to under $7. Stew is just over $3; fried chicken and veal cutlet with spaghetti are a little over $4; fried clams and fried shrimp are just over $7. *Credit cards:* None. *Hours:* Sunday through Thursday, 4:30 A.M. to 11 P.M.; Friday and Saturday, closes 12:45 A.M. Closed Christmas Day. *Owner:* Andy Galanis. *Directions:* From Newburyport, take Route 1 south to the intersection of Routes 133 and 1. It is on your right.

THE LYCEUM
43 Church Street
Salem, Massachusetts 01970
(508) 745-7665

This restaurant has an elegant decor to match its American contemporary cuisine. As you enter, the bar and lounge are to the right and the dining room to the left. You can get some items in the bar at lower prices. However, we always eat in the main dining area or on the back patio. The Portobello mushrooms for an appetizer are delicious. We recommend the seafood and pastas. The sautéed sole with lobster and crab ravioli and the lemon cucumber chicken are especially good. California wines are featured.

Average prices: Lunch, $3–$8; dinner, $10–$15. *Credit cards:* MasterCard and Visa. *Hours:* Monday through Saturday: lunch, 11:30 A.M.–3 P.M.; dinner, 5:30–10 P.M. Sunday brunch, 11 A.M.–2:30 P.M. *Owner:* George Harrington. *Directions:* Take Route 128 to exit 25E and follow Route 114 into Salem. Two blocks after you pass over the overpass, turn left onto Lynde Street; at the end of Lynde, cross Washington onto Church Street. The Lyceum is the second building on your right.

MIKE PURCELL'S RESTAURANT & SPORTS LOUNGE
90 Washington Street
Salem, Massachusetts 01970
(508) 745-1630

This is a new spot in Salem and a real favorite of Frank's. It's where he takes his college friends for a special occasion. His friend Paul Girard, a Salem native, recommended it, and Frank has never been disappointed. The chef, David Rowand, gets the fish fresh from his family's fish market in Beverly. The Caesar salad is a standout and big enough for four. The pasta dishes are excellent. Both traditional favorites and gourmet dishes are delicious, ample, and attractively presented. Lunch and dinner menus are varied, extensive, and very reasonable. Service is excellent. Decor is restful and pleasant, with linen tablecloths and candlelight.

Average prices: Lunch, $4–$7; dinner, $8–$13, with half orders available on pasta entrees. Lots of good appetizers, soups, and salads. Wines and imported beers available. *Credit cards:* Visa, MasterCard, and Discover. *Hours:* Monday through Saturday: lunch, 11:30 A.M.–4:30 P.M.; dinner, 5–9 P.M. *Owners:* Marianne and Mike Purcell. *Directions:* Take Route 114 south from Route 128 at North Shore Shopping Center. When you enter business district with courthouse on left and Masonic Hall on right, you are on Washington Street. Purcell's is on right a few doors after Masonic Hall, a tall gray building.

STROMBERG'S
2 Bridge Street
Salem, Massachusetts 01970
(508) 744-1863

Stromberg's is a very relaxed, reasonably priced restaurant, just before the bridge to Beverly. It has pleasant views of Salem Harbor and very jovial waitresses. They all have worked here for years, which shows that the owners are good managers. Their specials are à la carte, but you get french fries or rice pilaf and salad with all of them. Fresh fish is their specialty; other entrees include a half-pound broiled sirloin steak, shish kebab, fried chicken, chops, broiled halibut, baked stuffed shrimp, fried clams, lobsters (any style), and homemade New England chowder. The deluxe hamburger is inexpensive. All the food is fresh, tasty, and nicely served with smiles and often a little joke. Children enjoy watching the fish in the huge aquarium. There is also a small cocktail bar.

Average prices: Same menu at lunch and dinner, $5 to $10. *Credit cards:* MasterCard and Visa. *Hours:* 11 A.M. to 8:30 P.M. sharp! You will be served if you get in the door before the 8:30 closing. Closed Monday except holidays and closed last two weeks in December every year. *Owner:* George Kastrinakis. *Directions:* From Route 128, take Route 1A going toward Beverly. The restaurant is on the left before the bridge.

Also recommended:

There are a variety of restaurants and small stands that serve ethnic foods and short-order dishes in Salem. **The Commons,** a cafeteria at Salem State College on Lafayette Street, is a good place to get a reasonably priced meal. Breakfasts are served from 7:30 to 10:30 A.M. at low cost, and there is a good variety of deli sandwiches plus a salad bar; the soup and sandwich is under $3. A large hamburger is just over $2. Lunch is served from 10:30 A.M. to 2 P.M., and the restaurant is open winter and summer, except for holidays and school breaks.

Another place to save your pennies while eating out is at the **Cabot Place,** on Cabot Street in Beverly (just over the bridge). They feature twenty entrees between $6 and $8.50, most served with rice pilaf and salad, some with a vegetable, too. Shish kebab and fish are their specialty, all fresh and very well cooked. At lunch these are all $1 less! Sandwiches are $2 to $4. Specials run about $6. Owned by Tony Adoniou, this great bargain is open Monday through Friday from 11 A.M. to 9 P.M. and Saturday and Sunday from 7 A.M. to 9 P.M. Its location is 256 Cabot Street, Beverly; telephone (508) 927-3920.

The Galley at Pickering Wharf (the corner of Derby and Congress streets) is a fun place for folks who like variety! Fashioned after the very successful Quincy Market in Boston, there are small takeouts of four different types and tables in sunny windows, all enclosed in one building, which is clean and nicely decorated. For information, call the main number: (508) 745-9540. It opens at 7:30 A.M. and closes at 6 P.M. in winter and 10 P.M. in summer. There is Chinese food at the **Hong Kong Star,** pizza and subs at **Ceronel's,** and creole dishes at the **Creole Corner.** For dessert try a pastry at the **Bavarian Strudel Shop.**

Try the **Salem Diner** on the corner of Loring Avenue and Canal Street. They have specials every day for $3, including coffee and many other delicious entrees in the $3 to $5 range, such as Yankee pot roast and fish dishes. Frank says it has the "best pea soup in the U.S." Join us, along with many other loyal patrons in this folksy, very typical American diner. The restaurant opens at 5 A.M. every Monday through Friday and closes at 8 P.M.; Saturday 5 A.M. to 1:45 P.M. (closed Sunday). It is located at 326 Canal Street, and the telephone is (508) 744-9776.

We'd like to mention two more places for quick, enjoyable, very reasonably priced breakfast and lunch in Salem. One is **Boyle's Elm Tree Diner** on Boston Street. Go west on Essex Street to the monument and turn right. Boyle's is on your immediate right.

Bowman's Bakery on lower Essex Street in Salem is a great place to pick up lunch! For sandwiches, they feature avocado melt, ham and Jarlsberg, roast beef, and turkey. Try their good salads: mixed garden, cottage cheese and fruit, spinach, chef's, and pear and ginger. For delicious snacks, coffee and a dough-nut are reasonable, or choose from turnovers, muffins, crois-sants, cakes, cookies, rolls, and breads. Their big fruit cup in summer is sensational.

Dube's is great for seafood on Friday. It's a small, inexpensive restaurant with a great, longstanding track record. Find it at 317 Jefferson Avenue, Salem, on the left going south after St. Ann's Church.

"10 BRIDGE STREET"
10 Bridge Street
Shelburne Falls, Massachusetts 01370
(413) 625-6345

This restaurant is a marvelous eating spot along the Mohawk Trail. Frank's sister loves this place and put us on to it. It certain-ly will make your day if you hit the prime-rib special on Saturday night. Breakfast, lunch, and dinner are served at street level, while the 10 Bridge Street Cafe offers more intimate dining downstairs. Everything is homemade on the premises—all the pies and breads; the turkey is roasted right here . . . you get the idea. A great lunch is the roast beef sandwich on homemade bread with gravy, peas, and real whipped potatoes. The service is excellent.

Average prices: Breakfast around $3.50. Lunch and dinner, $5–$10. Lunch and dinner use the same menu except for daily specials advertised at your table or booth. *Credit cards:* None; per-sonal checks accepted. *Hours:* 6:30 A.M. to 10 P.M. daily, year-round. *Owner:* David Holstein. *Directions:* Exit off Route 2

(Mohawk Trail) to Shelburne Falls, then get on Route 2A. The restaurant is on the right, in the center of town just before the bridge.

JOY'S LANDING RESTAURANT
Water Street
South Dartmouth, Massachusetts 02748
(508) 992-8148

Joy's Landing Restaurant is small, very reasonable, and has good food. We ate there twice while in the vicinity. At dinner, we tried the linguica sandwich and kale soup, both Portuguese specialties, with coffee at the end of the meal. Fish and other delicious meals with a potato and vegetable or salad and bread are offered. Fish and chips are their specialty, and lobster rolls are very popular these days. We had super breakfasts of French toast and bacon or sausage for a good price. Across the street you can feed the ducks by the water.

Average prices: Breakfast, about $2. Sandwiches are $2 to $5 and dinners are under $4 to $10. *Credit cards:* None. *Hours:* Every day from 8 A.M. to 9 P.M.; open twenty-four hours on weekends for fishermen. *Owner:* Joyce Cousen. *Directions:* From New Bedford, take Dartmouth Street all the way to the end (St. Mary's Church). This leads into Prospect Street. At the stop sign, take a left onto Elm Street and your first right onto Bridge Street. The restaurant is on Water Street next door to Padanaram Guest House, which is at the corner of Bridge and Water streets.

Also recommended:

Joyce Williamson of the Padanaram Guest house suggested we try the very good gourmet cuisine of **The Bridge Street Café** at 10A Bridge Street in South Dartmouth. We found it moderately expensive. Call (508) 994-7200.

CRABAPPLES
Haynes Street
Sturbridge, Massachusetts 01566
(508) 347-9555

Crabapples is part of the Publick House complex. It is very charmingly decorated in plaids with white tablecloths and colorful stained-glass hanging lamps. Farm tools and antiques from old estates hang from the rafters, and a new room called the "Chicken Coop" is catchy with its chicken wire and pretend chickens peeking out at you. There are some good low-priced lunches such as quiche and salad, soup and sandwich, and an eight-ounce burger. Fried ice cream with fudge sauce is a special dessert. For dinner, try the delicious seafood pie or turkey dinner, both reasonably priced entrees.

Average prices: Lunch, $5 to $12; dinner, $5.50 to $12. *Credit cards:* All major. *Hours:* Sunday through Thursday: lunch, 11:30 A.M. to 5 P.M.; dinner, 5 to 9 P.M.; Friday and Saturday, open until 10 P.M. (snack menu till 11 P.M.). *Owner:* Noel Hennebery. *Directions:* Take the second right off Route 131 south, into the Publick House orchard.

ROM'S RESTAURANT
Route 131
Sturbridge, Massachusetts 01566
(508) 347-3349

Rom's Restaurant, specializing in Italian foods, is a favorite of many area natives. They have won several awards in New England. Their homemade pasta and delicacies are outstanding! In the medium price range are specialties of veal parmesan and veal cacciatore. They feature a smorgasbord on Wednesday from 5 to 9 P.M. with twenty-eight Italian-American dishes if you'd like to splurge. The dining room is comfortable and roomy with lots of windows, maple captain's chairs, and tables. Children's menu is available, groups are encouraged, and cocktails are served.

Average prices: Lunch, $4 to $6; dinner, $6 to $14, many in $6 to $8 range. *Credit cards:* American Express and Visa. *Hours:* Daily,

11:30 A.M. to 10 P.M. except Sunday when they close at 9 P.M. Open year-round. *Owner:* Romaldo Roscioli. *Directions:* Take Route 131 off Route 20. Rom's is a short way past the Publick House, on the right. It is 1½ miles from Old Sturbridge Village.

THE SUNBURST
484 Main Street, Box 555
Sturbridge, Massachusetts 01566
(508) 347-3097

The Sunburst is in an attractive 150-year-old yellow house on the main road featuring homemade goods and fresh fruits and vegetables in season. The inside is decorated with hanging plants and cheerful white and yellow checks. We had trouble choosing between the quiche with fruit, the egg o'muffin and the eggs with scrumptious, puffy, warm muffins for breakfast. They serve healthy lunches of cottage cheese and fruit with granola; soup and salad; chef's, egg, and tuna salads; and yummy sandwiches. Choose a box lunch of a muffin, fruit, yogurt, and/or soup, plus a drink, for about $3.50. Jean Dahler was very accommodating and her polite son was our waiter. She and her partner ran the business for four years in Brookfield before moving to Sturbridge.

Average prices: Breakfast, $2 to $4. Lunch: pockets, omelets, salads, quiche, and sandwiches, under $3 to $5.00. *Credit cards:* None. *Hours:* All year, every day from 7 A.M. to 3 P.M. *Owners:* Jean Dahler and Sylvia Sullivan Moore. *Directions:* Take Route 20 to Arnold Road. The restaurant is on the corner, across from The Sweater Outlet.

THE WHISTLING SWAN
502 Main Street
Sturbridge, Massachusetts 01566
(508) 347-2321

The Whistling Swan is a family-run restaurant in the center of town. The building, impressive with its white columns, is one of the prettiest we've seen. Restaurant owners eat there, which is a very good recommendation. There is entertainment on weekends in the lounge. Their specialties are homemade soups and desserts. We are accenting the menu in the Ugly Duckling Loft for you budget-minded folks, as you can eat a light but adequate meal at any time of the day. They have the same menu for lunch and dinner, which offers a half-sandwich and soup, fancy sandwiches, broiled scrod, beef stew, broiled scallops, and rum-honey-glazed barbecued spare ribs. French fries, cole slaw, vegetables, and fresh French bread are served with these light dinners. The service is fine and the atmosphere is great! Reservations are recommended.

Average prices: Lunch, about $4–$5. Dinner is the Ugly Duckling Loft, $7–$16. In the main restaurant, dinner prices are $9–$18. *Credit cards:* All major. *Hours:* Lunch, 11:30 A.M. to 2:30 P.M.; dinner, 5:30 to 9:30 P.M. Open Tuesday through Sunday. In the Loft, meals served 11:30 am. to 11:30 P.M. *Owners:* Carl and Rita Lofgren and family, Karen, Leslie, and Kim. *Directions:* Take Route 20 (Main Street) to the center of town. The restaurant is on the right, across from the Sturbridge Heritage Motel.

Also recommended:

Another wonderful buy is right in the Old Village at **The Sturbridge Village Tavern** in the great buffet room. If you don't mind having your big meal at midday, try the delicious "Colonial meal" consisting of country ham, baked beans, tavern chicken pie, succotash, tuna salad, baked macaroni and cheese, tossed salad, many corn and pickle relishes, jellied fruit salad with cottage cheese, marinated bean salad, and homemade bread, with deep dish apple pie or Indian pudding for dessert. All this, for a reasonable price, is served 11:30 A.M. to 3 P.M. daily from mid-June through Thanksgiving and in the winter on weekends only. Call (508) 347-3362 for reservations and information.

THE CHATEAU
195 School Street
Waltham, Massachusetts 02154
(617) 894-3339

The Chateau is recommended by *Boston Magazine* as the best Italian restaurant west of Boston. We knew it as a good spot when we lived in this area. You can get all the standard items from a listing of forty to fifty selections on the paper placemat they put on the table. It's that sort of place. It's great for the family or for a couple. It is handsomely decorated and doesn't seem noisy although it does a high-volume business. The lasagna, manicotti, and ravioli are all very tasty. Seafoods, chicken, and steak are also available if someone in your party doesn't like Italian food. A cocktail lounge with oak paneling and furniture has been added.

Average prices: Lunch or dinner, $5 to $9; spaghetti and meatballs are $5. Almost all entrees are under $7, and salads, soups, sandwiches, pizza, and takeout are available. *Credit cards:* All major. *Hours:* Monday through Thursday, 11 A.M. to 11 P.M.; Friday and Saturday, 11 A.M. to 11:30 P.M.; Sunday, noon to 8:30 P.M. Closed on Sunday during July and August. *Owner:* Lou Nocera. *Directions:* Exit off Route 128 to Route 20 and drive into Waltham. Take a left after the Shell gas station onto School Street. Turn right, and the Chateau is a few blocks up on your left.

RITCEY'S SEAFOOD KITCHEN
560 Moody Street
Waltham, Massachusetts 02154
(617) 893-9342

Ritcey's Seafood Kitchen is a favorite with locals and an establishment that we have enjoyed over the years. It has seafood in all styles of cooking. You can have it in a roll, in a stew, fried, baked, or caked. In case you bring someone who is not a seafood lover, they have hamburgers and chicken dishes. You may order small or large portions, which makes Ritcey's a good place to bring children. Also, if you are on the run, you can take out a medium box of delicious fried clams and eat them on the road. There is a small counter and ample table space for those who like to relax during lunch or dinner. Ritcey's can be a jumping-off point for a tour of the Minuteman National Historical Park in Lexington and Concord situated north of Waltham. Remember, though, that between 5 and 6 P.M. on Fridays, Ritcey's is mobbed and only takeout is offered.

Average prices: Lunch sandwiches are $1 to under $4. Fifteen sandwiches are priced under $2. Dinner prices range from $4 for smelts to $6 to $9 for lobster, clams, haddock, and scallops (lobster prices fluctuate according to the market). Specials in the $2 to $3 range for kids are chicken wing dings and franks and beans. *Credit cards:* None. *Hours:* Tuesday, 11 A.M. to 7 P.M.; Wednesday, Thursday, and Saturday, 11 A.M. to 8 P.M.; Friday, 11 A.M. to 9 P.M. Closed on Sunday and Monday. *Owner:* Kevin Ritcey. *Directions:* From Route 128, take Route 20 into Waltham. At the town center, turn south onto Moody Street. Ritcey's is ½ mile farther on the left. Look carefully because the sign is quite small.

BAYSIDE RESTAURANT
1253 Horseneck Road
Westport, Massachusetts 02790
(508) 636-5882

Bayside Restaurant, on a backroad toward Horseneck Beach, was one of our "happenings" in this area. We were visiting our daughter at Southeastern Massachusetts University and wanted to try something different for breakfast. She and her roommate took us on a winding drive through gorgeous countryside, with fields and farms at every turn. Finally we reached an absolutely hallowed place, where we could see a bay and waving marsh grass; the sun was new and the breezes fresh—what a morning! And there in full view of all this beauty was the little Bayside, with picnic tables on a deck with umbrellas. We ate our pancakes, sausage, and coffee from paper dishes, and feasted on both the meal and the wonderful morning outdoors. It was crowded, but the waitress was gracious and kind, and the prices were great, too.

Average prices: Breakfast, $1 to $3. Lunch: hamburger and other sandwiches, $1 to $5. Dinner: spaghetti, $5; meatloaf, mashed potatoes, and a vegetable, $6; large fish and chips, $6; lobster,

$16. *Credit cards:* None. *Hours:* Winter: Tuesday through Sunday, 8 A.M. to 8 P.M. Summer: every day, 8 A.M. to 9 P.M. *Owner:* Robert E. Carroll. *Directions:* From Route 6, take the road to Westport. In town, ask for directions to Horseneck Road. It's only about twenty minutes from the university and is on the right, near the water.

CAPE COD & THE ISLANDS

Cape Cod has an interesting geologic history. In the last Ice Age, the glacier deposited a flat ridge of earth called a terminal moraine as it melted northward. Many of the lakes are called kettleholes, where a large cake of ice settled and melted, causing the round shape peculiar to New England ponds and lakes. Other physical phenomena are the great tidal salt marshes, which attract hundreds of varieties of shore birds for feeding, and some ponds near the ocean that were once bays and still have a degree of salt water. The Gulf Stream, flowing up from the south, causes the waters of Nantucket Sound to be extremely warm in the summer, making it a very popular vacation spot for New Englanders, New Yorkers, and folks from many other states. Indigenous to the Cape are cranberry bogs, good flat bicycling roads, numerous seductive little roads that end at the sea, bays and beaches for great sailing and swimming, and miles of sand and dunes on which to catch some rays!

Traveling from Boston, you can use either the Sagamore or the Bourne Bridge to cross the canal. Be sure to visit the Cape Cod Canal, 17 miles long and manmade, with great fishing from its banks and unusual sights of huge ships and barges passing through. In the spring, watch the herring fighting to spawn upstream at herring runs in Bournedale and Red Beach Harbor. You'll find Chamber of Commerce booths for information and maps at Bourne, Sagamore, and West Barnstable, at the junction of Routes 6 and 132. Generally, there are three main roads: The Cranberry Highway or Route 6A runs along the northern coast to Orleans; Route 28 runs to Falmouth and along the southern part; and Route 6 starts at the Sagamore Bridge and runs along the center of the Cape, meets the other two routes in Orleans, and continues along by itself to Provincetown. Many routes connect the north and south, but the less traveled are Phinney's Lane and Station Avenue. It's only an hour-and-a-half drive from the Canal to Provincetown. There is a 70-mile segment of the Boston Cape Cod Bikeway marked by arrows and signs. For information and map, send a self-addressed, stamped envelope and 37 cents to Cape Cod Map, CTPS, 27 School Street, Boston, MA 02108.

Being so popular, the Cape has higher prices than other parts of New England, especially for lodgings. We have sought out as many reasonably priced ones as possible. If you're looking for low prices, consider coming to the Cape in Indian summer, late

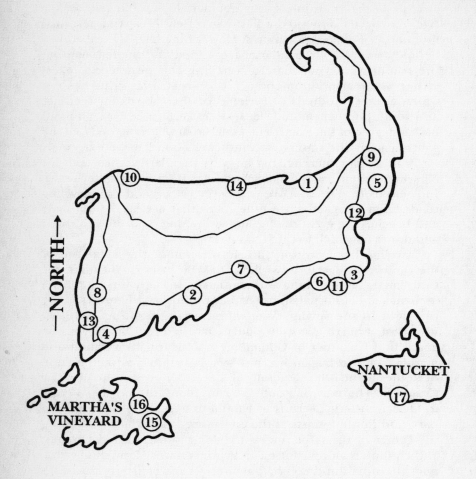

CAPE COD &
THE ISLANDS

	🛏	🍴
1. Brewster	117	—
2. Centerville	117	—
3. Chatham	119	130
4. East Falmouth	121	—
5. East Orleans	121	—
6. Harwichport	122	—
7. Hyannis	123	130
8. North Falmouth	—	132
9. Orleans	124	133
10. Sandwich	124	136
11. South Harwich	125	—
12. South Orleans	126	—
13. West Falmouth	126	—
14. Yarmouthport	127	137
15. Edgartown, Martha's Vineyard	140	142
16. Oak Bluffs, Martha's Vineyard	—	142
17. Nantucket	145	—

fall, or early spring. The weather's not bad then (it's delightful in Indian summer) and you'll be able to find off-season rates at many lodgings.

One alternative for those who like to rough it are the American Youth Hostels, which are all dormitory style but super reasonable. For information, write them at 1020 Commonwealth Avenue, Boston, Massachusetts, or phone (617) 731-5430. There are also excellent campgrounds on the Cape. One of the best, Nickerson State Park, always has a waiting line, so we'd like to suggest our favorite—Sweetwater Forest, off Route 124 in Brewster. It has a good swimming pond and is so large that it is the best bet to try at the last minute. You can reserve here whereas you cannot at Nickerson. Call (508) 896-3773.

Good luck! We hope we've helped you find the essence of the Cape, which is, most of all, its natural simplicity!

WHERE TO STAY ON CAPE COD

OLD SEA PINES INN
2553 Main Street, Box 1026
Brewster, Massachusetts 02631
(508) 896-6114; (800) 242-6114

Old Seas Pines Inn, a stunning gray building with twenty-one guest rooms, is one of the prettiest inns on the Cape. The gracious young hostess showed me all her sparkling "pin-neat" rooms with wallpapers, antiques, and quilts. There is a wonderful feeling of space in all the common rooms, especially the big dining room, outdoor porch, and enclosed porch. The three and a quarter acres of woods and lawns will give you room to walk and lounge. This nineteenth-century charm school is very close to Point of Rocks Beach. It is also a great spot for a large party or wedding! The inn has a full liquor license. The "North Cottage" has seven non-smoking rooms with shared baths. One suite in the main building is handicapped accessible.

Average rates: Double, $40–$90; suites, $85–$125. $10 for cot. All rates include full breakfast. *Credit cards:* Diner's Club, MasterCard, Visa, and American Express. *Open:* All year. *Owners:* Steve and Michele Rowan. *Directions:* Take exit 10 off Route 6 (Mid-Cape Highway). Go north on Route 124. Take right on 6A and go 1 mile past the Brewster General Store. The inn is on the left. *Children:* Yes, ten and over. *Pets:* No. *Smoking:* Restricted.

LONG DELL INN
436 South Main Street
Centerville, Massachusetts 02632
(508) 775-2750

Long Dell is an attractive, 140-year-old home. There are six rooms, all with private baths and very beautifully decorated, many with floral stencils. Blue and white are prevailing colors, especially in the pretty Victorian living room with its oriental carpet, white fireplace, wide board pine floors, and high ceiling. A full three-course breakfast is served in the blue and white breakfast and dining room. There are also two rooms in a carriage house in the rear of the yard. This home is within walking distance of Craigville Beach. Special honeymoon and weekend packages are available. Inquire for current prices.

Average rates: Double or twin bedded room, $60–$75. *Credit cards:* None. *Open:* All year. *Owners:* Joy and Roy Swayze. *Directions:* Take Route 6 to Route 132 to Phinney's Lane. Turn right and go all the way to Centerville. Take Main Street toward Craigville Beach. Go right on South Main about 1 block, and the house is on the right. *Children:* Fourteen and over. *Pets:* No. *Smoking:* No.

THE OLD HUNDRED HOUSE
1211 Craigville Beach Road
Centerville, Massachusetts 02632
(508) 775-6166

The Old Hundred House is a very special place—we feel it is the find of the Cape. Situated in this wonderfully peaceful, shady town, very close to the lovely Craigville Beach and surrounded by the beautifully subtle tidal marshes, there are only eight rooms to rent. The back yard, with water within yards of the house, is a delight for birdwatchers. Ducks, geese, herons, and even swans frequent the area daily. You may enjoy them from the huge porch, which is breezy all summer. The very best guest room in the house is on this mellow back side, where "you wake to bird sounds," as the congenial Mrs. Downes explains. The rooms all have brightly flowered wallpaper, really old four-posters, and antique coverlets. Two of the rooms are quite large and have fireplaces. All rooms share baths. The complimentary continental breakfast includes "homebaked goodies." The name of the house comes from a hymn Captain Andreus Bearse, the builder, used to whistle. The doxology in those days, 160 years ago, was also called the "Old One Hundred Hymn." Children are welcome.

Average rates: Rooms, $38. *Credit cards:* None. *Open:* All year (in winter only when the owners are home). *Owners:* Marina and Jack Downes. *Directions:* Take Route 132 south off Route 6. Go right on Phinney's Lane, which goes directly south to Centerville. The house is just a few hundred yards beyond Centerville Corners. *Children:* Yes. *Pets:* No. *Smoking:* Restricted.

ADAMS TERRACE GARDENS INN
539 Main Street
Centerville, Massachusetts 02632
(508) 775-4707

Adams Terrace Gardens Inn, another sea captain's house (Captain John Baker), has a screened porch, an open porch, and a truly spectacular garden, full of shade trees, roses, and yellow daisies. The surprise is a pool in the lower yard. The inn is near the center of town, but you may still walk to the beach. The rooms are all large with colonial decor and nicely coordinated colors. One has a private entrance and one a fireplace. Guests are welcome to use the large sitting room. All eight rooms have cable television. A full breakfast is served.

Average rates: Double with private bath, $75; with shared bath, $65. *Credit cards:* None. *Open:* All year. *Owners:* Pat and John Veracka. *Directions:* Take Route 132 off Route 6 and turn right onto Phinney's Lane, which goes directly to Centerville. The inn is just before the Country Store on Main Street. *Children:* Yes. *Pets:* No. *Smoking:* Yes.

BOW ROOF HOUSE
59 Queen Anne Road
Chatham, Massachusetts 02633
(508) 945-1346

Bow Roof House is an enchanting sea captain's house built 200 years ago, but very well kept up. Captain Solomon Howe built this "best standing example" of a "bow roof" (in the shape of a ship's bow) with well-seasoned timbers like those used in ships. It has the feel of an English cottage with the narrow staircase and many old slanted fireplaces and chimneys. Upstairs the rooms are snug with slanted, attic ceilings, velvety blankets, handsome spreads on four-posters, and dainty wallpaper. Downstairs

119

guests may mingle in the relaxing sitting room with a television, huge fireplace, and cathedral ceiling. All rooms have private baths. Mrs. Mazulis allows kitchen privileges and loves to talk about her home, Chatham and its history, and the high points of the town. The yard has a lovely patio with chairs, and a small beach is just a two-minute walk down Pond Street. Continental breakfast is included in the room price.

Average rates: Double, $45–$50. *Credit cards:* None. *Open:* All year. *Owner:* Vera Mazulis. *Directions:* Go off Route 6 at exit 11 (Route 137 to Route 28). Continue on 28 to the stoplight. Take a right at the stoplight; you're now on Queen Anne Road. The house is 1 block up on the right, across from the Queen Anne Inn. *Children:* Yes. *Pets:* No. *Smoking:* Yes.

CHAT-HAM HOUSE
49 Queen Anne Road
Chatham, Massachusetts 02633
(508) 945-3274

Chat-Ham House is just down the road from Bow Roof and is quite a different style. The rooms are immaculate, wood paneled, good looking, and motel-style with cable television, roomy private baths, and private entrances. Coffee makers are in each room, and picnic tables and a fireplace are in the back yard for guests' enjoyment. There are two king- and two queen-sized beds.

Average rates: Double, $45. *Credit cards:* None. *Open:* April–October. *Owners:* Paul and Patricia St. John. *Directions:* Go off Route 6 at exit 11 (Route 137 to Route 28). Continue on Route 28 to the stoplight. Take a right at the stoplight and you're now on Queen Anne Road. The house is 1 block up on right, across from the Queen Anne Inn and next to the Bow Roof House. *Children:* Yes. *Pets:* No. *Smoking:* Yes.

Also recommended:

Cranberry Inn in Chatham is a homey, large guest house with a refined, handsome living room filled with plants. The inn has been recently renovated. It is very centrally located at 359 Main

Street and has a huge porch for people-watching. The Morris family gives guests a lot of attention, and the rooms are clean and comfortable. The inn is open from early May to late October and the rates are reasonable. Telephone (508) 945-9232 or (800) 332-4667.

GREEN HARBOR MOTEL
134 Acapesket Road
East Falmouth, Massachusetts
(508) 548-4747

Green Harbor Motel has beautiful surroundings bordering on Green Pond. There is a boat deck and ramp, free rowboats and paddleboats, and an adult and a child's pool! The rooms are clean, comfortable, and fitted out with color television and air conditioning. The Dineens hold clambakes for their guests to give them a true Cape Cod experience. If you like exercise and scenery, you can bike or walk to Menauhant Beach.

Average rates: Double, in season $74–$88; off-season, $56–$64. *Credit cards:* MasterCard, Visa, and American Express. *Open:* April 15 to November 1. *Owners:* The Dineen family. *Directions:* Cross Cape Cod Canal on Route 28. Follow 28 to the Brick Kiln Road exit and East Falmouth. Turn left at the end of the exit ramp. Proceed on Brick Kiln Road to the end. Go left on Route 28. Proceed ½ mile to Acapesket Road. Turn right, and go ½ mile to the motel on the left. *Children:* Yes. *Pets:* Yes. *Smoking:* Yes.

THE NAUSET HOUSE INN
Beach Road, P.O. Box 774
East Orleans, Massachusetts 02643
(508) 255-2195

This charming 1810 inn with fourteen rooms is a little higher priced than most of those we recommend, but not terribly high for the Cape. It has special qualities such as a gorgeous big dining room with a beamed ceiling, stucco walls, a huge fireplace, a painted oval table, and conservatory that is glassed in and sunny and houses many plants and flowers among the wicker furniture.

It also is very near Nauset Beach. The bedrooms are cozy, some with slanted ceilings and all with lovely antique beds and covers; the oversized living room with the fireplace is a welcoming sight. Some rooms have hand-painted floral designs on the furniture done by Diane Johnson. Music lovers will enjoy the piano in the little alcove. Breakfast is extra.

Average rates: Double with shared bath, $55–$65; double with private bath, $85–$95; double with bath and balcony or large double with bath and sitting area, $95. Full breakfast, $5; continental breakfast, $3. *Credit cards:* MasterCard and Visa. *Open:* April 3 to October 31. *Owners:* Diane and Al Johnson. *Directions:* From Route 6 take exit 12 and turn right at the first set of stoplights. Go two more lights and turn right again onto Main Street. Follow the signs to Nauset Beach. The inn is halfway down the beach on the right. *Children:* Yes, twelve and over. *Pets:* No. *Smoking:* Tolerated.

COUNTRY INN
86 Sisson Road
Harwichport, Massachusetts 02646
(508) 432-2769

Country Inn is an engaging 1773 colonial on six and a half acres of land about a mile from Harwichport. There are seven pleasant rooms, one a suite, all with private baths, plus three tennis courts and a pool. Some of the inn's eleven fireplaces are in the bedrooms. The inn is very homey and beautifully decorated and has plenty of space for guests to enjoy the company of one another.

A continental breakfast, which is included in the price of the room, is served buffet style in the tavern room. The inn also serves elegant and delicious evening meals, including seafood and steak, at reasonable prices. Homemade breads and desserts are the specialties. They cook with an emphasis on the native Cape Cod cranberry.

Average rates: In-season double, $55–$65; off-season double, $5 less. $12.50 for an extra person in the room. *Credit cards:* MasterCard, Visa, and American Express. *Open:* All year except

January. *Owners:* Jim and Lois Crapo. *Directions:* From Route 6, take exit 10 to Harwichport. Go right on Route 124, cross Main Street in Harwichport, and continue on Routes 124 and 39, which becomes Sisson Road. The inn is on the right about a mile from Main Street. *Children:* Twelve and over. *Pets:* No. *Smoking:* Yes.

Also recommended:

Dunscroft Inn, on 24 Pilgrim Road in Harwichport, is another bed & breakfast with three hundred feet of private beach. In summer it is over our price limit, but off-season, a double is reasonable. It's really a gorgeous home with lots of care and attention from the amiable Cunninghams. All rooms have private baths, and you may use the large living room with a television or socialize in the spacious sun room. It is open year-round. Full breakfast is included in both summer and off-season rates. A cottage that sleeps four is available in season. Call Wallace and Algie Cunningham at (508) 432-0810.

SALT WINDS BED AND BREAKFAST
319 Sea Street
Hyannis, Massachusetts 02601
(508) 775-2038

Salt Winds is a homey, traditional house with seven rooms furnished in early American and country decor. Some rooms have canopy beds. There are pleasant areas for picnics and cookouts in the yard, and it's only a short walk to Orin Keyes Beach or to town. Four rooms in a separate house in the back have private baths. This B&B serves a full breakfast. The hosts offer free transport to island ferries. A new pool is also available.

Average rates: Double, in season $55–$75; off-season, $50–$55. Efficiency apartment: one bedroom, $395 per week; two bedrooms, $495 per week. *Credit cards:* None. *Open:* April to November. *Owners:* Virginia and Craig Conroy. *Directions:* Take Route 6 to Route 132 south to Hyannis. Take Barnstable Road to Main Street, turn right, and go less than a mile to Sea Street. Turn left, and a short way down is Salt Winds, a gray house with pink shutters on the right. *Children:* Yes. *Pets:* No. *Smoking:* Restricted.

ACADEMY PLACE BED & BREAKFAST
8 Academy Place
P.O. Box 1407
Orleans, Massachusetts 02653
(508) 255-3181

This 1752 colonial is one of Orleans's oldest homes. It is now owned by Charles and Sandy Terrell, but we stayed there with our children many years ago when Charles's mother ran it. It has been very nicely renovated to show more of its post and beam construction and wide pine boards as well as Sandy's choice of fine flower-printed wallpapers. The beautiful antique blue and white platters on the walls hold to traditional early American decor. There are five rooms, three with private and two with shared baths. The narrow stairway with a railing around the top and the slanted ceilings give you a feeling of being in Gramma's attic. The property was once a working farm, and you may sit and rock on the old farm porch or lounge under the sycamores in the yard. You can also walk to town. Sandy serves a wonderful breakfast of cereal, fruit, her own delicious warm muffins and breads, coffees, and teas of all flavors.

Average rates: Double, $50 to $70. *Credit cards:* MasterCard and Visa. *Open:* Memorial Day to early October. *Owners:* Charles and Sandy Terrell. *Directions:* Take Route 6 past Hyannis to exit 12 toward Orleans. Turn right at end of exit onto Route 6A and go through one light. At the next light, at the center of town, turn right onto Main Street, then go to the next light at the intersection of Main Street and Route 28. Academy Place is across the Village Green; look for its flagpole and sign. Go through the light and turn left around the far side of the green into their driveway. *Children:* Six and over. *Pets:* No. *Smoking:* No.

THE CAPTAIN EZRA NYE HOUSE
152 Main Street
Sandwich, Massachusetts 02563
(508) 888-6142; (800) 388-2278

The Captain Ezra Nye House is a hip-roofed Georgian-Federal style home, built in the 1820s. You'll enjoy reading in the den and socializing in the elegant living room with the charming Dicksons. The whole house is decorated in Williamsburg colors and antique furniture; some of the beds have high Victorian headboards, and two have canopies. The blue room with a king-sized bed has a working fireplace. The walls are covered with soft watercolors (some done by Elaine), bird pastels, marvelous charcoals, pastoral oil paintings, and some oriental works. The full breakfast, served in the dining room, consists of fresh fruit, melon or baked apple, muffins, coffee cake or cobblers, quiches, and soufflés.

Average rates: Double, $50–$75; 10 percent discount for stays of five nights or more. *Credit cards:* Visa, MasterCard, Discover, and American Express. *Open:* All year. *Owners:* Harry and Elaine Dickson. *Directions:* Take Route 6 to exit 2, then proceed to Sandwich center. The house is in the village center on the right. *Children:* Yes, six and over. *Pets:* No. *Smoking:* No.

THE HOUSE ON THE HILL
968 Main Street, P.O. Box 51
South Harwich, Massachusetts 02661
(508) 432-4321

We were driving along Route 28 when we spotted this bed & breakfast off the beaten path, stopped, and conducted our usual inspection and interview. What a pleasant surprise to discover such a nice and reasonable place on this very popular area of the Cape. Carolyn Swanson showed us her pretty, restored country colonial and its antique furnishings and explained how they had remodeled the bathrooms and beautifully decorated the guest rooms. We were impressed. Not only is the ambience pleasing but the hosts and their family are charming. A living room with a television is available to guests. There are four bedrooms, one a single. One has a private bath; the rest share a bath. Continental breakfast is served.

Average rates: Double, $50–$65; single, $35–$40. Off-season, $40–$50. Special rate for family suite. *Credit cards:* None. *Open:* All year. *Owners:* Allen and Carolyn Swanson. *Directions:* Take exit 10 off Route 6. Head south on Route 124. Turn left on Route 39

125

and proceed a short while to Bank Street on your right. Go south on Bank Street to Route 28, then turn left and drive for 1.4 miles. The House On The Hill is on your left. *Children:* Yes. *Pets:* No. *Smoking:* No.

HILLBOURNE HOUSE
Box 90; Chatham Road
South Orleans, Massachusetts 02662
(508) 255-0780; (508) 755-3647 (weekdays off-season)

This beautiful house on a hillside overlooking Pleasant Bay is a great find on the eastern edge of the Cape. It is a historical house with a motor inn added to it. The rooms, in Williamsburg blue, green, and mauve, all have private baths. From the lawn chairs, surrounded by gardens out front, you can enjoy the fantastic water view. Barbara serves a good-sized breakfast of fruit, French toast, waffles, and baked goods. The attractive common room is great for reading or talking with other guests. There are also two vacation cottages, one with a fireplace, and the motel rooms all have cable television.

Average rates: Double, $60 to $80. *Credit cards:* None. *Open:* End of May to end of September and off-season weekends. *Owners:* Jack and Barbara Hayes. *Directions:* From Route 6, take exit 11, turn left onto Route 137 and almost immediately left again onto Pleasant Bay Road. Follow it to its end at Route 28. Go left and proceed ½ mile to Hillbourne House. *Children:* Twelve and over. *Pets:* No. *Smoking:* Restricted.

SJÖHOLM BED AND BREAKFAST INN
17 Chase Road
West Falmouth, Massachusetts 02574
(508) 540-5706

This 125-year-old cape with ten rooms is on a quiet dead-end street in a pastoral setting. A delightful surprise is the complimentary, full breakfast buffet every morning, composed of fresh fruit, two or three types of cereal, homemade bread, muffins,

126

bagels, and coffee, which is on all day! There is a common living room with a television, and a bright, colorful sun porch for guests. The inn rooms are very pretty. Barbara has added five rooms with private baths, all with a lovely country motif. One is in the main house; four are downstairs in the Carriage House.

Average rates: Double: in season, $55–$85; off-season, $50–$75. Discounts for longer stays. *Credit cards:* None. *Open:* All year. *Owner:* Barbara Eck. *Directions:* From Bourne Bridge, take Route 28 south to the Thomas Landers exit. Make a right at the bottom of the ramp, then go left and drive ½ mile on 28A to Chase Road. The inn is on the right. *Children:* Five and over. *Pets:* No. *Smoking:* Restricted.

COLONIAL HOUSE INN
Route 6A
Yarmouthport, Massachusetts 02675
(508) 362-4348

The Colonial House Inn is a buy in all seasons because the rates include breakfast and dinner for two!

The inn is an immense Victorian mansion on three lovely acres with gardens, a pond, and a fountain. The bedrooms are charming with antique pineapple four-poster beds and private baths. There are three dining rooms, one a large, screened, green and white veranda; continental cuisine is served in all.

Average rates: Off-season, from Columbus Day to Memorial Day, Sunday through Thursday, $60 for two, including breakfast and dinner. Friday and Saturday in the winter, $80 for two. In-season double is $80–$95, including breakfast and dinner. Two-night minimum on weekends. Holiday and other special rates are available. *Credit cards:* MasterCard, Visa, American Express, and Discover. *Open:* All year. *Owner:* Malcolm Perna. *Directions:* The inn is on the south side of Route 6A, just over the line in Yarmouthport, as you drive east. *Children:* Yes. *Pets:* Yes. *Smoking:* Yes.

OLD YARMOUTH INN
223 Main Street, P.O. Box 212
Yarmouthport, Massachusetts 02675
(508) 362-3191; (508) 362-3130

Old Yarmouth Inn, the oldest inn on the Cape, dates back to 1696 and is full of tradition, from charming, sagging floors to spool beds. Fireplaces, wicker antiques, and stenciled walls take you back to olden times. The full breakfast includes everything but eggs. The inn also houses a very popular restaurant. All rooms have color television and air conditioning. Maid gratuities are included in the price.

Average rates: Double with private bath, $80–$90; off-season, $60–$70. *Credit cards:* All major. *Open:* All year. *Owners:* Carl Manchon and David Madison. *Directions:* The inn is on the north side of Route 6A near the center of town. *Children:* Over twelve. *Pets:* No. *Smoking:* Yes.

ONE CENTRE STREET INN
1 Centre Street
Yarmouthport, Massachusetts 02675
(508) 362-8910

One Centre Street Inn is a charming single home with four guest rooms. The house has a really old flavor with Shaker-like sparseness and subdued colonial creamy colors, like the colors of buttermilk. The antique high-back beds are covered with quilts, and every room has braided or oriental rugs. There is a comfortable public sitting room and a Gaelic welcome sign over the door. The Wrights offer a full breakfast of fruits, baked goods such as blueberry nutcake or fruit kuchen, Belgian waffles, cheese strata, and homemade granola. Beaches are nearby and four bicycles are available to guests. There is a nice table and chair in the backyard garden for you to enjoy. The inn is AAA-approved.

Average rates: Double, $50 to $85. *Credit cards:* MasterCard, Visa, and American Express. *Open:* All year. *Owners:* Stefanie and Bill

Wright. *Directions:* The inn is on the corner of Route 6A and Centre Street near the center of Yarmouthport. *Children:* Yes. *Pets:* No. *Smoking:* No.

THE VILLAGE INN
92 Main Street (Rt. 6A), P.O. Box 1
Yarmouthport, Massachusetts 02675
(508) 362-3182

The Village Inn is a beautiful, rangy, old sea captain's house with ten guest rooms, six with private baths. The rooms are large and handsome with unusual features, such as a fireplace in one of the bathrooms as well as in the bedroom, and pine walls in another room. There are two large sitting rooms, a great old piano, and a spacious screened porch for guests. The complimentary continental breakfast is served in a cozy family room with a fireplace.

Mrs. Hickey, the owner since 1952, is a warm, generous lady, who shows her guests very special attention. She loves to help them find just the right place to eat or to give them directions to beaches.

Average rates: Double: in season, $60–$75; off-season, $55. *Credit cards:* None. *Open:* All year. *Owners:* Mac and Esther Hickey. *Directions:* Take exit 7 north from Route 6 (Willow Street) to Route 6A. Go right. The inn is on the left (north side) between the Christmas Tree Shop and the two banks. (Route 6A is Main Street.) *Children:* Yes (reservation necessary). *Pets:* Yes (reservation necessary). *Smoking:* Restricted.

WHERE TO EAT ON CAPE COD

OLD HARBOR BAKERY AND COFFEE SHOP
75 Old Harbor Road
Chatham, Massachusetts 02633
(508) 945-4380

Old Harbor Bakery and Coffee Shop is a bright, clean spot for breakfast or lunch. Full breakfasts of eggs, bacon, sausage or ham, and home fries are favorites, and two eggs cost less. There are also pancakes, French toast, and omelets. We had bowls of delicious, homemade minestrone soup. The grilled cheese, hamburger, and fancier things like Reubens are served with pickles and chips. Luscious coffee rolls, muffins, and fresh doughnuts are available. It's worth it just to walk in the door and smell the fresh, hot, enormous bran, blueberry, or orange-cranberry muffins. All may be eaten at a long counter or at tables in a raised dining area. Jim took over as owner in 1991, so expect some special changes in the menu.

Average prices: Great muffins are low in price! Sandwiches run from $1 to a little over $3. *Credit cards:* None. *Hours:* Monday through Saturday, 6 A.M. to 2 P.M.; Sunday, 6 A.M. to 1 P.M. *Owner:* James Tserpes. *Directions:* Take Route 28 to the rotary at Chatham and turn left. The bakery is in Old Harbor Plaza, 1 block up on the left. This is at corner of Depot Road.

JOHN'S LOFT
8 Barnstable Road
Hyannis, Massachusetts 02601
(508) 775-1111

John's Loft is attractive and comfortable with wooden beams, antiques, and an immense fireplace. Many reasonable specials are offered, such as the early-bird specials between 5 and 6:30 P.M. When we were there, the specials were seafood, various casseroles, and boneless breast of chicken for fair prices. The salad bar is always an option. The newest feature is an exciting international menu. Other delectable entrees are petit filet mignon, scrod, lobster, prime rib, and king crab. There is a cock-tail bar. Ample parking is just across the street.

Average prices: Dinner, $12–$24; early-bird specials, $2 less for anything, including lobster. *Credit cards:* MasterCard, Visa, Diner's Club, and American Express. *Hours:* All year, 5 to 10 P.M. *Owner:* Nick Joakim (for 30 years). *Directions:* Take exit 6 to Route 132. Continue to the airport rotary. Take the second right onto Barnstable Road. The restaurant is 1 mile farther on left, before Main Street.

MURPH'S RECESSION
12 Thornton Drive
Independence Park
Hyannis, Massachusetts 02601
(508) 775-9750

Murph's is a must for Cape travelers. This very popular, fairly priced restaurant is comfortable and attractively decorated, with beams, plants, and lots of wood. It seats about forty people. They offer fifteen different blackboard specials daily. New York sirloin, roast lamb, char-broiled pork chops, and swordfish are some of them. The beef stew was super! You'll appreciate the casual atmosphere; the barnboard makes for warmth and coziness. "Murph" calls it "the Durgin Park of the Cape." Not recommended for very young children. There is a small bar.

Average prices: Lunch sandwiches are over $3 to over $4. Dinner, $5 to $12. Haddock au gratin, over $7; New York sirloin and roast lamb, $8. *Credit cards:* None. *Hours:* Monday through Thursday, 11 A.M. to 10 P.M.; Friday and Saturday, 11 A.M. to 11 P.M.; Sunday, 4 to 9 P.M. *Owner:* Nancy Hickey. *Directions:* Turn off Route 132 into Independence Park. Go to the stop sign and take a left. You'll see Murph's on the right next to the U.S. Spring Company.

SUNNYSIDE RESTAURANT
304 Main Street
Hyannis, Massachusetts 02601
(508) 775–3539

Sunnyside is a fabulous bargain for breakfast and lunch. Homemade soups and sandwiches are offered, as well as daily specials. The food is excellent.

Average prices: Breakfast, $2.20 to $7; lunch, $1.90 to $4.25. *Credit cards:* None. *Hours:* Open Monday to Saturday, 6 A.M. to 3 P.M.; Sunday, 6 A.M. to 1 P.M. *Owner:* Arthur Beatty. *Directions:* Go to center of Hyannis. The restaurant is at the east end of Main Street across from the Cape Cod Bank and Trust.

Also recommended:

Baxter's Fish and Chips at 177 Pleasant Street in Hyannis features tasty fried fish, clams, shrimp, scallops, and fritters. Their chowders are super! It is very casual with good food, and you may watch the boats from the wharf or the ferry boat. Prices are very reasonable. They're open from May to October, every day but Monday. Hours are 11:30 A.M. to 10 P.M. Call (508) 775-4490.

THE SILVER LOUNGE
Route 28A
North Falmouth, Massachusetts 02556
(508) 563-2410

The Silver Lounge is right next to Uncle Bill's Country Store in North Falmouth. It has a rustic and nautical decor, and the food is terrific. Just ask a local resident. This place is known for its great sandwiches, steaks, and seafood. Scallops and a big lobster pie are some of the favorites, and there is a special every night.

Average prices: Sandwiches, $2.40 to $6.50. Dinner, $6.75–$13. Many dishes are in the $9.50 to $11 range. *Credit cards:* None. *Hours:* 11:30 A.M. to 1 A.M. daily. *Owner:* Bill Weaner. *Directions:* Take Bourne Bridge to Otis Air Force rotary. Take first right off rotary and left at stoplight. Continue through next stoplight. It's ¼ mile on the right on Route 28A.

CAPT'N ELMER'S SEAFOOD RESTAURANT
18 Old Colony Way
Orleans, Massachusetts 02643
(508) 255-7221; (508) 255-3350 (takeout)

Capt'n Elmer's Seafood Restaurant is a favorite of the natives. The atmosphere is casual, with booths, tables, soft orange walls, and a cozy woodburning stove in the middle of the floor. There are specials every day. Their tasty homemade breads are a specialty. There is a children's menu, and they have takeout orders. Dinners are served on Friday and Saturday. It seats a hundred people. Cocktails are served; fresh fish, shellfish, and live lobsters are for sale.

Average prices: Breakfast, under $4 to under $6. Lunch: sandwiches in the $2 range; fish and chips, $6. Dinner: fried clams, haddock, and swordfish range from $6 to $12. *Credit cards:* MasterCard, Visa, and American Express. *Hours:* Off-season, Sunday through Thursday, 6 A.M. to 3 P.M.; Friday and Saturday, 6 A.M. to 8 P.M. In summer, 8 A.M. to 8:30 P.M. every day. *Owner:* Elmer Costa. *Directions:* From Route 6, take exit 12 to Orleans. At the stoplight turn left onto West Road, then turn right onto Old Colony Way. Elmer's is 1 mile up this road.

HOMEPORT RESTAURANT
Main Street, P.O. Box 1228
Orleans, Massachusetts 02653
(508) 255-4069

Homeport Restaurant has a warm atmosphere and is centrally located. You can get a full breakfast for a reasonable price, and coffee is a set charge with refills any time of the day! For lunch there are numerous sandwiches, such as a charbroiled hamburger; chicken or tuna salad; bacon, lettuce, and tomato; corned beef; roast beef; pastrami; and an Alpine burger with sautéed onions, melted Swiss cheese, tomato, lettuce, pickles, and fries. All sandwiches are served with pickles and chips on dark or white bread or a bulkie roll, and you can make a meal of it with a choice of two of the following: fries, baked potato, beans, cole slaw, cottage cheese, vegetable, or lettuce and tomato. The possibilities are stupendous! The dinners are chicken, ham, fish, clams, scallops, baked stuffed haddock, and fancy steaks or seafood combinations. The specials on the board the night we were there were crock of clam chowder, baked stuffed clams, and half a roast beef sandwich; grilled Reuben with fries and cole slaw; and hotdogs or ham and beans with brown bread. Other specialties are European coffees, homebaked pies, and cocktails or beer. You may eat at tables or at a diner-like bar.

Average prices: Lunch, under $2 to over $5; dinner, $7–$15. Board specials offer much in the $5–$10 range. *Credit cards:* None. *Hours:* Every day, 6 A.M. to 8 or 9 P.M. *Owner:* Jack Shields (for ten years). *Directions:* In Orleans, take Main Street to Ellis Market (in the mall across from the post office). Homeport is next door.

THE LOBSTER CLAW
Route 6A
Orleans, Massachusetts 02643
(508) 255-1800

The Lobster Claw, a big, informal, airy place on Route 6A, has been operating since the Berigs's children were small, fifteen years ago, and still offers a wonderful variety for families, with children's specials. This happy affair, run by the Berig family, has a nice surprise for early diners: chowder, beverage, and ice cream are free with any regularly priced dinner from 4 to 5:30 daily! Other good buys are native steamed clams or mussels with drawn butter (small order and large order available); fried sole or ham steak; fried scrod or broiled chicken; fried shrimp or oysters; and excellent cold plates of turkey, tuna, or julienne salad or cold ham or turkey that include potato salad, tomato, egg wedges, and cottage cheese.

Average prices: Lunch until 5 P.M., under $3 to $10 and over. Dinners are $8 to $15. Early diners (4 P.M. to 5:30 P.M.) have many offers in a lower range. *Credit cards:* All major. *Hours:* April 1 to November 12, every day from noon to 9 P.M. *Owners:* The Berigs and their two charming daughters. *Directions:* Go north on Route 6A. The restaurant is about 2 blocks past Main Street on the left.

OLD JAILHOUSE TAVERN
28 West Road
Orleans, Massachusetts 02653
(508) 255-JAIL

We visited this place on a recent trip to Cape Cod and found it a pleasant surprise. There are so many items to choose from, such as chicken pie made in a warm bread bowl, veggie pizza, quahog pie, lobster salad, and barbecued ribs; some good Italian fare includes veal marsala and chicken parmigiana. There are many options for soups or salads, and a light menu is served from 11 A.M. to midnight. Nightly specials are offered, too. The atmosphere is jolly and the service is delightful. The building is old but much of it has been renovated. Stone and oak and the greenhouse room with its hanging plants attracted our attention. There seemed to be many different levels to the house. The story goes that in the late 1800s it was the home of a constable who used one of his rooms as a Saturday night lock-up.

Average prices: Light meals, $5 to $7; regular meals, which include salad, hot bread and potato, rice or linguine, over $12 to $17. *Credit cards:* Visa and MasterCard. *Hours:* Every day. Lunch 11:30 A.M. to 5 P.M.; dinner, 5 to 10 P.M.; lighter meals until midnight. *Owner:* Lynne W. Hirst. *Directions:* From Route 6, take exit 12. Bear right. Go left at traffic light onto West Road. The tavern is 1 block farther on your right.

Also recommended:

Nonnie's Country Kitchen on Route 6A in midtown Orleans is still great after twenty-two years. We tried the eggs, marble toast, and seafood chowder, which were excellent. There are daily specials featuring homemade soups, shrimp, chicken, ham, and hamburger dishes. It is bright and cheerful with fancy plates decorating the walls. It's open from 6 A.M. to 3:30 P.M. Monday through Saturday, seven days a week in summer.

HORIZONS ON CAPE COD BAY
98 Town Neck Road, Box 2019
Sandwich, Massachusetts 02563
(508) 888-6166

Horizons is an extra special place to eat and enjoy panoramic views of Cape Cod Bay all year round. It overlooks the ocean and has open skylights and big windows for perfect views. Inside there is a lot of brass and beach club decor—very romantic! Meals are reasonable. Teriyaki beef tips, New York sirloin, barbecued chicken, and a lovely fresh ocean crab salad are the favorites. Also, see the new menu this year. All meals are now served in the upstairs beach club grille. They have high chairs, and children of all ages are welcome.

Average prices: $8 to $11 for above-mentioned meals. Lobster costs more. Sandwiches are about $5 (ocean crab salad sandwich served on Portuguese bread is still $3.95). *Credit cards:* MasterCard, American Express, and Visa. *Hours:* Summer from 11:30 A.M. to 11 P.M. or midnight. *Owner:* Frank Kelleher. *Managers:* John Maynard and David Sedita. *Directions:* Take Route 6A east from the center of Sandwich to Tupper Road. Then go to Town Neck Road, bear right on both forks on Town Neck Road, and you'll see the restaurant at the end of the road.

SANDY'S
Route 6A
Sandwich, Massachusetts 02563
(508) 888-6480

Sandy's is a longtime favorite of the area and was originally located only on the Canal in Buzzard's Bay. Now we are lucky enough to have two to choose from; one is in Sandwich. This one used to be an old house. It has a fireplace, maple furniture, and a more relaxed atmosphere. The capacity is 200; there is a lounge and waiting room, and cocktails are served. The restaurant serves two meals and offers specials every day, such as broiled salmon or halibut steaks with baked potato and vegetable. Chowders and soups are homemade and delicious. They also serve casseroles, baked stuffed haddock, shrimp, steaks, and chicken. They are open all year. Visit the Buzzard's Bay Sandy's

136

(508-759-3088) when convenient. It has the same fare and prices, does not serve breakfast, and is open 11:30 A.M. to 9 P.M. It is beside the Bourne Bridge on the Buzzard's Bay side and is busier than the Sandy's in Sandwich. There are a counter and tables.

Average prices: Lunch and dinner, $7–$14; many dishes in the $6.95, $8.95, and $10.95 range. Takeout available. *Credit cards:* MasterCard and Visa. *Hours:* Every day, 11:30 A.M. to 9 P.M. Closed on Tuesday in the winter. *Owner:* Neil Bisset. *Directions:* Take Route 6A to Sandwich. Sandy's is across from Angelo's Shopping Center.

Also recommended:

A suggestion for saving money at lunchtime would be to go to the **West Harwich Deli,** where you'll find a tempting assortment of salads and sandwiches for decent prices. Then head for a beach! The deli is on 216 Main Street (Route 28). Call (508) 432-5827.

OLD YARMOUTH INN
223 Main Street
Box 212
Yarmouthport, Massachusetts 02675
(508) 362-3191; (508) 362-3130

Old Yarmouth Inn used to be the Sears Hotel, owned by the brother of the great Boston merchant in the 1800s. Henry Thoreau stayed here in 1849. This very popular restaurant features salads, quiche, and other daily specials at lunchtime. All are served with a potato, vegetable, dessert, and beverage. The sandwiches are large and come with a fresh slice of melon and soup or a beverage. They feature New England cooking with a continental flair. Dinners are a bit highly priced and quite fancy, except for the hot roast beef and the Reuben sandwich with peddlar potatoes and salad bar. A classical jazz group plays in the lounge. Be sure to reserve ahead!

Average prices: Lunch is $7 to $8 and includes many extras. Dinner is $14–$20; early-bird specials are 15 percent off regular prices. The children's menu offers full dinners for $9 to $10.

Credit cards: All major. *Hours:* All year, Wednesday through Sunday, 11:30 A.M. to 8 P.M. Closed January. *Owners:* Carl Manchon and David Madison. *Directions:* The inn is on the north side of Route 6A near the center of town.

Also recommended:

Colonial House Inn (508-362-4348) is another place with decent lunch prices. Choose from the colonial room with stenciled walls, the oak room, or the beautiful green and white veranda. Here you can enjoy chicken pie, chicken piccata, spinach or lobster salad, sole almandine, a scrumptious Monte Cristo, or a creative deli sandwich. The dinner menu is extensive. Lunches are $5 to $10. Dinners are $10 to $19. It is located on Route 6A and the owner is Malcolm Perna.

The Harbor Point Restaurant and Lounge in Barnstable has especially good budget prices in the lounge, a big open room with candlelight and a large fireplace. Excellent music is featured on Friday and Saturday nights. We heard a young couple on guitar and bass playing soft rock with mellow, out-of-the-ordinary tunes by Stevie Nicks and Kenny Rankin. Dinner is served between 3 and 9 or 10 P.M. Dinners are priced in the $13 to $19 range, with most costing around $16. Lunch, served 11:30 A.M. to 3 P.M., costs $4 to $10; about ten items run between $4 and $8. The restaurant is on Harbor Point Road overlooking Barnstable Harbor. Call (508) 362-2231.

The Scargo Cafe in Dennis was mentioned to us by two bed & breakfast owners. It is an older home with five dining rooms, some formal and some contemporary and casual; one has a fireplace. The fare is American-Continental and features beef, chicken, and seafood, in pasta dishes or charbroiled. It's open every day, lunch is served 11 A.M. to 3 P.M. and costs $3 to $9. Dinners, served 4:30 to 10 P.M., run $8 to $16. There are early-bird specials. The owner is David Troutman. Phone (508) 385-8200.

MARTHA'S VINEYARD

Many people feel that this beautiful island is off limits to them because of high costs. But with the help of Shirley Craig, born and raised on the island, we've found ways to see the sights, eat fine food, and stay overnight there for fairly reasonable rates. The best savings start right at the ferry. We urge you to take bicycles, especially for adults, as a couple can save a bundle. All the roads are flat and easy to ride on; plus, there are protected bike paths right along the ocean between Oak Bluffs and Edgartown. There's a ferry charge for passengers and also for their bicycles. The area changes every year. You can also rent bikes near the ferry building on the island. For nonbikers, there is an island bus that runs between the main towns about two times every hour in the summer. To see the whole island, take a bus tour. Of course, the best way to save money staying overnight is to stay at family campgrounds, which we have done with our three kids. We stayed at **Martha's Vineyard Family Campground** on Edgartown Road in Vineyard Haven for a very low cost, and found it quite clean and convenient. Another way to go is to join the American Youth Hostel, so you can stay in dorms for very little cost.

The island is definitely worth a visit—it has an old charm and dignity of its own, and the miles of beaches with free parking seem heavenly to us after living on the North Shore of Massachusetts. You'll find Edgartown sophisticated with art galleries and smart shops; while in Oak Bluffs and Vineyard Haven, people let their hair down and loosen up more. Some very famous people sing in taverns there. We just missed a concert by the whole family of James Taylor! Tisbury is residential and peaceful, and Gay Head is impressive with sweeping cliffs and colorful Indians dressed in costume to sell their unusual crafts.

WHERE TO STAY ON THE VINEYARD

THE ARBOR
222 Main Street
Edgartown, Massachusetts 02539
(508) 627-8137

This beautiful white house is tastefully decorated in an eclectic style with a mix of antiques and traditional furnishings. It also has a pretty garden with chairs and a hammock for relaxing outside. Setups are provided for drinks and sherry is offered for evening get-togethers. Of the ten guest rooms, eight have private baths and two share a bath. A bike path runs in front of the house and you can walk to town in five minutes. A shuttle bus from the ferry will drop you off here. Continental breakfast is served on china on a linen tablecloth with linen napkins. Minimum stay in season is three days. Housekeeping unit in the rear.

Average *rates:* In season, $75–$125; off-season $55–$90. *Credit cards:* MasterCard and Visa. *Owner:* Peggy Hall. *Open:* Spring, summer, and fall. *Directions:* From the ferry, head toward Edgartown Center. The Arbor is just past the A&P grocery store, on the right. *Children:* Over twelve. *Pets:* No. *Smoking:* Restricted.

CHADWICK INN
67 Winter Street
Edgartown, Massachusetts 02539
(508) 627-4435

The Chadwick was built in 1840, but the new owners have put on a new addition. Rooms have king- or queen-sized beds, some with canopies. Twenty-one rooms and five suites with working fireplaces give you plenty of selection. All guest rooms have private baths, and three of the suites have Jacuzzis. This elegant inn has Laura Ashley appointments, a sherry decanter, and fresh flowers in each room. The surrounding grounds are beautiful, complete with porches and a secluded courtyard for trysts. The romance of it all has made The Chadwick a favorite for weddings and honeymoons. Raspberry crepes and fancy omelets are two inn specialties served in the breakfast room. Beach towels are provided to guests. The in-season minimum stay is two or three days. During "Christmas in Edgartown" weekend, the inn hosts an open house with chamber music.

Average rates: In season, $95–$250 (the higher rates are for suites); midseason, $75–$220; off-season, $65–$195. *Credit cards:* American Express. *Open:* Year-round. *Owners:* Peter and June Antioco. *Directions:* Go to Edgartown Center. Take left on Pease's Point Way. Turn right onto Simpson's Lane. Parking is behind the inn on Simpson's Lane. *Children:* Over ten. *Pets:* No. *Smoking:* Restricted.

KATAMA GUEST HOUSE
166 Katama Road
Edgartown, Massachusetts 02539
(508) 627-5158

This New England-style farmhouse is the birthplace of the father of our close friend Shirley Prado Craig. (Shirley screens all our Vineyard selections.) Anyway, this bed & breakfast is run by a charming couple, the St. Pierres, originally from Salem, Massachusetts. There are four rooms—two with private baths and two sharing one bath. Lorraine has a little den where she displays her arts and crafts, which are for sale. This establishment once was a farm and is next to a farm stand, so it has a rural feel. There is a bike path across the street, so bring your bikes, or ride the trolley that stops out front. A side yard with a swing and chairs is for guests. Breakfast is "super continental," with home-made breads and muffins and such. Off-street parking is available. Minimum stay in season is two nights.

Average rates: In season (Memorial Day through Columbus week-end), $75–$85; off-season, $60–$70. *Credit cards:* None; personal checks accepted. *Owners:* Raymond and Lorraine St. Pierre. *Open:* Year-round. *Directions:* Head toward Edgartown Center. Go right on Pease's Point Way to Katama Road. It is ¼ mile farther on the right. Shirley points out that the traffic pattern in Edgartown will change soon, so stop and ask for help if these directions don't work. *Children:* Over ten. *Pets:* No. *Smoking:* Restricted.

WHERE TO EAT ON THE VINEYARD

OCEAN VIEW RESTAURANT
Chapman Avenue
Oak Bluffs, Massachusetts 02557
(508) 693-2207

This new nautical restaurant replaces the old Ocean View Hotel and is noted for its incredible lobster prices—the best on the island! They also serve chicken, fish, and steaks at lower prices than most. The restaurant is very comfortable, and the food is good. Dinners include salad bar, bread, and choice of potato. The bar was made from the mast of the ship *Manxman,* and the dining room is spacious, with great views. If you like to eat your main meal at lunch, this is the place for you, as you can get chicken in a basket, clam plate, steak sandwich, or fried haddock very reasonably. Lunch is served in the tavern.

Average prices: Lunch, $4–$9; dinner, $14–$18. Appetizers are free chicken wings and all the popcorn you can eat. *Credit cards:* None. *Hours:* Lunch in tavern, 11:30 A.M. to 3 P.M. daily except Sunday. Dinner, 6 P.M. to 10 P.M. *Owners:* Ron and Peg Jackson. *Directions:* Take Lake Avenue out of Oak Bluffs toward East Chop. The second right after the harbor is Chapman Avenue. The Ocean View is on the left.

Also recommended:

Linda Jean's on Circuit Avenue, in Oak Bluffs, is popular with the locals.

Tony's, on State Road out of Vineyard Haven, is a good place for sandwiches and spaghetti. Like a diner, it is frequented by townspeople.

The **Dock Street Coffee Shop,** on Dock Street in Edgartown, is a favorite of the natives. Great breakfasts are served, featuring Portuguese omelets.

The Barbershop Deli, also in Edgartown, on North Water Street, is a favorite of Fran's for breakfast and lunch. It is quite small but offers most delicious breakfasts and great sandwiches with many goodies to choose from as fillers. They have cheese plates with generous servings of Brie or Camembert on crackers with lettuce and tomato, and yummy salads. Cheesecake and other outrageous delights are available, too. They're open year-round, 9 A.M. to 9 P.M.

NANTUCKET

Nantucket is . . . rows of weathered gray houses with white trim, long white beaches extending to the horizon, old New England elegance, history preserved, flowers, fishing, bicycling, and . . . pride. You'll find a special sense of peace and solitude, a feeling of adventure and awe at being 30 miles out to sea, and of wonder at the solid folks who make their living here.

To travel to Nantucket, you'll find that boats leave much more frequently from Hyannis than from Wood's Hole. If you are on a tight budget, pack your bike on the ferry. It costs much less than a car, and the island isn't much over 10 miles long. You can bike to your lodging—it's fun, and you'll want to bike to the beaches anyway.

For restaurants, **The Woodbox** and **Ship's Inn** on Fair Street are both highly recommended for their good food and decent prices.

WHERE TO STAY ON NANTUCKET

HOUSE OF SEVEN GABLES, B&B
32 Cliff Road
Nantucket, Massachusetts 02554
(508) 228-4706

This one-hundred-year-old Victorian home in the historic district is only ¼ mile from Nantucket Sound. It has the feel of a Victorian summer home. Most of the ten rooms, decorated in soothing, muted colors, have private baths. The period antiques include a sleighbed and nice oak furniture, and some of the rooms have water views. The fireplace in the parlor is very enticing in the off seasons. Sue and Ed serve a continental breakfast of croissants, muffins, juice, and coffee. Walk to beaches and town.

Average rates: Double: in season, $70–$140; midseason, $55–$95; off-season, $35–$65. *Credit cards:* MasterCard, American Express, and Visa. *Open:* All year. *Owners:* Sue and Ed Walton. *Directions:* From Straight Wharf, take Main Street to South Water Street, turn right, and go to Broad Street. At Broad Street, go left, then right on North Water, and cross Eaton onto Cliff Road. The house is 1 block up on the left (a ten-minute walk). *Children:* Over eight. *Pets:* No. *Smoking:* Yes.

STUMBLE INNE
109 Orange Street
Nantucket, Massachusetts 02554
(508) 228-4482

This beautiful colonial house was built in 1704 by a whaling patriarch's daughter, Abigail Howes. All thirteen rooms are tastefully furnished in fine antiques and are unique in character. All the rooms at Starbuck House, part of the inn but just across the street, have fireplaces (no fires allowed by law), a private bath, and antique beds with handstitched quilts and wide pine floors. Double, triple, and quadruple accommodations are available; cable television and refrigerators are in selected rooms. The inn has spacious grounds and is away from the noise of town. It is a short bike ride away from the surf beaches.

You will partake of an elegantly served continental breakfast in the gracious dining room. The fruit, muffins, pastries, and coffee are served on crystal; homemade cereals are offered, too. Carol Condon describes the island as a perfect place for a second honeymoon or special getaway in the slower-paced off-season. Spring blooms, autumn colors, or Christmas stroll—all will delight you.

Average rates: Off-season, \$35–\$68; midseason, \$45–\$88; in season, \$75–\$115 (includes special weekends). Extra adult, \$20; extra child, \$10. *Credit cards:* MasterCard and Visa. *Open:* All year. *Owners:* The Condon family. *Directions:* Take ferry from Hyannis, from Steamboat Wharf; take South Water Street to Main Street. Turn left onto Orange at the bank. The inn is on the right. *Children:* Yes, in specific rooms. *Pets:* No. *Smoking:* Yes, except in dining room.

VERMONT

Vermont is a wondrous collage of history, nature, man's creativity, and independent, captivating people. Its greenery, alpine views, and enigmatic folks with their conservative ways and liberal ideas will charm you and give you refreshing viewpoints on life. You cannot understand the serenity and peacefulness of mind until you have traveled the backroads, poked around in the local country store, or gazed out on the many beautiful vistas. It speaks of an era long forgotten in the hustle and bustle of city life to the south.

In southern Vermont you will find old New England beauty in the artisans, artists, antiques, old homesteads, factories, mountains and rivers, and covered bridges.

Brattleboro, the gateway to Vermont, is tucked between the foothills and the joining of the West and Connecticut rivers. It was Vermont's first permanent community, begun in 1724. Fort Dummer, as it was then called, was built to protect Massachusetts colonists from raids by the French and the Indians. It is named after a wealthy physician from Harvard, William Brattle (Brattle's borough), who was a proprietor of the old Plymouth Grant at Sheepscot.

To the west, Bennington still has a look of newness about it and a hustle and bustle not found in most southern Vermont towns. Here Ethan Allen and the Green Mountain Boys defended their land against the British in 1777. There's a wealth of fine colonial buildings, historic landmarks, and impressive views and tourism abounds.

Continue north along Route 7A; we'd hate to have you miss the two charming old New England towns of Shaftsbury and Arlington. The splendid Battenkill River (loaded with trophy trout) meanders here and there as you drive on to Manchester, another bustling tourist town. The village section is elegant, the fresh mountain air is marvelous, and towering Mount Equinox gives one a sense of humility. As you continue on to northern Vermont, you'll pass through many more unbelievably beautiful and peaceful towns.

When we think of northern Vermont, we think of skiing, covered bridges, and small rural towns nestled in scenic valleys with white church spires evident from a distance. This kind of land-

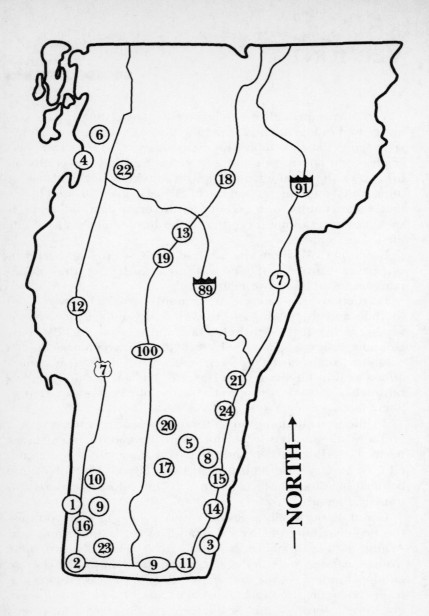

VERMONT

	🛏	🍴
1. Arlington	151	175
2. Bennington	153	175
3. Brattleboro	153	177
4. Burlington	—	178
5. Chester	154	—
6. Colchester	—	179
7. Fairlee	155	—
8. Grafton	155	—
9. Manchester	158	180
10. Manchester Center	158	181
11. Marlboro	159	182
12. Middlebury	160	183
13. Moretown	162	—
14. Putney	—	183
15. Saxtons River	163	184
16. Shaftsbury	163	—
17. South Londonderry	164	—
18. Stowe	164	185
19. Waitsfield	167	188
20. Weston	168	—
21. White River Junction	169	—
22. Williston	169	—
23. Wilmington	170	189
24. Woodstock	171	190

scape gives the region a charm found nowhere else in the United States. The recreation here revolves around the mountains.

To the west the Champlain Valley is dotted with red barns and silvery silos because of the flatlands that have given rise to a vigorous dairy industry. They say there are more cows in Vermont than people, which is probably true. These farms have produced the famous Vermont cheddar cheese and rich ice cream that delights the visitor.

The rugged mountains of the north are dominated by Mount Mansfield (4,393 feet), which provides the East with one of its major ski resorts. The fast-moving streams still yield many trout, and deer hunting is the best in the Northeast.

Stowe is the center of activity in northern Vermont. There seems to be plenty of room for tourists, shops, and miles of gorgeous mountain scenery. It truly is a winter wonderland in the cold months. Most proprietors must be happy with their work, as they take a lot of time to talk about it and are very comfortable to be with. The hour or two extra it might take you to get there is well worth it!

Waitsfield and Sugar Bush, the forgotten part of Vermont, is certainly the most breathtaking and magnetic, with green hills sweeping up to the mountains and the rushing Mad River commanding the town. It's great to know there's a spot where you can really "get away from it all" right in New England. We seriously considered moving up there to wake up to those glorious views every morning.

WHERE TO STAY

CUTLEAF MAPLES MOTEL
South Main Street
Arlington, Vermont 05250
(802) 375-2725

Cutleaf Maples Motel has rooms in the main house and very attractive, clean, large rooms in the little motel attached. The maple furniture is all new. Mrs. Cullinan, a native Vermonter, has owned the motel for forty years and serves free coffee, but breakfasts cost extra. There is a very homey, large living room. Cable television and air conditioning are available. The host allows pets, and children stay for free. It is on right on Route 7A near the center of town.

Average rates: Double, $35–$45; family room (sleeps four), $42–$50. *Credit cards:* MasterCard, Visa, and American Express. *Open:* Year-round. *Owner:* Dorothy Cullinan. *Directions:* Take exit 3 going north on Route 7 to 7A. Turn north on 7A. The Cutleaf Maples is about ¾ mile north on your right in the village. *Children:* Yes; cribs free. *Pets:* Yes. *Smoking:* Yes.

THE IRA ALLEN HOUSE
R.D. 2, Box 2485
Arlington, Vermont 05250
(802) 362-2284

This inn has recently been restored to its 1905 look. The hosts have gone all out to remodel and preserve the original decor by exposing beams, wallpapering the rooms in period prints, furnishing them in oak, and appointing them with beautiful antiques. Across the street from the inn's own picnic area, you can fish for trout on the Battenkill, swim, or take a leisurely canoe trip. This is a delightful place to spend a few days enjoying the historic Manchester-Bennington area. There are nine bedrooms. Ten acres in back are for hiking. A full country breakfast is included in the price. Two fireplaces add to the coziness.

Average rates: $28–$35 per person. *Credit cards:* American Express, Visa, and MasterCard. *Open:* May–March (closed April). *Owners:* Roland and Sally Bryant. *Directions:* From I-91, take the Brattleboro exit to Route 30 north; continue on Route 30 all the way to Route 11. Turn left and follow Route 7A toward Arlington. The inn is 5 miles south on the right. *Children:* Yes, over ten years old. *Pets:* No. *Smoking:* Restricted.

WEST MOUNTAIN INN
Arlington, Vermont 05250
(802) 375-6516

This spectacular inn is located high on a hill, and most of the rooms have an amazing mountain view. The charming host, Wes Carlson, who has ties to the Arlington area, showed us many of the rooms, all named for famous people, such as Grandma Moses and Robert Frost. Our favorites were the Norman Rockwell, or Tree Top, Rooms—one super cozy with window seats, and the other a gorgeous modern room with the bed on a raised area. All the decorations are tasteful and creative. You'll find fresh fruit and chocolate llamas in all the rooms, and all have private baths (one is barrier-free). There are several spacious public rooms, too, including a sun room. The day we visited, they'd collected fiddleheads and tried cooking and eating them. Apparently, they have frequent nature hikes and other surprise happenings for their guests. One featured event is a fly-fishing weekend. There are 150 acres on which to hike or cross-country ski from the doorstep, and the Battenkill River is right here. There are also llamas and sheep on the property. This inn was featured in both *Vermont Life* and *Country Inn* magazines in fall 1991. Its prices are a little high for our range, but it's still a bargain with the beautiful rooms and views. Country gourmet dinners and breakfasts are included in the price for two people.

Average rates: Double: two B&B rooms, $92; suites, $165; others, $142. Extra person, $50–$60; 15 percent service charge additional. *Credit cards:* MasterCard, Visa, and American Express. *Open:* Year-round. *Owners:* Wes and Mary Ann Carlson. *Directions:* Take Route 313 west from Arlington center. Take the road ½ mile along on the left, and follow signs along River Road to the inn. *Children:* Yes. *Pets:* No. *Smoking:* Restricted.

MOUNT ANTHONY GUEST HOUSE
226 West Main Street
Bennington, Vermont 05201
(802) 447-7396

Mount Anthony Guest House is a spacious, cool, clean Victorian home owned by two families on the west side of town. We were greeted by Mr. Grenier's grandson, who was most gracious and showed us the house. Most of the large rooms are decorated with antiques. Baths are shared or private. No breakfast is served. An old-fashioned porch adorns the front.

Average rates: Double, $45–$60. *Credit cards:* None. *Open:* Year-round. *Owner:* The Grenier and Woodbridge families. *Directions:* Entering Bennington from the west, you descend the hill from the Bennington Museum on the right. About 200 yards along on the left is the Mount Anthony. Or, from the intersection of Routes 7 and 9, go west on 9. Look for a large white Victorian 2 blocks up on your right. *Children:* Yes. *Pets:* No. *Smoking:* No.

MOTEL 6
Putney Road
Brattleboro, Vermont 05301
(802) 254-6007

This motel is a member of one of the new economy motel chains. It is an extraordinary bargain. Neat and clean, with wall-to-wall carpeting, color television, and air conditioning, it has everything that's in the expensive motels, only on a less lavish scale. We find these budget motels very satisfying. They even have swimming pools. This one had a very friendly desk clerk. She showed us the washer and dryer, the ice machine, and other amenities, and also pointed out that this motel has golf and tennis available nearby.

Average rates: Single, $27.95; double, $33.95; three people, $39.95; four people, $45.95. Children under twelve are free. *Credit cards:* All major. *Open:* All year. *Owner:* Motel 6. *Directions:* Take exit 3 off I-91 at the north end of Brattleboro. You quickly come to a set of lights where Route 5 intersects. Turn left on Route 5, and the motel is on your left within a ¼ mile. This is also known as Putney Road. *Children:* Yes. *Pets:* Yes. *Smoking:* Some nonsmoking rooms.

The Stone Hearth Inn
Route 11
Chester, Vermont 05143
(802) 875-2525

The Stone Hearth Inn is lovely, informal, and charmingly restored to show the beams, fireplaces, and wide pine floors. There are ten rooms, all with private baths. The cozy common room in the converted barn has a fieldstone fireplace, table tennis, and pool table. A Jacuzzi is in the game room. The inn is near Magic Mountain and Timber Ridge. This is a great place for a family, especially for those with teenagers—you know how antsy they get—because of all the things to do; they can even play soccer out back!

The complimentary full country breakfast features freshly baked pastry, eggs, sausage, and waffles. The pub offers relaxation and sandwiches at lunchtime.

Average rates: $30 to $80 per person, double occupancy; $15 per extra person. *Credit cards:* MasterCard, Visa, and Discover. *Open:* All year. *Owners:* Janet and Don Strohmeyer. *Directions:* Take exit 6 from I-91 and head west on Route 103 to Chester. Continue on Route 11 west to the inn, which is 1 mile from the center of town. *Children:* Yes. *Pets:* No. *Smoking:* Restricted to first floor.

SILVER MAPLES LODGE & COTTAGES
RR1, Box 8, Route 5
Fairlee, Vermont 05045
(802) 333-4326; (800) 666-1946

This quaint village farmhouse has fourteen attractive rooms, all quite spacious, and it's the best bargain in the area. Some rooms have flowered wallpaper, some have newly refinished floors, and some have antiques. Many of the beds and bureaus are matching and very handsome. Twelve rooms have private baths. There are also six cottages, four with air conditioners. Continental breakfast is served with juice, coffee, tea, fruit, and homemade breads. Picnic tables sit out under apple trees, and there are mountain views all around; enjoy the wraparound porch also. Lake Morey and a golf course are within a mile. This has been an inn for sixty years, and the Wrights are only the second innkeeping family to operate it. It was built as a farm in the 1790s.

Average rates: Double, $42–$62; single, $40–$60; rates are the same year-round. *Credit cards:* MasterCard, Visa, and American Express. *Open:* All year. *Owners:* Scott and Sharon Wright. *Directions:* From I-91, take exit 15 and go ½ mile south on Route 5. The inn is on your right. *Children:* Yes. *Pets:* No. *Smoking:* Restricted.

THE OLD TAVERN
Grafton, Vermont 05146
(802) 843-2231

Grafton Village is the epitome of old colonial elegance; it is like a smaller Williamsburg. It was completely restored by the Windham Foundation, and you should visit the Old Tavern whether you stay there or not.

We decided to give it a whirl as we found it had some reasonably priced doubles. We stayed in an annex called "The Homestead," which was super clean and quite plush with very expensive antiques in every corner. Although it was early in the season when we visited, there were many groups and families wandering about and people to talk to. It was a little like being in a movie. It's fun to feast your eyes on the gorgeous woodwork

155

and perfect antiques. There are enormous lounges with a color television and reading areas, pianos, and entertainment in full season. There are many extras such as tennis courts and rackets, a swimming pool, and even a stable where you may house your own horse! In the winter there are sleds, toboggans, and snow-shoes available and cross-country ski trails right on the property. Rates include a free continental cold buffet breakfast.

Average rates: Double, $95, $115, and $135. There is a great variety of family houses or cottages with kitchens available for rent, but some are above our price guidelines. *Credit cards:* MasterCard, Visa, and American Express. Personal checks accepted with proper identification. *Open:* All year except April and Christmas. *Owner:* The Windham Foundation. *Directions:* Take exit 5 off I-91. Proceed north on Route 121 through Bellows Falls to Grafton. It's about 12 miles from Bellows Falls. The Old Tavern will be up the hill in the center of Grafton on your left. You check in there for all the accommodations. *Children:* Yes (certain areas). *Pets:* Yes (certain areas). *Smoking:* Restricted.

THE HAYES HOUSE
Box 92, Water Street
Grafton, Vermont 05146
(802) 843-2461

This 1803 colonial bed & breakfast is a charming farmhouse on two acres within walking distance to the famous Grafton Village. You can rest on the porches or in the yard overlooking the large gardens. Inside you'll find flowered wallpaper, quilts, and hooked rugs; and you'll be able to chat with other guests in the large common room with fireplace. One bathroom, papered in stock-market wallpaper, will give you a chuckle. Enjoy the household cats and dogs. Marjorie will serve you her homemade breads, jams, and jellies for a continental breakfast. Sightseeing in the restored village, biking, and shopping are the activities.

Average rates: Double, $65–$75. *Credit cards:* None. *Owner:* Marjorie Hayes Heindel. *Open:* All year. *Directions:* From I-91, take exit 5 in Vermont, get onto Route 121, and go west 12 miles. Go over the village bridge; as soon as your wheels are off the bridge, turn left. The blue Hayes House is next to the covered bridge. *Children:* Under one and over four. *Pets:* Dogs only. *Smoking:* Restricted.

WOODCHUCK HILL FARM
Middletown Road
Grafton, Vermont 05146
(802) 843-2398

Woodchuck Hill Farm is tucked away in a wooded area and has been operating for twenty-four years. The warm innkeeper, Frank Gabriel, took the time to show us the lovely rooms with antique beds and soft colors and the big open porch with wicker furniture and a 75-mile view. There are accommodations for twenty guests. An antique shop is on the premises, as is a new lounge that serves beer and wine. We think the best bargain here is the barn-loft bedroom, with a kitchen and living room for four. All rates include extended continental breakfast. This might include boiled eggs and always includes scrumptious French pastries. In the evenings they serve complimentary Grafton cheddar cheese and crackers.

Average rates: Double: shared bath, $69; private bath, $89. New suite, $95. Studio apartment, $98. Barn-loft bedroom: two people, $115; four people, $185. *Credit cards:* None. *Open:* May to October. *Owners:* Anne and Frank Gabriel. *Directions:* Take exit 5 off I-91 and proceed west on Route 121 through Bellows Falls to Grafton. It's about 12 miles from Bellows Falls. Take Middletown Road off Route 121 after you have passed through the center of Grafton. The Middletown Road branches to your left from Route 121 going west just at the edge of town. The farm is 2 miles down on Middletown Road from where you leave 121. This is a dirt road. *Children:* In barn-loft only; must be over eight years old. *Pets:* No. *Smoking:* Restricted.

THE INN AT MANCHESTER
Route 7A, Box 41
Manchester, Vermont 05254
(802) 362-1793

The Inn at Manchester is an old restored home with twenty rooms, all beautiful with country-colonial and Victorian decor, and with great views. They are graciously decorated in matching colors. The complimentary breakfast specialties are blueberry pancakes, muffins, and omelets, which are served at a lovely long harvest table in the dining room. You may swim in the private pool. The inn is conveniently located in the village of Manchester on Route 7A. They hold weddings and family-style dinners for groups. At Christmastime they conduct tours, dress in costumes, dress up the inn, and offer special dinners.

Average rates: Double; $65–$100; suite, $115–$130. Extra person, $20. *Credit cards:* MasterCard, Visa, and American Express. *Open:* All year. *Owners:* Harriet and Stan Rosenberg. *Directions:* Take Route 7A south from Manchester center for 1 mile. The inn is on your right. *Children:* Eight years and over. *Pets:* No. *Smoking:* Restricted.

BROOK-N-HEARTH BED AND BREAKFAST
Box 508
Manchester Center, Vermont 05255
(802) 362-3604

This lovely home is clean, refreshing, and fully air-conditioned. The three trim rooms have pine wood, antiques, and wonderful braided rugs on every floor. You'll love the new dining room that Larry added with its big oval table, maple furniture, a bay window, muted colors, and fresh flowers. We shared conversation about our grown children with the Greenes while we enjoyed our complimentary full country breakfast in this room. They were very amiable and helpful. They showed us a nice little walk in the woods behind their house. They have a swimming pool and lawn games.

Average rates: Double, $50–$70; single, $36–$40. Family suite with two bedrooms, $60–$80 for two people; $16–$20 for extra person. Reduction for multiple-day stay at off-peak times. *Credit cards:* MasterCard, Visa, American Express, and Discover. *Open:* All year except three weeks in early November, late April, and early May. *Owners:* Larry and Terry Greene. *Directions:* The inn is 1 mile east of junction of Route 7 and Route 11/30. *Children:* Yes. *Pets:* No. *Smoking:* Restricted.

THE GOLDEN EAGLE MOTEL
Route 9, Box 108
Marlboro, Vermont 05344
(802) 464-5540

This is a reasonable, eighteen-room motel with a gorgeous alpine 100-mile view, just 2 miles west of Marlboro on Route 9. The rooms are nicely decorated and very clean, each with private bath and color television. There is a large meeting room with booths, a bar (BYOB), and a pool table. There is also a lovely restaurant on the second floor, which is open in winter only, but breakfast is available all year for an extra charge.

Average rates: Double, $42–$55 (less off-season); extra person, $7. *Credit cards:* MasterCard, Visa, and American Express; no personal checks. *Open:* All year. *Owners:* Manny and Maureen Santa Maria. *Directions:* The motel is 11½ miles from exit 2 of I-91 in Brattleboro, west on Route 9. It is at the top of a hill. *Children:* Yes. *Pets:* During off-season only. *Smoking:* Yes, some rooms.

THE WHETSTONE INN
Marlboro, Vermont 05344
(802) 254-2500

This eighteenth-century country inn, once a stagecoach station, with cozy fireplaces and several large, pleasant common rooms, is situated amongst trees and fields, with an unusual, seductive feeling of relaxed elegance. Its unique, caring owners, Jean and Harry Boardman, offer stimulating, intellectual conversation and one hundred percent service such as breakfast and

159

dinner served on the lawn on nice days, with soft violin music playing on the stereo. Other guests are apt to be musicians, students, or visitors to the famous Marlboro Music Festival in the summer. The day we were there, the sound of a piano floated through the halls. Books on how to relax and enjoy life are thoughtfully placed in each room. The rooms are large, with colonial decor, and a very handy feature is a sink in most rooms and extra little "water closets" for busy mornings. The breakfasts, not included in the price, are wonderful selections of raspberries and cream, melons, crisp waffles, and bacon. Children will be very comfortable here as the innkeepers have two young boys of their own.

It is exceptionally beautiful in full autumn color and offers many cross-country ski trails for the winter. There is swimming in a pond on the property, tennis and golf available nearby, and the hosts offer dinner to the public by reservation.

Average rates: Double: shared bath, $50–$60; private bath, $65–$80. Single with private bath, $30–$55. *Credit cards:* None. *Open:* Year-round. *Owners:* Jean and Harry Boardman. *Directions:* Take exit 2 off I-91 in Brattleboro. Go west on Route 9 about 9 miles. At the top of the hill, turn left to Marlboro village (very small). Marlboro is signposted. It's about ½ mile to the village. The inn is next to the large white church on the right. *Children:* Yes. *Pets:* Yes. *Smoking:* Restricted.

OCTOBER PUMPKIN BED & BREAKFAST
Route 125, P.O. Box 226
Middlebury, Vermont 05740
(802) 388-9525; (800) 237-2007 (out of state and Canada)

This colorful 1850 farmhouse with huge sugar maples in front would tempt the most discriminating traveler. The pumpkin theme is carried to the color of the house and many of the sweet gifts inside, handmade by the Roeders. The rooms are adorned in antiques (one has a canopy bed) and whimsical wicker and are accented by quilts and hand-stenciling throughout. All are air-conditioned, and both private and shared baths are available. There is a guest parlor with a piano for your use. Not far away you can ski at the Snow Bowl. Also nearby are Frog Hollow—a

160

haven for Vermont craftspeople—the Shelburne Museum, the summer cabin of Robert Frost in Ripton, concerts on the green, and summer theater. Breakfast is continental with corn sticks, homemade breads or muffins, juice, and coffee (regular or decaffeinated). Full breakfasts are extra. Visit the Craft Corner in the hall with stenciled and quilted items.

Average: Double, $50–$70. *Credit cards:* Visa and MasterCard. *Open:* All year. *Owners:* Eileen and Charles Roeder. *Directions:* Four miles south of Middlebury, go east on Route 125 for 1 mile. The inn is on the left, or north, side. The Waybury Inn is ¼ mile beyond it. *Children:* Yes. *Pets:* Yes, if well behaved. *Smoking:* Restricted.

THE SUGAR HOUSE RESTAURANT AND MOTOR INN
Route 7, Box 525
Middlebury, Vermont 05753
(802) 388-2770

This motel has fourteen clean and pleasantly decorated rooms, each with air conditioning, color television, wall-to-wall carpeting, combination bath and showers, and a telephone. It's all you can expect in a modern motel. There are two large double beds in most rooms. It is set back from the highway on a rural stretch just north of Middlebury. The surroundings are pastoral, so it should be relatively quiet with little traffic, and the air is very fresh. Nearby one can visit the famous Morgan Horse Farm, Shelburne Museum, the State's Craft Center, Fort Ticonderoga, or Middlebury College. If you arrive late and want dinner near at hand or want to walk to breakfast, try the Sugar House Restaurant main dining room or coffee shop. Both have been recommended to us by a friend.

Average rates: Double, $48–$54; lower in winter. No extra cost for children in two-bedded rooms. *Credit cards:* Visa, MasterCard, and American Express. *Open:* All year. *Owners:* Douglas and Mary Baker. *Directions:* Take Route 7 north from Middlebury. The motel is 2 miles up on your right, on the east, or mountain, side. Or head south about 12 miles from Vergennes on Route 7. *Children:* Yes. Porta-crib available. *Pets:* Yes. *Smoking:* Yes.

THE CARPENTER FARM
Meadow Road, Box 2710
Moretown, Vermont 05660
(802) 496-3433; (800) 253-0796 (USA only)

This very homey, working dairy farm is out in the scenic countryside. Mr. Carpenter was born in this enormous house, which now has nineteen guest rooms. The inn has been in the same family since 1893. They grow their own vegetables and still harvest hay. Both breakfast and dinner are generally served to the guests, but you can stay for a price that includes just breakfast. Dorothy showed us through all the rooms, which are color-coordinated with blues, reds, and rusts. There are also dorm rooms. Some baths are shared and some are private. The inn is very clean and in good repair, and the dining room is huge. It's a perfect place for a large group of skiers, hikers, fishermen, or bicyclists. They have a fixed dinner menu that changes every night, offering dishes such as pork chops, T-bone steak, turkey, pot roast, fresh vegetables, and homemade cakes, pies, and breads.

Average rates: $23–$26 per person with breakfast; $36 per person with breakfast and dinner. Extra child $14. Dorm rooms are $36 and up per person with breakfast. Rates are lower in summer. *Credit cards:* None. *Open:* Year-round. *Owners:* Dorothy and George Carpenter, daughter Marla, and Robert Durnham. *Directions:* Take exit 9 south off I-89 onto Route 100B. About 200 yards south of Moretown center, take a left on the dirt road (Austin Road). Carpenter Farm is about 1½ miles farther on your left. When driving from Waitsfield on Route 100, look for the Carpenter Farm sign about 1 to 1½ miles on the right. Exit right onto the dirt road (Meadow Road). The farm is about 1.3 miles farther on the right. *Children:* Yes. *Pets:* By prior arrangement. *Smoking:* Restricted.

THE INN AT SAXTONS RIVER
Main Street
Saxtons River, Vermont 05154
(802) 869-2110

The Inn at Saxtons River is a fascinating turn-of-the-century inn on Main Street. The comfortable porches are decorated with bright flowering plants in baskets. The special features of this inn are the attractive soft floral wallpapers in every room and the bright breakfast room. There are lovely antiques and classy posters in the rooms, and they have one suite of two rooms. Children are welcome. The handsome dining room serves fancy foreign cooking. All rates include a full breakfast. Breakfast and lunch are served in the dining room to the public, too.

Average rates: Double, $50–$70. *Credit cards:* MasterCard and Visa. *Open:* All year. *Owners:* Sandy and Ilene Frieman. *Directions:* Take exit 5 off I-91 to Route 5. Go north on 5 and take a left onto Route 121 west to Saxtons River. This inn is about ⅔ of the way down Main Street on your right. *Children:* Yes. *Pets:* No. *Smoking:* Yes.

GOVERNOR'S ROCK MOTEL
Route 7A, RD 1, Box 282
Shaftsbury, Vermont 05262
(802) 442-4734

This blue and gray motel is nicely situated with a mountain view, and the rooms have a cross breeze. They are clean and modest. The owners offer you coffee in the office when you arrive. Try their hibachi, picnic area, and play area. All rooms are brightly decorated and have a color television. Some rooms are air-conditioned. The rates are slightly higher for two double beds in a room with additional people. If you stay seven days, one day is free. A complimentary breakfast of coffee and blackberry and other homemade breads is served in August.

Average rates: Double, $35–$45. *Credit cards:* MasterCard and Visa. *Open:* May to November 1. *Owners:* Sylvia Burrill and Cynthia Wiesner. *Directions:* The motel is 8 miles north of

Bennington on historic Route 7A, on the left, 1 mile from Shaftsbury Lake. *Children:* Yes. *Pets:* No. *Smoking:* Yes.

LONDONDERRY INN
Route 100, P.O. Box 301
South Londonderry, Vermont 05155
(802) 824-5226

Londonderry Inn was a dairy farm 150 years ago, and it retains this old charm. It is in the National Historic District. Set on nine acres overlooking the West River, it also features a view of Mount Glebe. It has twenty-five guest rooms, a cozy sitting room with a huge fireplace, and a lovely dining room, which formerly was a woodshed. There are table tennis, billiards, and a pool on the property. In the winter, enjoy sledding, sleigh riding, and cross-country skiing. The rates include a buffet continental breakfast, which includes three-minute eggs. Dinners are served every night in summer and winter but Tuesday. The dining room is closed in the late spring and late fall.

Average rates: Double: in summer and on winter weekdays, $45–$60; on holidays and winter weekends, $60–$75. Additional person, $10–$20. *Credit cards:* None. *Open:* Year-round. *Owners:* Jim and Jean Cavanagh. *Directions:* Take Route 30 south from Manchester, Vermont (15 miles). Or take Route 30 north from Brattleboro, Vermont (39 miles), to Rawsonville, then go just 4 miles north on Route 100. It's a white building on a hill. *Children:* Yes. *Pets:* No. *Smoking:* Yes.

FIDDLER'S GREEN INN
4859 Mountain Road
Stowe, Vermont 05672
(802) 253-8124; (800) 882-5346

This very carefree inn is set back off the road, giving you a sense of privacy and serenity. The huge yard has a trout stream bubbling along behind. The inside is tastefully decorated in colonial decor with lots of pine furniture, and the restful living room is paneled in knotty pine and has a giant fieldstone fireplace.

164

The McKeons are thoughtful and very pleasant to be with. The greatest saving here is in the summer and during ski weekdays, especially in January. Dorm prices are also excellent all year.

Average rates: Winter, $38–$60 per person; breakfast and dinner included, ski week discounts. Summer, $20–$30 per person; does not include breakfast or dinner. *Credit cards:* All major. *Open:* Year-round. *Owners:* Bud and Carol McKeon. *Directions:* The inn is 4½ miles from Stowe village toward Mount Mansfield on the left. Mountain Road is Route 108. *Children:* Yes. *Pets:* No. *Smoking:* Yes.

SKI INN
Route 108, Mountain Road
Stowe, Vermont 05672
(802) 253-4050

Primarily a winter inn, this wonderful colonial house that hugs the ski slope also caters to summer guests. The Heyers have run it for more than twenty-five years, and Harriet will give you a lesson how to "vaidle." She keeps the inn immaculate, and Larry does the laundry. They have some good conversation around the fieldstone fireplace. There is a lot of knotty pine throughout, and the rooms are spacious and decorated nicely with matching colors. There are Ping-Pong and other games in the big game room downstairs. Mount Mansfield has intermediate to advanced trails and some of the steepest and longest trails in the East. You can cross-country ski right from the front door. A continental breakfast is served in the spring, summer, and fall.

Average rates: Winter: $20–$25 per person; $40–$50 per person with breakfast and dinner. Off-season: $20–$25 per person; $30 with full breakfast. *Credit cards:* None. *Open:* All year. *Owners:* Larry and Harriet Heyer. *Directions:* Get off exit 10 on Route 89 and follow signs to Stowe on Route 100. Turn left at Route 108, just after two gas stations. The inn is the last house on the left before the mountain. *Children:* Yes, over one year. *Pets:* By prior arrangement. *Smoking:* Yes.

TIMBERHÖLM INN
452 Cottage Club Road
Stowe, Vermont 05672
(802) 253-7603; (800) 753-7603

This wonderful inn has cheerful new innkeepers, Kay and Richard. The highlights of a stay include talking to the innkeepers, sitting in the bright dining room where you can watch birds in the woodsy yard through the many windows, and relaxing in the big secure living room with the stone fireplace where Kay offers you warm soup on your return from skiing. You can cross-country ski right from the door. The rooms are spic and span, and each has brightly colored bedspreads. There are a suite of rooms for families, a game room with bumper pool, and a ski room. The four surrounding acres are beautiful, and carefully tended flower gardens greet you in the spring. A full buffet-style breakfast is served, featuring quiches and eggs Florentine. All rooms have private baths, air conditioners, and a hot tub!

Average rates: Double, $50–$80; extra person, $10. *Credit cards:* MasterCard and Visa. *Open:* Most of the year; closed spring and November. *Owners:* Kay and Richard Hildebrand. *Directions:* After turning onto Mountain Road from Stowe center, go 2 miles to Cottage Club Road. The inn is in ½ mile on the right. *Children:* Yes. *Pets:* No. *Smoking:* Yes, limited.

THE YODLER MOTOR INN
Route 1, Box 10
Stowe, Vermont 05672
(802) 253-4836; (800) 227-1108

This converted 180-year-old farmhouse lends itself well to bed and board. The rooms are large and airy with homemade quilts, television, and private baths. The dining room is cheerful and big. Paige is a natural innkeeper, good-natured and engaging, and she works hard to make guests feel welcome and comfortable. The inn is located conveniently at the beginning of the Mountain Road and has a pool, clay tennis courts, and swings for the children. The bar is open only in the summer and fall. No breakfast is included in spring, summer, and fall. In the winter breakfast and dinner are included. A hot tub is available to guests.

Average rates: Summer and fall: double in the lodge, $25–$57; double in the motel, $40–$80; higher in July, August, and foliage season; extra person is a small amount more; reductions for seven-day stays. Winter: double in the lodge, $36–$55 per person; double in the motel, $65–$80 per person; all rates include breakfast and dinner. Add 15 percent gratuity. **Credit cards:** All major. **Open:** All year. **Owners:** Wolfgang and Paige Kier. **Directions:** Take Route 100 into Stowe and turn north onto the Mountain Road. The large white inn is about 1 block up on the left. **Children:** Yes. **Pets:** In motel only. **Smoking:** Yes.

WAIT FARM MOTOR INN
Route 100, Box 206-C
Waitsfield, Vermont 05673
(802) 496-2033

This motel has a spectacular view of the mountains and into the woods. The rooms are large and very clean, and they contain paintings and colonial decor. Each room has a table, chairs, and a television. The pond out back has ducks, but you can swim in the river nearby. The inn is very close to shopping, tennis, golf, and all the ski lifts in the area. The motor inn offers special low five-night ski rates.

Average rates: Double, $40–$60; extra person, $6. **Credit cards:** MasterCard and Visa. **Open:** All year. **Owners:** Paula and Paul Lavoie. **Directions:** Take exit 9 off I-89. Go south on Route 100 for 14 miles. The motor inn is on the left side. **Children:** Yes. Porta-crib available. **Pets:** No. **Smoking:** Yes.

Also recommended:

Another lovely little place you might want to try is **The Millbrook,** a country inn on Route 17 in Waitsfield. This warm, very homey place usually includes a full breakfast and dinner in the room rate, and you can order off the menu. They use all local products, make their own pasta, and feature some American

Indian dishes. The prices are $25 to $30 per person in summer and $42 per person on winter weekdays. The inn is on Route 17, less than a mile from Route 100, on the left. You may call owners Thom and Joan Gorman at (802) 496-2405 for particulars.

THE DARLING FAMILY INN
Route 100
Weston, Vermont 05161
(802) 824-3223

The Darling Family Inn is an idyllic 160-year-old farmhouse set in a picturesque valley in the unbelievably beautiful town of Weston. The inn is run by a couple who fusses over you as Grandma used to. The sachet on your pillow and cookies by the bed at night are just a few of the pleasantries you experience with the Darlings. Joan, a talented artist, is delightful company, as is Chape, who keeps the fire going in the wood stove and puts on tapes of soothing music. They should write a book on how to comfort and relax people. Enjoying breakfast in the dining room; watching chickadees, redstarts, and an occasional deer; and sipping wine or tea at night—all are experiences you won't forget. A full country breakfast is complimentary at this family inn, which was recently covered in several gourmet magazine articles that highlighted Chape's delightful berry pancakes. The rooms take you back in time with handmade quilts, braided rugs, special antique furniture, and knickknacks. There are fields and hills to climb over and bobolinks in the meadow to cheer you with their merry notes. A swimming pool is available in the summer. All baths are private. Dinner is served with advance notice. The famous Weston Priory is located 3 miles north of the inn.

Average rates: Double, $75–$95; housekeeping cottages available for two, $85; each additional person, $20. Two-night minimum. *Credit cards:* None. *Open:* Year-round. *Owners:* Joan and Chapin Darling. *Directions:* Traveling east on Route 11, take a left onto Route 100 in Londonderry to Weston. Go ¼ mile north beyond the center; the inn is on the right. *Children:* Yes, in cottages only. *Pets:* Yes, in cottages, with deposit. *Smoking:* Restricted.

HOWARD JOHNSON MOTOR INN
Junction of Routes 91 and 89
White River Junction, Vermont 05001
(802) 295-3015; (800) 654-2000

Although this motel is part of a national chain, we include it here because it is the one good bargain for families in this area. The rooms are large and attractive, and it has a lovely indoor swimming pool. There is a dining room with a lounge right in the building. When our children were young, they loved the place! It is very close to Woodstock, which has very few reasonably priced places to stay.

Average rates: $65–$95; children under eighteen stay free; extra adult, $6. *Credit cards:* All major. *Open:* All year. *Directions:* Take I-91 to the north and turn onto I-89 to White River Junction. The motel is at this intersection. *Children:* Yes. *Pets:* Yes. *Smoking:* Yes.

SUNRISE TAVERN
RD 2, Box 454
Route 2A (St. George Road)
Williston, Vermont 05495
(802) 482-3135

This is a new find: a delightful, restored colonial tavern with innkeepers who have had a lot of experience in the hospitality profession. As you enter you are greeted by an open-hearth fireplace with a musket above. You feel the colonial ambience all around. The bedrooms have their own open baths, two with clawfoot tubs and one with an old-fashioned copper tub. The loft where we stayed allowed one to bathe while looking out the window at the pastoral scene in the meadow behind the tavern. This room is a suite with a couch and queen-sized bed. The Sunroom and Delia's Room are equally bright and distinctive. Breakfast is a treat—granola loaded with a variety of nuts, fruit beautifully presented, fresh-squeezed orange juice, and coffee from fresh-ground beans. You are about fifteen minutes from Burlington and a half hour from Shelburne Museum. Restaurants are nearby, so this is an ideal place to use as a base camp while exploring the Burlington area.

169

Average rates: Double, $65; single, $50. *Credit cards:* None; personal checks accepted. *Open:* May through October. *Owners:* Michele and Andy Rose. *Directions:* From I-89, take exit 12 south onto Route 2A. Go 4 miles. You will pass a sign for St. George. Don't worry. The inn is in St. George, although the mailing address is Williston. The white inn is on your left, right on the road as are most colonial taverns. *Children:* Ten and over. *Pets:* No. *Smoking:* No.

Also recommended:

In the Burlington area, try **On the Lamb** in Colchester. Call innkeeper Audrey Chetti at (802) 879-1179 (home) or (802) 879-8681 (work). The three rooms cost $70 to $85, and a continental breakfast is served. **Charlotte's Web,** on Greenbush Road in Charlotte, 12 miles south of Burlington, is an elegantly restored nineteenth-century barn near Shelburne Museum. Call Gretchen and Stan Semuskie at (802) 425-3341.

SLALOM LODGE
Shafter Street, P.O. Box 27
Wilmington, Vermont 05363
(802) 464-3783

Slalom Lodge is a very large, clean Victorian house (five rooms) with the flavor of old Europe. It is generally open only in the winter for skiers but will occasionally take travelers in the summer. The hosts are extremely congenial. These are spartan accommodations but clean and comfortable. Full breakfast is served.

Average rates: Double, $65. *Credit cards:* MasterCard and Visa. *Open:* Year-round. *Owners:* Walter and Maria Schneider. *Directions:* Take a left at the light in Wilmington, when traveling west on Route 9. Take a right if coming east. Once over the bridge, take your first right. It's a dark brown, two-family house with white trim on your right about 200 yards in. *Children:* Yes; no babies. *Pets:* No. *Smoking:* Yes.

THE VINTAGE MOTEL
Route 9, P.O. Box 222Z
Wilmington, Vermont 05363
(802) 464-8824

The Vintage is very close to Mount Snow and has a heated pool in the summer. The rooms are pretty with colonial prints and two comfortable chairs in each. All units have cable color television. A light continental breakfast of juice, coffee, and muffins or coffee cake is included in the price. A very appealing feature that most motels lack is a cozy common room with a wood stove and couches where you may enjoy conversation, television, and breakfast with other travelers. There is some practice cross-country ski mileage on the property. Inquire about the five-day, midweek ski package. Seven rooms have air conditioning.

Average rates: Double: summer, $49–$54; winter midweek, $50; winter weekends, $64; holidays, $68. *Credit cards:* MasterCard, Visa, and American Express. *Open:* All year. *Owners:* Joy and Grant Moyer. *Directions:* The motel is 1 mile west of the center of Wilmington on Route 9. *Children:* Yes. *Pets:* No. *Smoking:* Yes.

THE APPLEBUTTER INN
Route 4, P.O. Box 4
Woodstock, Vermont 05091
(802) 457-4158

This bed & breakfast in the countryside east of Woodstock with an old barn out back lies up a side street away from the traffic, making it a restful place to hang out. The interior, decorated with period antiques, suggests the Spartan conditions in which our forefathers lived. You'll want to stay because of both the early American look and the comfortable beds and modern bathrooms. We liked the porch on the second floor where you can sit in the shade and take in the scenery. The formal parlor and sitting room with a fireplace are an important part of the guest accommodations. There are six guest rooms. A "hearty and healthy" breakfast is included in the room rate. This restored Federal house is located in Taftsville, east of Woodstock, near

Quechee Gorge, the Simon Pierce glassblowing shop, antique malls and galleries, and golf and skiing centers. Beverlee will soon begin to sell her own apple butter.

Average rates: Double, $70–$120 (four people). Single, $55. Lower off-season rates. *Credit cards:* None; personal checks accepted. *Open:* All year. *Owners:* Andrew and Beverlee Cook. *Directions:* Take Route 4 from I-89 to Woodstock. At Taftsville you will see a red brick general store; turn left. The inn is first house on the left. *Children:* Yes. *Pets:* No. *Smoking:* Restricted.

THOMAS HILL FARM
Rose Hill
Woodstock, Vermont 05091
(802) 457-1067

This is a charming bed & breakfast. The host is a friendly lady who moved up from Florida and remodeled and redecorated her new home and furnished it with lovely antiques, paintings, and flowers. As she said, if you see it, you'll love it. We agree. The quiet, rural setting makes it special. Fran loved the views of many distant, overlapping green mountains, an old barn behind the house, and cows and sheep at a neighboring farm—so many farm scenes to paint. There are four guest rooms, two with private baths, two that share. A "continental plus" breakfast is served.

Average rates: $65–$75. *Credit cards:* MasterCard and Visa. *Open:* All year except November and April. *Owner:* Marilyn Truitt. *Directions:* From I-89, take Route 4 to Woodstock. Go through town. At the farm stand on the left, just after the White Cottage Drive-In restaurant and before the Carriage House, take a sharp right. Up the hill about 100 yards, the B&B is on the left. *Children:* No. *Pets:* No. *Smoking:* Not in bedrooms.

THE VILLAGE INN OF WOODSTOCK
41 Pleasant Street (Route 4)
Woodstock, Vermont 05091
(802) 457-1256; (800) 722-4571

This inn is described in the Where to Eat section. It offers doubles with private or shared baths. Rooms are comfortably furnished in the country tradition, some with original marble washstands. You are in town here, so ask for rooms away from the street. Book early for the foliage season. Woodstock is a very popular town, and you can walk to the downtown shops and galleries from the inn.

Average rates: Double, $60–$80. On in-season weekends, $250 per couple buys two nights, one dinner, and two breakfasts for two. *Credit cards:* MasterCard, Visa, and American Express. *Open:* All year. *Owners:* Kevin and Anita Clark. *Directions:* Take Route 4 to Woodstock from I-89. After you follow a sharp bend to the right on to Pleasant Street, it is about 100 yards up on the left. Off-street parking is available. *Children:* Yes. *Pets:* No. *Smoking:* No.

THREE CHURCH STREET BED & BREAKFAST
Three Church Street
Woodstock, Vermont 05091
(802) 457-1925

Mrs. Paine has lived in this beautiful brick and clapboard home for thirty years; she brought up all eight of her children here. Built in 1800, the house is listed in the National Registry of Historic Places. The spacious rooms are lovely with many antiques and some canopy beds. Six of the eleven rooms have private baths. The three lovely acres include a swimming pool and tennis court, which guests may use. You may play the piano in the elegant music room, or peruse and rest in the very special library, living room, or gallery overlooking the Ottauquechee River and Mount Tom. Eleanor serves a full breakfast with some Southern surprises. Walk to town where there are many boutiques and restaurants. Woodstock also has superb fishing, hiking, and cross-country skiing, as well as downhill skiing at Suicide Six. The bed & breakfast now serves lunch to the public Monday through Friday.

Average rates: Double, $68–$95. *Credit cards:* MasterCard and Visa. *Open:* All year. *Owner:* Mrs. Eleanor Paine. *Directions:* From Route 89 north, take exit 1 to Route 4 west; go through Woodstock village. You'll pass the Village Green on the left and the town hall and movie house on the right. The B&B is next door. From Route 91 north, take Routes 5 and 12 north to Route 4 west; then follow the directions given above. *Children:* Yes. *Pets:* Yes. *Smoking:* Yes.

Also recommended:

Nancy and Jim Mills have just bought *Abbott House* at 43 Pleasant Street in Woodstock. It is a white colonial with five rooms in New England decor with antiques. Doubles cost $40 and $50. It is open all year and has air conditioning. No breakfast is served. No pets are allowed. All major credit cards are accepted. Call (802) 457-3631.

WHERE TO EAT

PHYLLIS' FOOD & ETCETERA
Old Mill Road
Arlington, Vermont 05252
(802) 375-9990

This warm and friendly place, raved about by many innkeepers, has visitors from all corners of the country. The 250-year-old house is all wooden pegged and has white Cape Cod curtains, beamed ceilings, and antiques. Phyllis serves your wine in cut glassware and uses delicate antique plates and glasses. Her absolutely best specialty is chicken and biscuits with homemade rolls, vegetables, and tossed salad. Roast lamb is also a favorite. Her soups and desserts are homemade, too. Try her pecan pie, and get her recipe for French silk pie. "It's easy!" she says.

Average prices: Lunch quiches and sandwiches are under $4 to under $6. Chicken and biscuits are over $6. Full dinners are $13 to $17 and include soup, a main course, and a light dessert. *Credit cards:* None; personal checks accepted. *Hours:* End of May to October. Tuesday through Saturday noon to 9 P.M. Closes 7 P.M. on Sunday. *Owner:* Phyllis Allen. *Directions:* From Route 7, take the East Arlington cutoff and continue until you reach the little village with the Candle Mill Village shopping center. Phyllis' is on the left across from it.

BLUE BENN DINER
Route 7 North
Bennington, Vermont 05201
(802) 442-8977

Blue Benn Diner is featured in the *Diners of New England* for those who like to visit some of the classic Silk City diners. This has vegetarian and health food as specialties. You will see the hand-painted signs posted above the counter advertising the spinach pesto omelet, the huevos rancheros, and the Greek omelet. It's mobbed for breakfast, especially on Sunday. It looks as though the students from nearby Bennington College had an influence on some of the offerings! However, the cook, Sonny Monroe, has developed some skill with omelets, salads, and desserts. Try the apple streusel coffee cake. A surprise are the Middle Eastern specials of tabouli and felafel. Breakfast is served all day. Fresh fruits and vegetables are available. This place is on our list of the five best diners in New England!

Average prices: Breakfast: continental, $2 and change; full, under $5. Pancakes and sausage under $5. Lunch and dinner, $3–$6. *Credit cards:* None. *Hours:* Monday and Tuesday, 5 A.M. to 5 P.M.; Wednesday to Friday, 5 A.M. to 8 P.M.; Saturday, 5 A.M. to 4 P.M.; Sunday, 7 A.M. to 4 P.M. *Owners:* Sonny and Marylou Monroe; Lisa Monroe is hostess. *Directions:* Take Route 7 north from the intersection of Routes 7 and 9. About 1 mile from the intersection as the road bends to the left, it's on the left, just before Deer Park.

GEANNELIS' RESTAURANT
520 Main Street
Bennington, Vermont 05201
(802) 442-9778

Geannelis' Restaurant is a bargain hunter's dream. It's a small but friendly family restaurant with inexpensive lunches and dinners. The owner scurries about seating customers and seeing to their needs. There is an ice-cream counter as you come in, and an L-shaped counter with stools for fast service. Many locals come here for lunch. The two of us ate heartily, and the home-made soup was excellent. You can take a homemade ice cream with you when you leave and walk about Main Street, looking at the shops and stores. Hearty Vermont breakfasts are served here for terrific bargain prices! The menu offers a good selection of American items.

Average prices: Lunch and dinner specials, from $3 up. Two people should be able to eat a substantial meal for $10 to $12. *Credit cards:* MasterCard and Visa. *Hours:* Monday through Saturday, 6 A.M. to 8 P.M.; Sunday, 7 A.M. to 8 P.M.; closed Thanksgiving, Christmas, and Labor Day. *Owners:* Jack and Holly Downey. *Directions:* From the intersection of Routes 9 and 7, go east on Route 9 about 100 yards. It is on the left.

JAD'S RESTAURANT
107 Canal Street
Brattleboro, Vermont 05301
(802) 257-4559

Jad's is a folksy, down-to-earth family restaurant with the hustle and bustle, good quality, and bill of fare you usually find in a diner. The waitresses make you feel right at home joking and teasing as in a regular diner. The man at the end of the counter spoke of Brattleboro to us with such pride and fondness that we envied him for living there. He told of its culture, concerned institutions for the handicapped and elderly, and wonderful playgrounds. We were impressed, too, by the warmth and loyalty of the owner and our waitress. This proved to us that to get to know the real spark of a town, you must meet its people.

If you look above the counter, you can see the original diner ceiling. The other rooms have expanded their capacity to accommodate the eager and satisfied patrons. Frank ordered a bowl of beef noodle soup for lunch. It was superb, homemade from last night's roast beef drippings! The dinner specials draw the locals to this top-bargain restaurant. Jad's has a full liquor license.

Average prices: Full breakfast, under $4. Lunch sandwiches, $2–$4. Chowder, under $2; soup of the day, under $1. Great dinners, $5 to $10; fried chicken, baked ham, pot roast, or roast pork are daily specials; prime rib on weekends. *Credit cards:* None. *Hours:* Wednesday through Monday, 7 A.M. to 8:30 P.M.; closes Thanksgiving and Christmas. *Owner:* Doug McLean. *Directions:* Take exit 1 from I-91, and go north on Route 5, which becomes Canal Street in Brattleboro. As you descend the hill, the restaurant is on your left.

THE TAVERN
Putney Road, Route 5
Brattleboro, Vermont 05301
(802) 254-9675

The Tavern is a pretty restaurant with hanging ferns, a green interior, and oak tables and chairs. The pretty waitresses scurry about bringing plates of freshly baked pastries, tantalizing quiches, and gigantic sandwiches on all sorts of breads and fresh rolls to their waiting patrons. Turkey, Vermont smoked ham, and roast beef are prepared fresh each day. In the background is classical music. The mood is romantic and chic. Take advantage of the lunch prices both on the menu and the blackboard. If it's a nice day, you might like to eat outside in the courtyard beneath an umbrella. This atmosphere is "just right for honeymooners." A pleasant cocktail lounge invites as you enter. The tavern employs a special pastry and dessert chef. An off-the-menu brunch is served on Sundays.

Average prices: Lunch, $4–7; dinner, $8–$16; brunch, $3–$7. *Credit cards:* All major. *Hours:* Monday through Friday, 10:30 A.M. to 9 P.M.; Saturday and Sunday, 11:30 A.M. to 10 P.M.; Sunday brunch served 9 A.M. to 3 P.M. *Owners:* Kyle and Carmen Tyler. *Directions:* Take exit 3 off I-91 to Route 5. Go south at the light. The restaurant is ½ mile farther on the left.

Also recommended:

The Country Kitchen has an excellent salad bar, blackboard specials, and a full dinner and lunch menu. Lunch is served 11:30 A.M. to 2:30 P.M.; dinner, 4:30 to 9 P.M.; Sunday dinner, noon to 9 P.M. The restaurant is on Western Avenue, 2 miles west of the I-91 Route 9 exit, in Brattleboro. Call owner Joanne Vulcano at (802) 257-0338.

BOVE'S RESTAURANT
68 Pearl Street
Burlington, Vermont 05401
(802) 864-6651

We heard about this very well-known restaurant from so many of our own guests and other folks that we have to introduce you

178

to it. They say Bove's makes the best spaghetti you'll ever taste! The restaurant serves strictly Italian food, and it's been in the same family for fifty years—three generations. Besides regular spaghetti and meatballs, steak, and super antipastos, Bove's features daily specials of lasagna, chicken cacciatore, stuffed peppers, or manicotti. They are also proud of their mushroom, clam, and garlic sauces. The restaurant is quite comfortable, seats seventy-five in cushioned booths, and has the same art deco front it has had for more than fifty years. A bar services tables only. You can take out any of their dishes.

Average prices: $3 to $7. Antipasto: $2.70 for one; $5.60 for eight. *Credit cards:* None. *Hours:* Tuesday through Saturday, 8:30 A.M. to 10 P.M. Closed Sunday and Monday. *Owner:* Richard Bove. *Directions:* From I-89, take East Avenue exit, turn right, and go to Colchester. Go left on Colchester for 1½ miles; it runs into Pearl Street.

Also recommended:

In Burlington, there are many good places to eat; here are only a few. **Carbur's** at 11 St. Paul Street is the best family sandwich place, although there are many to choose from; **Henry's Diner** and **Al's French Fries** are two other local favorites. Try **Sweetwater's** for "yuppie" type creative food. We ate lunch in **The Shanty** on the Ferry Docks because it was open on Sunday; we had good chowder and crab rolls there.

COLCHESTER REEF LIGHTHOUSE RESTAURANT
Mountain View Road
Colchester, Vermont 05446
(802) 655-0200

This is a very reasonable place to eat with some interesting touches not found in other restaurants. You get a bottomless bowl of salad already tossed with a delicious dill ranch dressing. If this isn't enough to fill you up, you are given the most delicious buttermilk biscuits. Both salad and biscuits come with your entree. Frank had the baked stuffed scrod (haddock, not cod) and Fran ate the sirloin tips. Both meals were served with potato or rice and vegetable. A special of prime rib and scallops was featured the night we were there. All items were very reasonably priced. The booths and tables are tiered to give diners a sense of privacy. It seemed a little noisy, but not bad. The service is excellent.

Average prices: Lunches, $4–$8; dinner, $9–$14. *Credit cards:* All major. *Hours:* Lunch: Monday through Saturday, 11:30 A.M. to 2:30 P.M.; dinner, 5–10 P.M.; Sunday brunch, 10 A.M. to 2:30 P.M.; Sunday dinner, 4 to 9 P.M. *Owners:* Tygate Corporation. Andy Rose is head chef. *Directions:* Take exit 16 off I-89. The restaurant is on the right beside the Hampton Inn. Look for the replica of a lighthouse.

GURRY'S RESTAURANT
Routes 11 and 30
Manchester, Vermont 05255
(802) 362-9878

Gurry's is a good family dinner place with many fish dishes and at least one beef dish in the medium range, plus many types of parmigianas. They also serve four different kinds of burgers. This place was recommended to us by innkeepers and other townspeople as having very good food. They have specials on the board each night also. Gurry's is attractive with a casual atmosphere and a cozy, quiet bar. The chicken is a house favorite. All dinners are served with potato, salad or cole slaw, and home-baked bread.

Average prices: Dinner, $8–$12. Half a roasted chicken and fried clams are under $7. *Credit cards:* MasterCard, Visa, Diner's Club, and American Express. *Hours:* All year except Christmas and Thanksgiving. Sunday through Thursday, 4 to 11 P.M.; Friday and Saturday, until midnight. *Owner:* Richard Gurry. *Directions:* From Manchester Center, take Routes 11 and 30 north about 3 miles. The restaurant is on your right just east of Manchester Depot.

THE QUALITY RESTAURANT
726 Main Street (Box 1168)
Manchester Center, Vermont 05255
(802) 362-9839

This restaurant in the center of town is highly recommended. The atmosphere is friendly, and the maple furniture and green and wine colonial prints give it a country flavor. It was the setting for Norman Rockwell's painting *War News*. It features fancy sandwiches (thirteen different ones) and nine hearty dinners for very reasonable prices. Breakfast is served every day until 11 A.M. A special dessert is served every day. They also have nightly specials.

Average prices: Breakfast, $3–$4; lunch, $4–$7; dinner, $9–$13. *Credit cards:* All major. *Hours:* All year. Daily from 7 A.M. to 9 P.M. *Owners:* Wayne and Debra Bell. *Directions:* It is ¼ mile north of the intersection of Routes 7 and 11-30, on the right in the center of town, next to Factory Point Bank.

Also recommended:

Ye Olde Taverne on North Main Street serves delicious seafood, lamb, and steak dinners for a moderate price. Call (802) 362-3770.

One way to beat those expensive lunch prices that somehow destroy your vacation budget is to buy some Vermont cheddar cheese sold in all Vermont general stores and groceries (pieces cut from a wheel of cheese are best). Then scout out a bakery— Vermont has many new ones run by a relatively young crop of creative bakers. Purchase your rolls or bread, and enjoy a super Yankee lunch. Two good bakeries we found in Manchester were the **Mad Batter,** on Route 7 on the left going north as you enter the town center, and the **Rolling in Dough Bakery.** Our favorite is Rolling in Dough, where we got coffee and a chocolate chip cookie for an all-time bargain. They also have spinach pie and quiche, which, with a little wine and a sunny day, could make a romantic picnic. You may sit at one of their indoor tables if the weather is bad and fill yourself on the spot. It is located on Center Hill Road across from Battenkill Meat Locker.

SKYLINE RESTAURANT
Molly Stark Trail, Route 9
Marlboro, Vermont 05344
(802) 464-5535

Skyline Restaurant has big country breakfasts and a view that, on a clear day, stretches a hundred miles to the south from the summit of Hogback Mountain (elevation 2,410 feet). Joyce Hamilton, the wife of the owner, must be the happiest and most cheerful woman in Vermont. Her dad, Harold White, started the whole complex, and it now has a major ski resort, lookout stations, a natural history museum, and a gift store. The Hamiltons have operated the restaurant for forty years, and it drew a big breakfast crowd the Sunday morning we were there. The interior is varnished knotty pine—a rustic look enhanced by a large stone fireplace. Big bay windows allow you to view the hills to the south from this mountaintop. Waffles and griddle cakes are the specialty. The location on Route 9 on the way from Brattleboro to Bennington makes a nice break in the driving. You can walk around and unwind if you've been behind the wheel too long. Skyline has a full liquor license and is accessible to handicapped. The Lumen Nelson Museum of New England Wildlife is across the street.

Average prices: Continental breakfast, about $3. Farmer's breakfast with eggs, under $8. Griddle cakes and waffles with meat, only around $7 (available all day). Lunch: club sandwiches, chef salad, and some plates around $6. Dinner, $10–$15, with salad, a potato, vegetable, relish tray, rolls, and datenut bread. *Credit cards:* All major. *Hours:* Summer: 8 A.M. to 8:30 P.M. every day. November 1 to April 30: Monday and Tuesday, 8 A.M. to 3 P.M.; Wednesday to Sunday, 8 A.M. to 8 P.M. Open year-round. *Owners:* Richard and Joyce Hamilton. *Directions:* Take exit 2 off I-91 in Brattleboro. Go west on Route 9 about 15 miles. It's on the right at the top of a mountain summit, across from Hogback Ski Resort.

THE SUGAR HOUSE RESTAURANT
Route 7, P.O. Box 525
Middlebury, Vermont 05753
(802) 388-2770

This large restaurant, attached to the motel, has very good prices. You'll be comfy around the big fieldstone fireplace in the center of the dining room. Old sugar molds and other equipment adorn the walls. At breakfast, of course, you'll get honest-to-goodness Vermont maple syrup on hot cakes or French toast. They have scrumptious sandwiches, and for their dinner specialties they offer great prime rib, sirloin, and tenderloin tips; a wide variety of fish, broiled or poached; and lobster in the summer; plus regular favorites as daily specials. Their many years of experience in palate pleasing is evident! High chairs are available.

Average prices: Breakfast, about $2.50 to $3.50; lunch, $3–$5; dinners, about $8 to $13. *Credit cards:* All major. *Hours:* June to October, daily, 7 A.M. to 9 P.M.; closes at 8 P.M. from November to May. *Owners:* Douglas and Mary Baker. *Directions:* This place is located exactly 2½ miles north of Middlebury on Route 7, on the right.

PUTNEY SUMMIT RESTAURANT AND LOUNGE
Route 5, P.O. Box 728
Putney, Vermont 05346
(802) 387-5806

This restaurant has the food to make your mouth water and reasonable prices to go with it. The locals rave about the cooking of the Narkiewicz family that makes this place such a standout. The dining room is finished in light pine and has large bay windows (especially nice during foliage time). The chef and owner, Mr. Narkiewicz, was the head chef at the Old Tavern in Grafton. He is abetted by his son and daughter. Dinner entrees include a cup of soup or fresh fruit, salad and vegetable, potato, roll, and butter. For the bargain hunter there is spaghetti and meatballs or an open steak sandwich. When we were there, the blackboard specials were prime rib-Summit cut and sole stuffed with crabmeat. They are especially creative with their menu. They even

183

have a Cape Cod special with lobster and steamed clams. The portions are generous. We were told by a patron at Jad's that this place was the best! A shy woman at the counter nodded her head in agreement as he spoke. This restaurant has a full liquor license, bar, and lounge. Lodgings are also available but not advertised.

Average prices: Full breakfast, $2–$8; lunch, $3–$8; dinner, $9–$18. *Credit cards:* MasterCard, Visa, and American Express. *Hours:* Every day of the year. Monday to Saturday, 8 A.M. to 9:30 P.M.; Sunday, 8 A.M. to 9 P.M. *Owners:* The Narkiewicz family. *Directions:* Get off exit 4 on I-91. Go a few hundred yards west, and pick up Route 5 north through Putney center. The restaurant is about a mile from the town center at the top of the hill on your left.

KATIE'S KITCHEN
Route 121, P.O. Box 435
Saxtons River, Vermont 05154
(802) 869-2383

Katie's Kitchen on Main Street is a pleasant surprise. It is a homey, down-to-earth, jolly restaurant—very clean with real home cooking. This is a good place to get information about the region, where things are, what's happening—all the gossip of small town New England. The meatloaf, soups, stews, baked beans, and homemade desserts are delicious. Counter service and tables are available. The waitresses maintain cheerful and humorous banter with customers.

Average prices: Full breakfast, $2 to $4; lunch sandwiches, $2 to $4; dinner, $5 to $8. Homemade pies are over $1 (we had the blueberry—yummy). *Credit cards:* None. *Hours:* Open every day, 7 A.M. to 7:30 P.M. *Owner:* Chuck Wood. *Directions:* Take exit 5 off I-91 to Route 5. Go north on 5 and take a left onto Route 121 west to Saxtons River. Katie's Kitchen is on the left about in the center of this small town. Route 121 is called Main Street here.

THE INN AT SAXTONS RIVER
Main Street
Saxtons River, Vermont 05154
(802) 869-2110

This is an old inn that has been fixed up and redecorated by the Friemans to its current country, Victorian splendor. Lots of color gives it a unique elegance. There is outside dining on the lawn, which adds a nice turn-of-the-century ambience. The dining room is large, and the cuisine has a gourmet flair—nouveau French. Fresh soups, homemade desserts, unique pastas, and enchanting appetizers make eating here a gourmet adventure. The inn is completely remodeled. Enjoy a cocktail or aperitif at the white lawn tables on the side lawn before your meal. Very elegant and relaxing!

Average prices: Breakfast, $4–$7; lunch, $4–$6; dinner, $12–$18. You can also get a special, very popular with locals, consisting of soup, salad, and bread for about $4. *Credit cards:* MasterCard and Visa. Checks accepted with proper identification. *Hours:* In season: Sunday through Thursday, 7:30 A.M. to 9 P.M.; Friday and Saturday, until 10 P.M. Off-season, closed Tuesday. *Owners:* Sandy and Ilene Frieman. *Directions:* Take exit 5 off I-91 to Route 5. Go north on Route 5 and take a left onto Route 121 west to Saxtons River. The inn is about ⅔ of the way down Main Street on your right.

FOXFIRE INN
Route 100 North (1606 Pucker Street)
Stowe, Vermont 05672
(802) 253-4887

Irene and Art Segreto make their Italian meals a work of art, and the resulting dining pleasure, part of the art of good living. The dining room is beautifully decorated with bright country prints, cloth napkins, and navy blue and beige tablecloths. The sun porch-dining area to the right of the cocktail lounge is bright yellow with white furniture and reminded us of a scene out of *House and Garden*. This eating place is a favorite with the local population, because the quality and price are right.

Lasagna, fettucine, ziti, linguine, and spaghetti with four different sauces available with or without sausages and meatballs.
Salad is included. Desserts are delicious and very reasonable.
Espresso and cappuccino are available. We urge that you take
plenty of time with your meal so as not to offend the owners-
chefs. In our conversation with Art we learned that he had been
a technical illustrator on Long Island; he described how art and
cooking are very much the same. He pointed out that the pre-
sentation of the plate should be an artistic creation. We were
impressed with his philosophy. Reservations are recommended.

Average prices: Pasta dishes, $7–$8.50. *Credit cards:* MasterCard
and Visa. *Hours:* 5:30 P.M. to 10 P.M., every day except Thanksgiving. *Owners:* Irene and Art Segreto. *Directions:* Take Route 100
north from Stowe Village for 1½ miles; the inn is on the right.

McCARTHY'S
Mountain Road
Stowe, Vermont 05672
(802) 253-8626

The food and the prices at this fantastic place have no equal
for breakfast and lunch. Muffins are very popular. Fran tried
their excellent homemade apple Danish, and Frank was bowled
over by the superb oatmeal with natural brown sugar. Homemade
doughnuts, waffles with strawberries, and eggs McCarthy are big
favorites. For lunch they have hot and cold sandwiches, clubs,
grinders, pockets, salads, and seafood platters. On Sunday they
serve a mean eggs Benedict. In the summer there are barbecued
hotdogs and hamburgers on the patio outdoors.

Average prices: Breakfast, under $2 to under $3. Lunch: $2–$4 for
sandwiches; grinders were $4, and club sandwiches $5, when we
visited. *Credit cards:* None. *Hours:* All year, every day, 6 A.M. to 3
P.M. *Owner:* Diane McCarthy. *Directions:* From Stowe center, turn
north onto Mountain Road (Route 108). Turn right into Baggy
Knees complex. McCarthy's is behind Front Four Sports and
next to The Cinema.

THE SHED RESTAURANT
1859 Mountain Road
Stowe, Vermont 05672
(802) 253-4364

The Shed, which offers the most varied menu in Stowe, is a big favorite of the natives and tourists. The interior is attractively done in floral tablecloths and many plants, with a large sunny greenhouse on the side. Breakfast is served on weekends, offering many different kinds of eggs and featuring Belgian waffles. On Sunday there's an option of a beautiful brunch with "add your own" style omelets, fresh fruits, and waffles. Their Shedburger for lunch or dinner is a prizewinner—marinated chuck served on a large English muffin. Other favorites are the chicken fingers and seafood or spinach strudel. They also serve chicken, steak, lamb, seafood, and pasta. Families are welcome, and there are three large smokeaters in the walls. Visit the original frontier-style room with a Wurlitzer that plays music from the '40s, '50s, and '60s.

Average prices: Breakfast, $3 to $5; sandwiches, $3 to over $7; dinner, $6 to $13. *Hours:* Breakfast: Sunday only, 8:30 to 11:30 A.M.; brunch, 9 A.M. to 2 P.M. Every day: lunch, 11:30 A.M. to 4:30 P.M.; dinner, 5 to 10 P.M. *Credit cards:* All major. *Owner:* Kenny Strong. *Directions:* The Shed is about 2 miles north of Stowe center on Route 108 (Mountain Road) on the left.

STOWE AWAY LODGE
3148 Mountain Road
Stowe, Vermont 05672
(802) 253-7574

We used to stay here with our kids to enjoy the downhill skiing at Mount Mansfield. The rooms have all been redecorated and subsequently the prices are above our limit, but we still recommend the Mexican cooking. Michael, the owner and chief chef, studied Mexican cooking in the Southwest and began offering this cuisine before it became popular. The atmosphere is like someone's home. There is a beautiful pool table in the bar that we enjoy playing on before the meal. The dining room area had

187

checkered tablecloths and candles when we were there. It is a small room—cozy and intimate. The usual Mexican dishes are offered plus an unusual and scrumptious variety of innovative dishes like crabmeat enchiladas and special tacos served with rice and beans. Our children fell in love with the sopapillas (fried dough with honey butter). A pretty patio at the rear provides a nice fair weather dining area.

Average prices: Dinner entrees in the usual platter style average from $7 to $12. Apertivos (appetizers), such as nachos verde and chili con queso dip, range from $4 to $6.50. *Hours:* Daily, 5:30–10 P.M. *Credit cards:* MasterCard and Visa. *Owner:* John M. Henzel (Michael). *Directions:* Take Mountain Road (Route 108) from the center of Stowe. It is a red, single-story building right on the road about 4½ miles down on the right.

D. W. PEARL'S
Route 100, Box 850
Waitsfield, Vermont 05673
(802) 496-8858

This restaurant caters to families and has a section set up like a diner with a counter and tables. It has a good-sized dining room on the side with red and yellow tablecloths, beamed ceilings, bright country prints, and Vermont barnboard on the lower walls. A fireplace is comforting in the winter. They bake all their own pies, cakes, and breads in a small bakery downstairs. In the summer you can eat outside. The most fantastic feature of this place is the extensive salad bar, which comes with all entrees, and includes along with a full array of crisp vegetables, a homemade soup and a pasta sauce! There are five specials every night, and they also cater to dieters. A children's menu is offered too.

Average prices: Breakfast, under $2 to just over $4. At lunch, sandwiches are mostly in the $2 to $3 range. Dinners run from under $7 to $11. During our visit a seafood special, fettucine with chicken and mushrooms, and prime rib were under $9 and included soup and salad. *Credit cards:* MasterCard, Visa, and Diner's Club. *Hours:* Monday through Saturday, 6 A.M. to 10 P.M.; Sunday, 7 A.M.

188

to 9 P.M. The lounge is open later. *Owner:* Dewey Dwinell. *Directions:* From Stowe follow Route 100 south to Waitsfield. About 1 mile south after the Route 17 turnoff, you'll see it on the left on Route 100.

DOT'S RESTAURANT
Main Street, Box 1415
Wilmington, Vermont 05363
(802) 464-7284

This is one of the best buys in this expensive town. It is where the locals go for breakfast and a reasonable lunch. There are oak tables, a counter with stools, and a fireplace at the end of the long dining area. Their blueberry muffins and cinnamon rolls are the best in Vermont. Pancakes are available with real Vermont maple syrup. Other home cooking and baking make it a must for bargain hunters. Lasagna and other hot dishes are available at very reasonable prices. Homemade soup and chowder are a specialty—both for low prices. Reasonable home-cooked dinners also are now available on Friday and Saturday. Beer and wine are available.

Average prices: Breakfast of eggs, toast, home fries, and coffee was just over $3 when we visited. Lunch sandwiches range from $3 to $4. Dinners average about $9. *Credit cards:* None. *Hours:* Sunday through Thursday, 5:30 A.M. to 3 P.M.; Friday and Saturday until 8 P.M. *Owners:* The Regan family. *Directions:* The restaurant is near the stoplight in the center of Wilmington. It is on the north side of Main Street (Route 9) on the Bennington (west) side of the intersection.

PONCHO'S WRECK
South of the Light in Wilmington
Wilmington, Vermont 05363
(802) 464-9320

Poncho's Wreck is a trendy restaurant with a second-floor balcony. Lots of atmosphere—dark and campy. The summer night we were there, a folk singer entertained the guests with ballads.

The decor is meant to look like a scene from Treasure Island. Our waitress, from Lexington, Massachusetts, had given up the fast pace of Boston for "something quiet." She was very understanding with us, as we were very tired after a day of searching out good bargain places and eateries. The specialties are either Mexican or seafood (Poncho owns a fish market next door and his own fishing boat). The bargains are in the Mexican entree list. Try the flauta, enchilada, and tacos. The ice-cold goblets of beer hit the spot on a hot, dry Vermont evening. The big salad placed on the table is free if you order an entree. They have barbecued steaks and chicken, too. There are early-bird specials and a children's menu. Live entertainment is offered in the evening.

Average prices: Lunch and dinner, chili is the best item at under $5. Plates of tacos, enchiladas, and the other Mexican fare range from $7 to $12, averaging about $9. Seafood, $10 to $19; steaks, $12 to $19. *Credit cards:* All major. *Hours:* Open every day. Lunch, 11:30 A.M. to 4 P.M.; dinner, 4 to 10 P.M. *Owner:* Poncho. *Directions:* Take Route 9 to Wilmington. Traveling west, take a left at the traffic light. It's about 50 yards along on the left.

THE VILLAGE INN OF WOODSTOCK
41 Pleasant Street (Route 4)
Woodstock, Vermont 05091
(802) 457-1255; (800) 722-4571

This Victorian home with fireplaces, rich oak wainscoting, ornate tin ceilings, and beveled glass is both a bed & breakfast and a restaurant or, technically, an inn, because it serves dinner as well. We enjoyed an Italian meal here—Italian cuisine is their specialty. Aside from the antipasti and pasta dishes on the menu, they offer traditional New England fare. The lamb, steak, duck, and other entrees are prepared with the flair of an Italian gourmet. Fran loved the half order of pasta, but Frank was disappointed that the turkey dinner was only the roasted breast. You have to have the whole bird to get the gravy and make a proper dressing. Even so, a homey, elegant ambience was ensured by candlelit tables set in different small rooms. We found this a very restful, relaxed place to eat. Reservations are recommended. A cocktail lounge and wine list are available. Some porch tables and garden benches are available for before-dinner drinks. Note: Rooms are available; see Where to Stay section.

Average prices: Dinner entrees range from $13 to $21; full-order pasta dishes, $10 to $12; half orders available. *Credit cards:* MasterCard, Visa, and American Express. *Hours:* 5 to 9:30 P.M.; closed off-season Sundays. *Owners:* Kevin and Anita Clark. *Directions:* Take Route 4 from I-89 to Woodstock. When you make the sharp bend to the right in town, you will be on Pleasant Street. The Village Inn will be on your left, brightly painted with loud Victorian colors.

Also recommended:

Downtown Woodstock has two good places, especially for lunch. One is the **Downtown Deli,** which is built right over a river, and the other is the **Mountain Creamery** on the opposite side of the road. In the Creamery we tried some very good homemade onion soup and a good-sized, reasonably priced sandwich. The pies are huge and taste fantastic. Both restaurants are on the main street of Woodstock.

The **White Cottage Snack Bar** on Route 4, West Woodstock, is on the left as you leave town going west. They serve very reasonable burgers and sandwiches, fried seafood, and ice cream. Picnic tables by the river make a beautiful spot for lunch or supper and save you money you might otherwise spend in expensive eateries in town. Woodstock is pricey!

NEW HAMPSHIRE

New Hampshire is pleasing in a thousand ways. The lakes are clear and warm; the mountains, inspiring and challenging; and the fly-fishing in rushing rivers in the spring, is excellent. You'll find the dairy farmers determined, good-natured folk; the cities, Manchester, Concord, and Portsmouth, dignified and proud; and the seacoast gentle. Country music abounds and artists are enchanting. You'll love its composure and constancy and its shy, amiable people with their wisdom and wit.

If you like mountains, the area around Mount Monadnock is lovely and worth a visit, even though the mountains aren't as high as in the north. The woods and serene lakes are natural and clean and the folks are quite laid back, though interested in talking and philosophizing. Farther north, the Mount Washington Valley in the White Mountains is certainly one of the most pleasing, enchanting, and appealing places to spend recreational time and restful hours in all of New England. The snowcapped mountains are great for skiing, hiking, and camping, and the little green villages in the valley are enticing.

North Woodstock, Plymouth, and Lincoln, on the west side of the White Mountains, have much to offer in dramatic natural beauty, such as gorges, waterfalls, and exquisite mountain views. There are thousands of trails to discover, and fishing is popular in the Pemigewasset River off the Kancamagus Highway.

If you like the seacoast, take a look at the area around Portsmouth. This city not only has colonial beauty and richness of history in its own right, but also is surrounded by numerous attractions. It is in the vicinity of miles of gorgeous beaches and is the gateway to Maine and the White Mountains. The whole coast to the north and south is an antiquer's dream.

Winnipesaukee and the Lake District, in about the center of the state, have a unique appeal, with rolling hills, woods, and water views everywhere. Except for Weirs Beach and some crowded camping areas along the lakes, it's still unspoiled and quiet in the small towns. In the summer there's plenty of swimming, boating, and fishing, and in the off-season it's very relaxing.

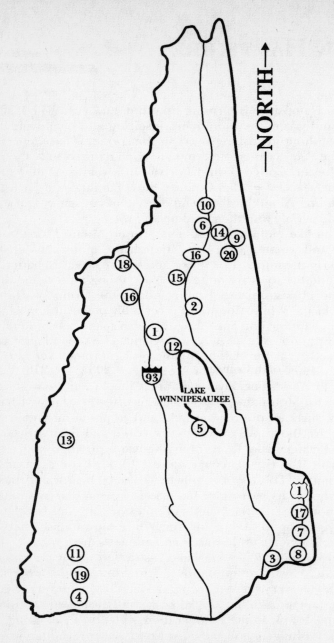

NORTH

10
6 14 9
16 20
16
15
2
1
12
93
LAKE
WINNIPESAUKEE
5
13
1
17
7
11 3 8
19
4

NEW HAMPSHIRE

New Hampshire

	🛏	🍴
1. Ashland	196	212
2. Chocorua Village	196	—
3. Exeter	—	212
4. Fitzwilliam	197	214
5. Gilford	198	—
6. Glen	—	214
7. Greenland	199	—
8. Hampton	199	215
9. Intervale	200	—
10. Jackson	201	—
11. Marlborough	202	—
12. Meredith	—	216
13. New London	—	217
14. North Conway	203	218
15. North Sandwich	207	—
16. North Woodstock	207	219
17. Portsmouth	209	221
18. Sugar Hill	210	—
19. Troy	210	—
20. West Ossipee	—	224

Where to Stay

Country Options Bed and Breakfast
27–29 North Main Street, P.O. Box 730
Ashland, New Hampshire 03217
(603) 968-7958

This bed & breakfast is a lovely splurge. Every room is fresh and new, and yet keeps the flavor of times past. The color coordination is dazzling! There is a yellow room with an antique painted headboard, matching bureaus, and one-hundred-year-old lace curtains. Claudia's Room is small and red and white. The blue and white room is soft and beautiful with different shades of light and dark blue. All have fresh flowers, as does the bright and airy common room with a wood stove on a brick hearth. There are a sink, a coffee maker, and a refrigerator for guests' use, and you may breakfast on the breezy porch in the summer. A full breakfast is included in the cost. A bakery is part of the property called Country Options. During March, April, and May, be sure to call ahead in case Sandy is away for the weekend.

Average rates: Double with shared bath, $45–$50; single, $35. Extra person, $10. *Credit cards:* None. *Open:* Year-round. *Owner:* Sandy Ray. *Directions:* Take exit 24 off I-93 into Ashland. About ¼ mile on the right in the town's center you'll find the white house with black shutters and a red oval sign. *Children:* Yes. *Pets:* No. *Smoking:* No.

The Farmhouse Bed and Breakfast
P.O. Box 14
Chocorua Village, New Hampshire 03817
(603) 323-8707

This beautiful old homestead, with a screened porch, a barn, and outbuildings, is surrounded by gardens, pastures, and giant maples on seven acres. Your stay here will seem like a visit to Grandma's—a comfortable reminder of yesteryear. The three sunny guest rooms are decorated with stenciling and handmade quilts. Crisp, old-fashioned furnishings and antiques add to the

196

country charm. Relax in the guest parlor with books, table games, and television, after hiking, sightseeing, or skiing in the White Mountains.

Kathie and John, former teachers, serve their own fresh eggs, or pancakes with their own maple syrup, country ham, bacon or sausage, homemade muffins, and fruit. Afternoon tea is served on the plant- and wicker-filled porch in summer and in the cozy guest parlor in winter. You may dine at several good restaurants nearby or walk to village shops. All rooms share baths.

Average rates: Double, $60 for two. Weekly rates are available. *Credit cards:* None. *Open:* May to end of October. *Owners:* Kathie and John Dyrenforth. *Directions:* Take Route 16 north to its junction with Route 113. Turn west at the flashing yellow light in Chocorua Village. It is the first farmhouse on the left. *Children:* Limited. *Pets:* No. *Smoking:* Yes.

FITZWILLIAM INN
Routes 12 and 119
Fitzwilliam, New Hampshire 03447
(603) 585-9000

This very old, lovely inn has been redecorated with new wallpapers or stenciling and new curtains. Some rugs are braided or needlepoint. We enjoyed the antique-decorated living rooms with a grand piano and fireplaces, and the cheerful, busy bar. All the attendants are friendly and help you to relax. Most of the rooms in the front are large and contain two double beds, and some have cozy slanted ceilings with dormers. We only recommend rooms 3, 4, 6, 8, and 10 (3 and 4 have fireplaces) or rooms on the third floor. Guests can use the large swimming pool with the attached playroom. No meals are included, but there is an excellent restaurant in the building that serves interesting breakfasts and specials each dinnertime. There is a handy little gift shop also. Free classical music concerts are held throughout the year in the large living room.

Average rates: Double, $45–$60. *Credit cards:* All major. *Open:* All year. *Owners:* Barbara Wallace and her children. *Directions:* Take Route 24 off I-91 to Keene, then Route 12 south to where it meets Route 119 in the center of tiny Fitzwilliam. The inn is right off the common. *Children:* Yes: crib available. *Pets:* No. *Smoking:* Yes.

CARTWAY HOUSE
Old Lake Shore Road
Gilford, New Hampshire 03246
(603) 528-1172

This lovely 1791 farmhouse sits on a hillside very close to Gunstock Ski Area and has great views from all the rooms. You'll like its nearness to hiking, skiing, swimming, fishing, and boating. The dining room is modern and brightly colored with a long, tiled table. Here wonderful full breakfasts, which are included in the room, are served. Television and games are available in the cozy sitting room. Some rooms have bunkbeds; groups are encouraged and will obtain special rates.

Average rates: Double, $52–$60; no extra charge for children in room. Senior citizen discount. *Credit cards:* MasterCard, Visa, and American Express. *Open:* All year. *Owner:* Gretchen Shortway. *Directions:* From Route 93, take Route 3 to Laconia then take the Laconia bypass. At the end of the bypass, take a left at the traffic light and your first right. The house is about ¾ mile up the hill. It is yellow with large columns. *Children:* Yes. *Pets:* Yes, with prior approval. *Smoking:* Yes.

Also recommended:

The **Christmas Tree Inn** in Gilford is new, yet it retains the charm of the 1800s, when it was built. Doubles are $60 to $70 a night. There is a restaurant on the premises with excellent gourmet cooking. It's open most of the year. Call Mary Lou and Kent Thompson at (603) 293-8155.

Olde Orchard Inn, in Moultonboro, has been recommended to us by attorney Stephen Wise of Connecticut. He tells us that the 1810 farmhouse has been beautifully restored, is only a mile from Lake Winnipesaukee, and is surrounded by apple orchards. It is directly across from the Woodshed Restaurant and has very reasonable rates. Call Charles or Virginia Litzell at (603) 476-5004.

AYERS HOMESTEAD
47 Park Avenue
Greenland, New Hampshire 03840
(603) 436-5992

The Homestead is a carefully restored, attractively furnished 1737 colonial with an ample measure of coziness, quiet, and privacy. The breakfast is a full English affair with muffins baked every morning. The hosts are warm, witty, and gracious. You will learn about the history of the area and may be treated to a tour of the house with architectural and decorative commentary. The Engels are happy to recommend places to visit and others to avoid. There are four rooms, one with private bath. A suite on the second floor can accommodate a family. A cottage with kitchenette is also available. Greenland is a suburb of Portsmouth, giving you a good base of operation for the seacoast area.

Average rates: Double, $50–$55; check price for suite; cottage, $125. *Credit cards:* None. *Open:* Year-round. *Owners:* David and Priscilla Engel. *Directions:* From I-95 go through Hampton tollbooth and take exit 3. At light go left on Route 101 toward Greenland. Go left at the third light, Route 151. This brings you to the center of Greenland. Beyond the church go left onto Park Avenue. The Avery Homestead, a yellow house with black shutters, is on left. *Children:* Yes. *Pets:* No. *Smoking:* Restricted.

THE INN AT ELMWOOD CORNERS
252 Winnacunnet Road
Hampton, New Hampshire 03842
(603) 929-0443; (800) 253-5691

John and Mary worked hard renovating this wonderful old 1870 house to get it ready for guests. John did all the refinishing of floors and carpentry, and Mary did the fine decorating. In the Rose Room she stenciled plump roses around the top of the walls. This room also has a charming handmade quilt of rose and pink squares. Most of the rooms have country touches such as braided rugs. When people have taken this much care to ready their home for you, you know you'll be very comfortable and relaxed there. John has cooked for the Oarhouse and the Codfish, both fine restaurants in Portsmouth, and he has some fine omelets, pancakes, and Belgian waffles dreamed up for you. Mary bakes pastries and breads. Their traditional New England breakfasts are heartier in winter and lighter in summer. The hosts give guests a choice of breakfast entrees. They also have provided an attractive sitting room on the second floor with television, books, and games. The stenciled dining room with its antique oak table has some great old pictures of the house, which used to be Elmwood farm—famed for once having the oldest elm tree in the state. You'll be minutes from beaches, antiques, apple picking, golf courses, and cross-country skiing.

Average rates: Double: $55 off-season; $65 in season; shared bath. Suites that sleep four with full baths and kitchenettes: $75 off-season, $90 in season. *Credit cards:* MasterCard and Visa. *Open:* All year. *Owners:* John and Mary Hornberger. *Directions:* From I-95, take exit 2 for Hampton. Bear left after toll onto Route 51 east and continue 3½ miles to stoplight. Go left onto Landing Road, go to the end of the street, and Elmwood will be right in front of you. From Route 1, turn onto Winnacunnet Road toward Hampton Beach (at the Galley Hatch). The Elmwood is .8 mile up on the left, at the second blinking yellow light. *Children:* Yes. *Pets:* No. *Smoking:* Restricted.

WILDFLOWERS GUEST HOUSE
North Main Street, Route 16
P.O. Box 802
Intervale, New Hampshire 03845
(603) 356-2224

Accessible to most tourist attractions and mountain sports areas, Wildflowers Guest House is a very popular place to stay. This hundred-year-old home has a cozy living room and a cheerful blue-and-white dining room where the complimentary continental breakfast is served. The guest rooms are all large and decorated in jaunty floral prints. There are antique satin cover-

200

lets on the beds, appealing old trunks and rockers here and there, and fireplaces in most rooms. Both private and semi-private baths are available. The easygoing hosts give this inn a homey atmosphere.

Average rates: Double $50–$85; single $40, when available. *Credit cards:* MasterCard and Visa. *Open:* May 1–October 31. *Owners:* Eileen Davies and Dean Franke. *Directions:* From the center of North Conway go 1½ miles on Route 16. The inn is on the left. *Children:* Yes. *Pets:* No. *Smoking:* Yes.

THE BLAKE HOUSE
Pinkham Notch Road, Box 246
Jackson, New Hampshire 03846
(603) 383-9057

The Blake House is a gracious home with many nice touches. Sarah serves a lovely, complimentary full breakfast in her new breakfast room, which looks out on the woods, birds, and a stream. All the rooms are snug and restful, with electric blankets in the winter. We enjoyed the twin beds in the upstairs rooms with slanted ceilings; all rooms have shared baths.

We were here right after Christmas, so the Maynards' tree was still up in the spacious, quiet living room. After a day of skiing, we all sat in here reading and enjoying the Christmas tree. Jeff was very helpful, giving us hints on ski conditions and places to eat lunch and dinner and making us feel very cared for.

The inn is open all year, and the rates are the same during the summer and winter. There is a two-night minimum on weekends.

Average rates: Double, including breakfast, $50–$80. *Credit cards:* American Express, Visa, and MasterCard. *Open:* All year. *Owners:* Sarah and Jeff Maynard. *Directions:* From North Conway, continue north on Route 16 to Jackson. The inn is 4 miles north of town on the right. *Children:* Yes, all ages. *Pets:* No. *Smoking:* Restricted.

ELLIS RIVER HOUSE
Route 16, P.O. Box 656
Jackson, New Hampshire 03846
(603) 383-9339; (800) 233-8309

Country living is the hallmark of this quaint bed & breakfast. You will relax in an atmosphere of period antiques set off with colonial colors, mostly blue. You'll find a wood stove, a gigantic country breakfast, and chickens clucking in the barn. All this is carefully managed by Barry (thirteen years' experience with Sheraton) and Barbara. You can access one of the best cross-country trails nearby and connect into the Jackson Touring Center trail complex. The mountain air in this Swisslike mountain village will invigorate the most frazzled nerves of the visiting city dweller all year round. Don't watch calories at breakfast, as your hosts will be serving up juice, fresh fruit, banana or cranberry fruit bread, eggs any style, ham, and sausage or bacon, plus homemade cinnamon, oatmeal, or beer bread, or French toast or cheese omelets, and other goodies. There are five rooms and a three-room suite. Enjoy the Jacuzzi spa in the atrium at the rear of the living room. A new cottage sleeps up to four people.

Average rates: $23–$50 per person, double occupancy; 10 percent service charge. *Credit cards:* MasterCard, Visa, American Express, and Discover. *Open:* All year. *Owners:* Barry and Barbara Lubao. *Directions:* Take Route I-95 from Boston, then Route 16, Spaulding Turnpike, north at Portsmouth. Continue on Route 16 all the way to Jackson. At the Exxon gas station in Jackson, take a left and follow the road 300 feet to Ellis River House. *Children:* Yes, all ages. *Pets:* In cottage only. *Smoking:* No.

PEEP WILLOW FARM
51 Bixby Street
Marlborough, New Hampshire 03455
(603) 876-3807

How could you resist that name? We had to look into it. A new colonial house on a seventeen-acre horse farm, it is very close to Keene and has views of Vermont mountains from most rooms. Noel serves a full breakfast all year, a favorite being French toast

202

with her own maple syrup! She runs a thoroughbred horse breeding and training farm. You may help with chores and pat the horses, but there is no riding. Often there are foals sprinting around in spring, a delight for children. There are common rooms, a living room, and a sitting room with a wood stove for guests to enjoy. The three bedrooms, some with flowered papers, have a colonial motif, simple and almost rustic. You may relax on the terrace certain seasons of the year.

Average rates: Double, $40; single, $25. *Credit cards:* None. *Open:* All year. *Owner:* Noel Aderer. *Directions:* Turn off Route 101 onto Route 124. Take the first left onto Pleasant Street; go up the steep hill to the stop sign. Turn right onto Bixby Street. Peep Willow is the second drive on the left. *Children:* Yes. *Pets:* By prior arrangement. *Smoking:* No.

THE CENTER CHIMNEY
River Road, P.O. Box 1220
North Conway, New Hampshire 03860-1220
(603) 356-6788

This lovely 1787 home is one of the oldest in North Conway. Set in the quiet woods just off the Saco River, it was once featured on calendars and post cards throughout the United States. The four guest rooms are cozy, with some antiques and pretty, decorative touches. One room has a sundeck. There is one whirlpool bath, also. All rooms share a bath. The living room is charming; you'll want to snuggle by the fire with a book or just sit around and talk. Farley serves her continental breakfast of homemade muffins in her kitchen. You may cross-country ski or skate in the area; swim, fish, or canoe on the river; watch rock climbing or ice climbing at Cathedral Ledge; or walk to the village shops. Of course you'll be near numerous downhill mountains in the area.

Average rates: Double; $49–$55 plus tax; single, $40 plus tax; extra bed, $10. Discounts in off-season and for midweek three-day stays. *Credit cards:* None. *Open:* All year. *Owner:* Farley Whitney. *Directions:* Take Route 16 to North Conway. Just after the Eastern

Slopes Inn on the left, turn left onto River Road at the Texaco Station. The house is about ½ mile down on the left across from the Nereledge Inn. *Children:* Yes. *Pets:* No. *Smoking:* Yes.

CRANMORE MOUNTAIN LODGE
Kearsage Road, P.O. Box 1194
North Conway, New Hampshire 03860
(603) 356-2044; (800) 356-3596

The Cranmore Mountain Lodge is beautiful and unique and has many extras, such as a forty-foot pool, basketball court, and outdoor Jacuzzi. It once belonged to Babe Ruth and has some Babe memorabilia, including his own furniture in room 2. In the winter, there are snowmobile rentals, a lighted toboggan hill, and an ice-skating pond. Minutes away are the downhill ski areas of Attitash, Wildcat, Cranmore, and Black Mountains. Meals are served on weekends in the winter and during holiday weeks. Guests are served a full breakfasts every day with chef specials on holiday occasions. This old farmhouse has sixteen rooms, a television and game room, and a large, pine-paneled living room with a grand piano and fireplace for its guests. They now have a calf, sheep, pigs, rabbits, and ducks, all with names. There are mid-week and seven-night specials with one night free, and group specials. The forty-bed bunkhouse is ideal for large groups.

Average rates: Double, $59–$99, breakfast included (higher in winter when dinner is also included). Group packages available. Bunkhouse is $26 per person with breakfast or $71 for a two-night package including breakfast and dinner. *Credit cards:* MasterCard, Visa, and American Express. *Open:* All year. *Owners:* Dennis and Judith Helfand. *Directions:* Take Route 16 north to North Conway. At the town center, turn east at the light onto Kearsage Street. Go past the Cranmore Inn to the dead end, turn left, and go 1.2 miles to the lodge. *Children:* Yes, all ages. *Pets:* No. *Smoking:* Yes.

THE NERELEDGE INN
River Road
North Conway, New Hampshire 03860
(603) 356-2831

The Nereledge Inn is a quiet, old-fashioned inn very near North Conway's center. All nine rooms are large, clean, and comfortable, and each one is different, with various combinations of bed sizes. Guests can use either of two sitting rooms, with a television, a piano, games, and books (one has a woodstove). Three rooms have private baths, one has a half-bath, and five share two baths. A full breakfast (chosen off the menu) is included in the price and is served in a separate breakfast room. A small English pub here has English beer on draft and a dartboard—it's always crowded.

Average rates: Double with breakfast, $59–$85; single with breakfast, $45. Extra adult or child over 12 in room, $15 (with breakfast). *Credit cards:* MasterCard, Visa, and American Express. *Open:* All year. *Owners:* Valerie and Dave Halpin. *Directions:* Take Route 16 to North Conway, and turn left at Eastern Slopes Inn onto River Road. Go less than a mile to the inn on the right. *Children:* Yes. *Pets:* No. *Smoking:* No.

SUNNYSIDE INN
Seavey Street
North Conway, New Hampshire 03860
(603) 356-6239

Sunnyside Inn has new owners whose previous home was in Cape Cod. This is a bright, enthusiastic young couple with the knack of making their guests feel comfortable. The inn is charmingly and lightly decorated with many flowers and paintings. The doubles are redecorated in colonial decor and have shared or private baths. In the evenings we shared the events of the day with some avid ice climbers who frequent the place.

The large dining room, with a blue and white floral theme and bright tablecloths, is heated by a woodstove. Their specialty is a full, creative, healthful breakfast, which is included in the cost of the room. Thick French toast is a new offering. We tried fluffy, buttermilk-blueberry pancakes with nuts and pure maple syrup, and our daughters had oatmeal with raisins, walnuts, and apples. The freshly ground coffee was super, as were the grapefruit and orange juices. They are open all year and encourage groups.

Average rates: Double, $45–$65; single, $30–$50. Special group rates. *Credit cards:* MasterCard and Visa. *Open:* All year. *Owners:* Chris and Marylee Uggerholt. *Directions:* In the center of North Conway, turn east onto Kearsage Street. At the top of the hill, turn right onto Seavey. The lodge is about 50 yards down on the left. *Children:* Yes. *Pets:* No. *Smoking:* Restricted.

YANKEE CLIPPER MOTOR LODGE
Route 16
North Conway, New Hampshire 03860
(603) 356-5736

The Yankee Clipper Motor Lodge has attractive, good-sized rooms, private baths, and color cable television, plus air conditioning in the summer. A miniature golf course and outdoor pool are on the premises. It has a convenient location, and amiable people work there. The Blueberry Muffin Restaurant is located on the grounds and serves delicious breakfasts and lunches; it opens at 7 A.M. each day. In nice weather you can take advantage of the patio dining area.

Average rates: Double, $45–$100. *Credit cards:* MasterCard, Visa, American Express, and Diner's Club. *Open:* All year, twenty-four hours a day. *Manager:* Cindy McInerney. *Directions:* Take Route 16 north to North Conway. The motel is just before the town center on the right. Here Route 16 is also known as Main Street. *Children:* Yes, all ages. *Pets:* No. *Smoking:* Yes.

STRATHAVEN BED AND BREAKFAST
Route 113
North Sandwich, New Hampshire 03259
(603) 284-7785

Strathaven is very homey, and the owners enjoy taking the time to show you the best swimming and fishing spots around. They encourage children and take great pride in their beautiful rooms decorated with plaids and flowers. The dining room is blue and white with chairs and a buffet hand-carved by Mrs. Leiper's father. One of the most pleasant rooms in the house is the big family room with a bay window overlooking Whiteface Mountain and the pond. The well-stocked feeders attract many birds of all colors. The Leipers have added a solar greenhouse to the family room, which creates a feeling of being outdoors. This is great country for canoeing, hiking, and cycling—and plenty of antiquing goes on. Mrs. Leiper gives embroidery lessons, and people stay here to take her course. A full and hearty country breakfast is included in the cost of the room. Pets are allowed, within reason.

Average rates: Double: with shared bath, $55; with private bath, $60. Additional guests, $10. *Credit cards:* None. *Open:* Year-round. *Owners:* Betsy and Tony Leiper. *Directions:* From I-93, take Route 3 to Holderness, then Route 113 to Center Sandwich. Continue about 3 miles east and you'll find the inn on the left in North Sandwich. *Children:* Yes. *Pets:* Well behaved pets only; kennel available. *Smoking:* Restricted to porch.

THREE RIVERS HOUSE
Route 3, South Main Street (R.F.D. 1, Box 72)
North Woodstock, New Hampshire 03262
(602) 745-2711; (800) 241-2711

This late nineteenth-century historic building recently has been renovated and furnished by the new owners, Brian and Diane. The comfortable lounge with fireplace, piano, and cable television provides a place to relax, while those who wish quiet can read a book in front of the fire in the cozy parlor. A bar that will be open to the public is to be added. The Moosilauke River runs behind the inn and makes a scenic addition to the majestic White Mountains in the background. The hosts offer to make the inn your home while you are there, which promises to make your visit a memorable one. There are thirteen rooms, each with full carpet, cable television, telephone, and a private bath. A full breakfast is included in the room price; dinner is extra.

Average rates: Double, $46 to $85. *Credit cards:* MasterCard and Visa; personal checks accepted. *Open:* All year. *Owners:* Brian Crete and Diane Brisson. *Directions:* From I-93 take exit 32 and turn right. Continue ½ mile until you get to Route 3; then turn left. The inn is 500 yards down the road on the right. *Children:* Yes. *Pets:* No. *Smoking:* Yes.

WOODSTOCK INN
80 Main Street, P.O. Box 118
North Woodstock, New Hampshire 03262
(603) 745-3951; (800) 321-3985

This one-hundred-year-old inn, restored to its original beauty, is a delightful place to stay. The seventeen rooms have been redecorated with quilts on the beds, matching drapes, and new and unusual antique pieces that take you back to life in a previous century. Accommodations range from double and twin beds to bedroom suites. The rates include a full breakfast, but to describe the selections available is a very difficult task because of the creativity and variety of the breakfast menu. Let us just say that the twenty-six items from heuvos rancheros to the blueberry brandy crepes are an adventure for any gourmet. When we were there, the owners were busy expanding the eating area to a sixty-seat dining room with a wrap-around glassed-in porch, to accommodate the increase in the dinner business. The rooms upstairs and the unusual breakfast menu make this inn a real treat in a beautiful area of New Hampshire.

Average rates: Double, $50–$79. *Credit cards:* All major. *Owners:* Scott and Eileen Rice. *Open:* Year-round. *Directions:* Take exit 32 off I–93 at North Woodstock, and take the first right into town. At the traffic light in North Woodstock, turn right (north) on Main Street. The Woodstock Inn is about 100 yards down on the left, or west, side of the street. *Children:* Yes. *Pets:* No. *Smoking:* Yes.

Also recommended:

In the region above Franconia Notch, which some people call the "Northern Kingdom," There is a bed & breakfast called the **Davenport Inn** run by Janet Leslie. You will get a superb view of the Presidential Range from this 1805 home decorated in English motif. All guest rooms have private bath and cost $60. The inn is located on Davenport Road in Jefferson. Call (603) 586-4320 for directions.

THE INN AT STRAWBERY BANKE
314 Court Street
Portsmouth, New Hampshire 03801
(603) 436-7242

You can feel colonial ambience all around you in this 1800 home built near the waterfront by Captain John Holbrook. The back yard borders the Strawbery Banke, a living museum reminiscent of Williamsburg, but much smaller. You can walk to many restaurants and shops without ever leaving the historic district. Prescott Park, site of the summer music series and arts festivals, is just down the street. The inn offers seven spacious guest rooms, decorated in colonial colors, all with private baths in the room or nearby. Some have queen-sized beds and fireplaces. Three rooms are downstairs, four are upstairs. A full country breakfast of sourdough pancakes and real maple syrup, an egg entree, or crepes, all with bacon, sausage, or ham, is a highlight of the morning. Enjoy it in a sunny breakfast room off the living or sitting room. You do not have to worry about noise on Court Street in this B&B. This backstreet location is a quiet place to relax while you visit Portsmouth or the surrounding region. Parking is free.

Average rates: Double: in season, $70–$85; off-season, $60–$75. *Credit cards:* MasterCard, Visa, and American Express. *Open:* Year-round. *Owner:* Sarah Glover O'Donnell. *Directions:* Exit off I-95 at exit 7. Drive into Portsmouth on Market Street and pass the Sheraton on the right. In the center of the city, where a big

209

church is on the left, turn left onto Church Street. Go 3 blocks to Court Street, turn left, and the inn is 2 blocks farther on your right. Park in fenced lot beside inn. *Children:* Ten and over. *Pets:* No. *Smoking:* No.

THE HILLTOP INN
Main Street, Route 117
Sugar Hill, New Hampshire 03585
(603) 823-5695

This 1895 Victorian home has been an inn since 1907. In the heart of the White Mountains, you'll be close to Franconia Notch, Cannon Mountain, Loon Mountain, The Flume, and other great places to visit. The six guest rooms are all furnished in antiques and handmade quilts and dressed in Victorian shades of deep forest green and rose. Some have private and some have shared baths. Relax in the large sitting room with its hand-stenciled flowers,and eat in the cozy dining room with a woodburning stove and glass doors and bay windows that over-look wonderful sunsets. You may eat outside or just sit and rock on the porches. A tasty, full country breakfast offered here might be French cinnamon toast, smoked bacon or sausage, and poached pears and raspberries. They now serve dinner four nights a week, too. Two dogs and two cats are part of the family.

Average rates: Double, $60 to $85. *Credit cards:* MasterCard, Visa, Discover, and American Express. *Open:* All year. *Owners:* Mike and Meri Hern. *Directions:* From Route 93, take exit 38 and turn right on Route 18 north. Go left on Route 117, and the inn is 2.7 miles farther on the right. *Children:* Yes. *Pets:* Yes. *Smoking:* Restricted.

THE INN AT EAST HILL FARM
Troy, New Hampshire 03465
(603) 242-6495; (800) 242-6495

This inn, where we took our children several years ago, is still operating in much the same way. Their starring items are the chickens, whose eggs the children can collect; calves, lambs, and

210

piglets to enjoy; and horses to ride. You can swim in the enclosed pool from which you can see stunning Mount Monadnock. You can hayride (sleigh ride in the winter) or boat, waterski, and fish at Silver Lake just a few miles away (you'll get a van ride to it). A tennis court is on the premises. There are also scheduled cookouts and square dancing. It's really quite a whirlwind of activities, and kids are always given high consideration. The rooms are plain and simple in the inn, and modern and fancy in the motel units. Some nights the adults have a cocktail hour (BYOB) and entertainment. Dave and Sally met here while working for the previous owner and decided to keep the same features. Prices include use of all facilities and entertainment.

Average rates: $112 for two includes three meals. This rate applies year-round except winter weekends; check on weekend, long-stay, and other special rates. *Credit cards:* None. *Open:* All year. *Owners:* Dave and Sally Adams and family. *Directions:* From Boston, take Route 2 west to Route 140 north to Route 12 to Troy center. Go right on Jaffrey Road (toward Mount Monadnock) and go 2 miles to the inn. (There are signs pointing the way up the hill to the inn.) *Children:* Yes, all ages. *Pets:* By prior arrangement. *Smoking:* Yes.

WHERE TO EAT

THE COMMON MAN
Main Street
Ashland, New Hampshire 03217
(603) 968-7030

This rustic place is in a handsome, restored, old brick building. Its character is casual, with antiques and blue tablecloths. The bargain here is at "sunset hour," when you can get everything, including one-half the main entree, for half price! Their soups are homemade and good. During regular hours, they still have a number of meals in our price range, including sole, scrod, thin London broil, and vegetable kabobs. Other meals are more expensive. Meals are served with a salad, potato, and fresh vegetables. They also have a children's menu.

Average prices: At the time of our visit, the lunch specials were quiche and soup or turkey pie for about $3. For dinner at sunset hour, you may find swordfish or stuffed shrimp at half price. Entrees range from $10 to $16. *Credit cards:* MasterCard and Visa. *Hours:* Tuesday to Saturday, 11:30 A.M. to 2 P.M. and 5 to 9 P.M.; Monday and Sunday, 5 to 9 P.M. only. *Owner:* Alex Ray. *Directions:* Take exit 24 off I-93 into the center of Ashland. You'll see the big colonial sign on the side of the brick building.

THE STARVING CHEF
237 Water Street
Exeter, New Hampshire 03833
(603) 772-5590

This restaurant moved down the street to a more interesting 1732 colonial building and the change to a large space gave the owners an opportunity to create a more elegant home for their creative dishes. It still stands out as an exciting epicurean pleasure to dine here. We had the green goddess dressing on our salad made with an avocado base—excellent. Our daughter had the mussels for an appetizer—also very tasty. Their standard entrees still delight the palate. The lamb bhuna, shrimp khaophat, baked scrod fromage, and chicken lemon are still hits.

The specials are listed on glass boards, and children have very reasonable items to choose from. The flowers and the warm mauve colors make this a special place to dine. The desserts are yummy, and you can sample a variety of coffees with your sweets. Beer and wine are also available. Lunch offers special savings. Aunt Lydia's chicken, soup and salad, and scrod fromage, though smaller portions, were good bargains. Also, early-bird prices apply before the regular dinner hour.

Average prices: Dinner entrees: $11–$18; children's menu, $3–$4. Lunch, $3–$9. *Credit cards:* All major. *Hours:* Lunch: Tuesday–Saturday, 11:30 A.M.–2:30 P.M. Dinner: Tuesday–Thursday, 5–9 P.M.; Friday and Saturday, until 10 P.M.; Sunday brunch, 11 A.M.–2 P.M. *Open:* Year-round. *Owners:* Kathleen Bryan and John Marley. *Directions:* From I-95 take Route 101 west and get off in Exeter. Go to T intersection in Exeter and turn right onto Water Street. Proceed through the business section. The restaurant is about 100 yards past the theater, on the right.

Also recommended:

The Loaf and Ladle in Exeter (and in York, Maine) is a very special place for those chasing the elusive healthy diet. They bake many different breads and pastries on the premises and make gourmet soups. You get a huge slice of bread with butter with the soup ($2–$3 for a cup, which is really the size of a bowl). The black bean is Frank's favorite. Salads are also available. This is an "earthy crunchy" place, and the sandwiches, soups, and desserts are all fantastic. It's at 9 Water Street in Exeter; call (603) 778-8955.

Alexander's Italian Restaurant in Dover is our all-time favorite for Italian food outside the North End in Boston. You will not believe the reasonable prices in these elegant surroundings—dim candlelight, framed prints on the walls, etc. But the food is what brings in the locals and new converts. Pasta dishes start at $8, veal dishes at $10. Spaghetti and meatballs cost a recession-proof $6, and the Italian bread—wow. You won't stop eating it. Alexander's is on Route 4 on the way from South Berwick to Dover, just as you break into the countryside on the right. Or, take the time to drive off the Spaulding Turnpike (Route 16) to Route 4 east. Run by the Alexander family. Call (603) 742-2650.

FITZWILLIAM INN
Routes 12 and 119
Fitzwilliam, New Hampshire 03447
(603) 585–9000

You'll enjoy the ambience at this very popular old inn and restaurant. They feature many different styles of chicken, steaks, seafood, and roast duck. One elegant meal Fran tried was veal Oscar topped with lobster, white asparagus, and Béarnaise sauce. Frank tried and liked a German veal dish similar to Wiener-schnitzel. All meals may be ordered complete or à la carte, but will in any case include a potato, vegetable, and bread. The lunch menu offers six entrees and some very fancy large sand-wiches. There are specials that change daily for lunch and din-ner, and on Sundays a lighter fare is offered. The desserts, all made on the premises and included in the price of the complete dinner, are delectable. Could you pass up apricot walnut cake or toasted coconut almond cream pie? Breakfast is also served from 8 to 9:30 A.M. every day.

Average prices: Lunch, $4–$8.50; dinner, $9–$18; à la carte, $3 less. *Credit cards:* All major. *Hours:* Lunch: Monday to Saturday, noon–2 P.M. Dinner: Monday to Saturday, 6–8 P.M.; Sunday, noon–8 P.M. *Owners:* Barbara Wallace and family. *Directions:* From I-91 take Route 24 to Keene, then Route 12 south to Route 119 in Fitzwilliam center. The inn is off the common.

MARGARITA VILLE
Route 302
Glen, New Hampshire 03838
(603) 383–6556

Margarita Ville is a fairly new restaurant not far from the Red Parka in Glen. It is family-run and although it was very busy the night we visited, Mrs. Rober took the time to explain how they got started and how they figured out all their good recipes. She runs the place all week with her five pretty daughters, and her husband works here on the weekends as his second job. The ser-vice is great, and the atmosphere is warm and happy. Our family enjoyed the chicken flautas (deep-fried, folded flour tortillas

214

filled with chicken), the beef tostado (a corn tortilla topped with beef, lettuce, onions, sauce, and cheese) with sour cream, the combination burrito and enchilada plate with rice and beans, and the chili-stuffed baked potato with rice, beans, and corn-bread. We all shared a delicious large guacamole salad (avocado and tomato) with an edible bowl of deep-fried flour tortillas. After dinner, we were too full to try their homemade cheesecake, Toll House sundae, or the apple and banana flautas fritters.

"Gringo" food such as sirloin burgers, chicken sandwiches, and barbecued sirloin tips are also available. There is a cozy bar attached with serapes and Mexican hats on the walls.

Average prices: Dinner and lunch, $5.50–$11. *Credit cards:* None. *Hours:* Every day, noon to 10 P.M. Open all year. *Owners:* John and Dorothea Rober and family. *Directions:* Go north on Route 16. Just after Route 16 turns off toward Jackson, go straight ahead (west) on Route 302. The restaurant is just ahead on the right, about 1 mile.

THE GALLEY HATCH
Lafayette Road, Route 1
Hampton, New Hampshire 03842
(603) 926-6152

This restaurant was voted the best all around restaurant by the readers of *Seacoast* magazine. It's also my sister-in-law's favorite. We think they do a great job on their cooking—very tasty, and it has something for everybody. It has one of those menus with four or five pages: hamburgers and pizzas on one page and gourmet entrees on another. It's great for families with children, yet it is also a dressy, special occasion place. You can order trendy dishes such as Cajun-style blackened fish. We are old-fashioned, so we go for the haddock, duckling, veal, and chicken dishes. You can eat light or heavy, whichever you prefer, or choose from among several special heart-healthy meals.

Average prices: Deli lunch of soup and sandwich, about $6; dinner with salad and choice of potato or vegetable, $10–$14. *Credit cards:* All major. *Hours:* 11 A.M.–midnight every day. *Owners:*

Michael, Kay, and John Tinios. *Directions:* Take Seabrook exit off I-95 to Route 1 north. Go 5 miles and Galley Hatch is on the right after Hampton Cinema.

JACK NEWICK'S FISHERMAN'S LANDING
845 Lafayette Road
Hampton, New Hampshire 03842
(603) 926-7646

Newick's is famous for its huge servings and great tasting fried clams, shrimp, and fish. We've visited it for years at its other location in Newington, New Hampshire. This new place, right on Route 1, has three dining rooms, all large and airy, with attractive tables and captain's chairs. In the summer, you'll need to get there early to avoid lines (about 5 or 5:30), but the hostess said there are so many seats that the lines move fast. There are small and large servings on many items and most can be bought as takeout.

Average prices: $3 for a chicken burger to over $5 for surf 'n turf. Clam plates were $6.50 to $7.50, and large fried shrimp were $8 to over $9. Chowder is over $2 for a bowl. *Credit cards:* None. *Hours:* Wednesday, Thursday, and Sunday, 11:30 A.M. to 8 P.M.; Friday and Saturday, 11:30 A.M. to 9 P.M. Closed Monday and Tuesday. *Owner:* Jack Newick. *Directions:* The restaurant is about 1 mile north of Hampton center on Route 1 (Lafayette Road).

INTERLAKES DAIRYLAND
Corner of Routes 3 and 25
Meredith, New Hampshire 03253
(603) 279-4833

This good old standby has been operating for over twenty-five years under the same owner and is great for lunches and small suppers. The soups and seafood chowders and pies and pastries are all homemade. There is a long counter and an attractive connected dining room. You can see it's a favorite of the townsfolk. The specialties are corned beef and cabbage and fried scallops

216

and clams, and a big seller is the lobster roll! All items on the lunch menu can be ordered until 8 P.M.

Average prices: Breakfasts are all very reasonable. Lunches run from over $1 for hamburgers and under $2 for BLTs to full meals at about $5 to $6. Chicken nuggets are $3, corned beef is $4.75, and clams and scallops are over $6. Coffee with pie or pastry is $1.50. *Credit cards:* None. *Hours:* Open all year, every day but Wednesday, 5 A.M. to 8 P.M. (a little later on Friday nights). Closes Sunday at 2 P.M. *Owner:* Winston Titus. *Managers:* Martha Titus and Frances Daigneau. *Directions:* From I-93, take Route 104 to Meredith. You'll find this restaurant at the crossroads in the center of town.

PETER CHRISTIAN'S TAVERN
Main Street
New London, New Hampshire 03257
(603) 526-4042

If you weren't going to stop in New London, which has some charming shops, do make a point of it. This authentic tavern takes you back to the late 1700s. Great rough beams, worn tables, and hand-hewn curved pine benches complete the fantasy. The atmosphere and good food are enhanced by unhurried, soft-spoken waiters. We sampled their crocks of beef stew and vegetable stew, which were delicious. Other items on the menu that sound enticing are seafood and asparagus puff and Peter's Russian mistress, a sandwich. Tuesday is Mexican night. This is the best place to eat if you're visiting Colby Junior College or any other college in the area. And if you want a good bed and breakfast in New London, several people highly recommend **Maple Hill Farm** (603-526-2248). There is a Peter Christian's in Keene and another in Hanover, New Hampshire, also.

Average prices: Lunch, under $4 to over $6; dinner, $7 to $11. *Credit cards:* All major. *Hours:* Lunch and dinner served daily 11:30 A.M. to 10 P.M. Only Mexican meals are served on Tuesday. Open all year. *Owner:* Murray Washburn. *Directions:* From I–89 take the turnoff to New London (about 25 miles northeast of

217

Route 93). Turn left onto Main Street; the tavern is on your right about 1 mile down.

HORSEFEATHERS
Main Street
North Conway, New Hampshire 03860
(603) 356-6862

Horsefeathers is for those who like variety! If you'd like the chance to choose between fresh charbroiled seafood of the day, prime rib, fettuccine, jambalaya, Szechuan chicken or scallops and shrimp, or seafood pie—all served with "horsefries" and a small green salad—you've come to the right place. Try a creative hors d'oeuvre like sesame chicken fingers. The atmosphere is made pleasant by mood music and old pictures. The service is cheery, and so is the bar.

The owners have another Horsefeathers restaurant at Attitash ski area in Bartlett, New Hampshire.

Average prices: Many lunch dishes cost between $4 and $8; a few are between $9 and $11. Dinners are $10 to $12.50. *Credit cards:* MasterCard, American Express, and Visa. *Hours:* Every day, 11:30 A.M. to 11:45 P.M. *Owners:* Ben Williams and Brian Glynne. *Directions:* Take Route 16 into North Conway. Horsefeathers is on the right at the light in the center of town.

MERLINO'S STEAK HOUSE
Main Street
North Conway, New Hampshire 03860
(603) 356-6006

Merlino's Steak House is a wonderful family Italian restaurant. The variety of offerings on the menu makes this place special. You can get Italian dishes as well as steaks, chicken, and other American meals. There is a lower dining room for families with little kids and an upstairs dining room for adults who cannot stand the noise. The veal specialties are excellent. Frank likes the veal piccata. Most dishes are served with spaghetti or potato and salad. Reserve ahead during a heavy tourist season, such as during the summer or in good skiing weather.

Average prices: Dinner, $5–$19. A "Junior–Senior Menu" offers lower prices—in the $3–$7 range—for children under twelve and adults over sixty-five. *Credit cards:* All major. *Hours:* Every day, 11 A.M.–10 P.M., but during slow season they close around 9 P.M. *Owner:* Rich Luciano. *Directions:* It is on the east side of Main Street (Route 16) across from McDonald's.

Also recommended:

Also in North Conway, **Bellini's,** on Seavy Street, at (603) 356–7000, is a hot new restaurant offering a delicious pasta entree with salad, the best dressing in town, and a loaf of bread for $9. Their white sauce is spectacular. Portions are huge. Go early or late on weekends or plan to stand in line. Seavy Street is 1 block south of the traffic light at north end of town.

THE CHALET RESTAURANT
Main Street
North Woodstock, New Hampshire 03632
(603) 745-2256

The Chalet is a large, airy family restaurant with maple tables, chairs, and booths, which can serve 110 people. Their specialties are boiled, baked, and broiled lobster (with a special every Friday). You may look at your lobster in the live lobster tank. For dessert there's a "make it yourself" sundae bar, with three sauces, whipped cream, and a wide variety of nuts and fruit toppings. Hot or cold sandwiches come with french fries and cole slaw. One of the dining areas looks like an enclosed greenhouse.

Average prices: Lunch sandwiches, about $4 and up; dinner about $5 and up. On Friday, the special is two lobsters for $10. Ice-cream sundaes are under $2. *Credit cards:* MasterCard, Visa, and American Express. *Hours:* Every day, 11:30 A.M. to 9 P.M. *Owner:* Ronald Claremont. *Directions:* Take exit 32 off Route 93 north. Make a right at the end of the ramp at the lights. Take a right at the next set of lights, and the restaurant is on the left.

PEG'S RESTAURANT
Main Street
North Woodstock, New Hampshire 03262
(603) 745-2740

This small restaurant in the center of town is great for breakfast or lunch, with its diner atmosphere and friendly waitresses. You can sit at the counter or at tables. This is where the local folks meet and talk over the day's happenings. The food is good and a fantastic bargain.

Average prices: Full breakfast, $2 to $5. Lunch: homemade soup, $2; sandwiches, under $2. Dinner, about $5 to $6. *Credit cards:* None. *Hours:* Every day, 5:30 A.M. to 2:30 P.M. *Owner:* Sue Fadden. *Directions:* Take exit 32 off Route 93 north. Turn right at the end of the ramp at the lights. Turn right at the next set of lights and the restaurant is 1 block north.

TRUANT'S TAVERNE
Main Street, Box 413
North Woodstock, New Hampshire 03262
(603) 745-2239

This pine-paneled place has a schoolhouse motif and lots of atmosphere. Every table is an old desk and the seventy-five seats are school seats. Their clever menu has "prerequisites," "fine arts courses," and a "dean's list"; the sandwiches are named "class bully," the "valedictorian," and the "trouble-maker." Some specialties are chicken artichoke, seafood fettucine, ten-ounce sirloin steak, and prime rib. All are served with salad or fresh vegetables and a potato or rice pilaf. There are daily blackboard specials, and all soups and dressings and some desserts are homemade. The very cozy bar is made of a number of desktops with inkwells and scratched-in words of schoolchildren still readable through the lacquer.

Average prices: Clam chowder, $2.75; fancy sandwiches, $5–$7; dinner, $9–$14.50. *Credit cards:* Visa, MasterCard, and American Express. *Hours:* Every day, 11:30 A.M. to 10 P.M. Open all year.

Owner: Bill Walsh. *Directions:* The restaurant is at the intersection of Routes 112 and 3. The entrance is at the back of the building.

THE GOLDEN EGG
960 Sagamore Avenue
Portsmouth, New Hampshire 03801
(603) 436-0519

The Golden Egg is one of the best breakfast places in Portsmouth, which has many competing for that title. You can have the most creative breakfast of your life, if you are tired of the usual ham and eggs. Coffee cake comes in amazing varieties, as do omelets, which are made of linguica or feta cheese. You'll love them. There are seats for fifty, including a counter if you are in a hurry, but plan to wait a bit on Sunday morning. Lunches are great; blackboard specials list tasty soups and scrumptious sandwiches. On your trip to the seacoast area put this restaurant on your gourmet calender. Very reasonable!

Average prices: Traditional breakfast, $5; super gourmet, up to $8. Lunch, $4–$6. *Credit cards:* None; personal checks accepted. *Hours:* 6 A.M. to 2 P.M. every day. *Owners:* Tom and Debbie Gosselin. *Directions:* Take 1A south from Portsmouth. You'll wind around a bit before you come to a bridge just about at the Rye-Portsmouth line. It is on your left just after the bridge—a very scenic spot.

KAREN'S RESTAURANT
105 Daniel Street
Portsmouth, New Hampshire 03801
(603) 431-1948

This very charming, cozy little restaurant in the heart of Portsmouth is a favorite of ours. When Karen first opened the restaurant, she served only homemade ice cream. Now she serves breakfast, lunch, and dinner seven days a week. The dining room is colonial green and white with graceful stenciling, and she features a different artist's paintings each month. An updated menu on the fireplace chimney is changed daily. You must get there early on a Sunday morning to get one of the thirty seats. Try her eggs Florentine, pancakes, crepes, granola, or—Fran's favorite—cardamom coffeecake. For lunch try a chicken fajita or smokehouse turkey club or a yummy vegetarian stir-fry. At dinner, Karen features chicken raspberry, New York steak au poivre, and crab-stuffed sole; all are served with veggies, potato or rice, and her own special cornbread.

Average prices: Breakfast, about $2–$6; lunch, $3–$6; dinner, $8–$13. *Credit cards:* American Express and Discover. *Hours:* Open all year, seven days a week, 7 A.M. to 3 P.M. and 5 to 10 P.M. *Owner:* Karen Wiese. *Directions:* From Route 95, get off at exit 7 and head toward Portsmouth on Market Street; follow this to Bow Street, go left, and continue till you reach Daniel Street. Go right, and Karen's is on the left across from the post office. *Note:* There are high chairs, and it is wheelchair-accessible.

Old Ferry Landing
10 Ceres Street
Portsmouth, New Hampshire 03801
(603) 431-5510

This appealing little restaurant is right on the water, where you can watch the tour boats and freighters go by as you sit on the covered porch and enjoy the sea breezes. Once an old ferryboat terminal, it has a variety of tasty items including reasonably priced daily specials. The clam chowder tasted fresh and homemade. The fried fish we had was fresh and plump—and more than we could eat. Their specials are lobsters and fresh haddock, any style. A full bar is available.

Average prices: Large sandwiches, around $5; chili, under $5. Daily specials were fish and chips with tiny fries for $5 (a great buy!) and swordfish steak for $7. Fried clams and fried shrimp were under $7. Other dinners were in the $9 area. *Credit cards:* MasterCard and Visa. *Hours:* Mid-April through September, 11:30 A.M. to 9 P.M. *Owners:* Richard and Janie Blalock. *Directions:* From exit 7 off I-95, take Market Street to Ceres Street. Go left and follow the water. The restaurant is next to the tugboats on the right.

The Rusty Hammer
49 Pleasant Street
Portsmouth, New Hampshire 03801
(603) 436-9289

One of the great finds for us has been this restaurant near Market Square. It has to be one of the best bargains in New England. The atmosphere is pub-like with lots of Victorian decor, but not overly done. Frank's favorites are the haddock and broccoli with cheese sauce and the barbecued chicken breast, both with choice of potato or rice and a salad on a large platter at an amazingly low price. Pitchers of beer are available. The bar is closed off from the downstairs restaurant area. Downstairs is inexpensive; entrees at the upstairs restaurant, the School House, cost about $7 to $13.

Average prices: Breakfast, $4–$5; lunch and dinner, $5–$9. *Credit cards:* MasterCard, Visa, American Express, and Discover. *Hours:* 7 A.M.–11 P.M. *Owners:* Bill MacMillan and Russ Hammer. *Directions:* Exit off I-95 going north, last exit before Piscataqua Bridge. Turn right onto Market Street into downtown Portsmouth. After Market Square, take the first left to State Street. Turn left on State. Go 2 blocks; it is on the corner of Pleasant and State, on the left.

Also recommended:

In Newington, a suburb of Portsmouth, the **1853 School House** on Woodbury Avenue offers a choice of formal dining on the first floor or casual dining upstairs in the loft. This restored schoolhouse with exposed beams and brick is a favorite of ours to catch a light supper before a movie or to lunch while shopping at the malls. The upstairs, where the bar is, has very reasonable prices. If you want the full menu at higher prices, eat downstairs. The restaurant is at 1465 Woodbury Avenue next to the K-Mart shopping center. Call (603) 431-4650.

The **Toucan,** an unusual restaurant in the heart of Portsmouth, has Cajun, Mexican, and barbecue specialties. They are open for lunch, and dinner is served till 11 P.M. seven days a week. They have a full bar. Located at 174 Fleet Street, you can reach them at (603) 431-5443. Good tacos!

Another recommended restaurant in Portsmouth is **Szechuan Taste** at 54 Daniel Street for all types of tasty Chinese food. **Cafe Brioche,** with all kinds of rich coffees and marvelous baked goods, is a fun place to stop while shopping in Market Square in summer. They have tables on the sidewalk. Another yummy little bakery is the **Ceres Bakery** on Penhallow Street. They serve soup, quiche, and fresh salads for lunch, with great rolls and bread. **Rosa's** on State Street has fairly good Italian-American food. **The Depot** on Market Street near the bus stop is great for pasta dishes.

THE YANKEE SMOKEHOUSE
Route 16
West Ossippee, New Hampshire 03890
(603) 539-7427 (RIBS)

The Yankee Smokehouse is recommended by a number of natives. All the cooking is done in an actual smokehouse, and the meats are cooked on wire mesh stretched over a bed of coals of selected hardwoods. Pork, beef, and "charburg" sandwiches are reasonably priced. Full dinners are half of a barbecued chicken, ribs, smoked beef, lean and juicy pork, and a half-pound "charburger." There are smaller servings for less and servings for hearty appetites for more. A "Smokehouse sample" dinner for two offers a little of everything. They serve wines and draft beer, and the desserts are a meal in themselves. You'll enjoy the cheerful, informal surroundings with picnic benches.

Average prices: Dinner, $7–$13. *Credit cards:* None. *Hours:* Thursday–Sunday, 11:30 A.M.–9 P.M.; closed April. Call ahead. *Owners:* Lloyd and Mary Anne Kerr. *Directions:* The restaurant is at the junction of Routes 16 and 25.

MAINE

Maine is vast, awesome, and dramatic. It is almost as large in land mass as Texas, awesome as you view the beautiful, rocky coastline where the conifers meet the sea, dramatic in its unique blend of quaint New England fishing villages, mountain towns, and rugged wilderness areas.

It is distinctive in its versatility. You can visit the long sandy beaches of Ogunquit and York, the freshwater lakes of Sebago, Mooselookmeguntic, Sebec, and Damariscotta; you can photograph exciting, rocky lighthouses and the curious points of land that dip down to the sea, such as Bailey's Island, Pemaquid Point, and the Blue Hill region; or you can explore the delightful natural wonders of Acadia National Park on Mount Desert Island. You can canoe on the great Saco River; climb splendid mountains such as Mount Katahdin and Bald Pate; fish in the pristine waters of Rangeley and Moosehead; talk to farmers and lobstermen who refuse to be hurried; pick wild blueberries and lush blackberries; inhale the unusually pure country air; see a myriad of stars at night, and yes—hear ice moan on the lakes in winter. Thousands pay homage every year to this miracle in today's fast-moving, industrialized, computerized society. Maine is one of the last vestiges of wilderness and life as we used to know it.

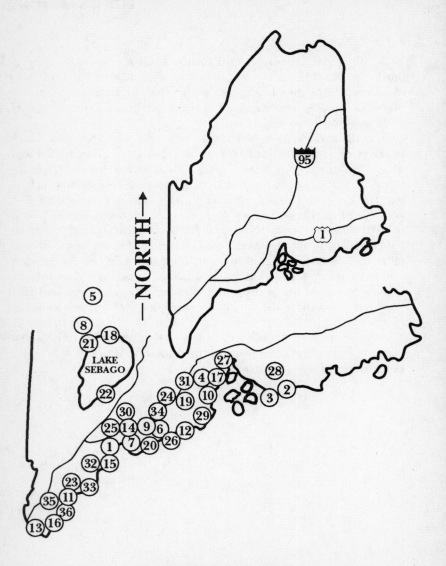

LAKE
SEBAGO

NORTH →

MAINE

		🛏	🍴
1.	Arundel	—	257
2.	Bar Harbor	228	257
3.	Bass Harbor	—	259
4.	Belfast	230	—
5.	Bethel	230	—
6.	Boothbay	231	—
7.	Boothbay Harbor	233	260
8.	Bridgton	233	—
9.	Brunswick	234	261
10.	Camden	235	261
11.	Cape Neddick (York)	237	—
12.	Damariscotta	237	262
13.	Eliot	—	265
14.	Freeport	239	265
15.	Kennebunkport	239	—
16.	Kittery	—	266
17.	Lincolnville	—	267
18.	Naples	242	—
19.	Newcastle	243	—
20.	New Harbor	243	268
21.	North Sebago	244	—
22.	North Windham	—	269
23.	Ogunquit	245	270
24.	Pemaquid Falls	246	—
25.	Portland	246	271
26.	Round Pond	—	272
27.	Searsport	247	273
28	Southwest Harbor	248	274
29.	Thomaston	249	—
30.	Topsham	250	—
31.	Waldoboro	251	—
32.	Wells	253	275
33.	Wells Beach	253	—
34.	Wiscasset	—	276
35.	York	254	278
36.	York Harbor	256	—

WHERE TO STAY

THE BASS COTTAGE
The Fields
Bar Harbor, Maine 04609
(207) 288-3705

This splendid Victorian home has belonged to the same family for over fifty years, and seeing it is like walking back in time to the early 1900s. The elegant original hall and dining room wallpaper, gold oak paneling and stairway, and Tiffany-type stained-glass windows are a wonderful sight. We sat and talked on the enormous, sunny porch and then visited the ten rooms with high ceilings and lovely matching furniture. Guests are asked to confine smoking to porches, which are enclosed. No breakfast is served here, but this B&B's downtown location gives access to many fine restaurants nearby. You can also walk to the ocean or the town beach near the pier and shore path.

Average rates: Double: shared bath, $50–$55; private bath, $66–$85. Single, $35 and up. *Credit cards:* None. *Open:* Memorial Day weekend to Columbus Day weekend. *Owner:* Anna Jean Turner. *Directions:* It is off Main Street, behind Bar Harbor Bank and Trust. *Children:* Yes. *Pets:* No. *Smoking:* Restricted.

THE COVE FARM INN
R.F.D. 1, Box 420
Bar Harbor, Maine 04609
(207) 288-5355

Originally built as a farm by the Jesuits for a Mrs. Degreguire in the 1780s, The Cove Farm Inn was acquired and restored by the Keenes in 1984 and then opened as a bed & breakfast. The farmhouse and barns, along with a trout pond and gazebo, give the five acres a pastoral ambience. Hearty breakfasts greet the guests in the country kitchen: oatmeal with brown sugar, raisins, and/or nuts, blueberry muffins, juice, and fruit. Who could call this a continental breakfast? The rooms are neat and clean with a plain but fresh decor. Early spring or late fall can be cool at the edges, but Barbara and Jerry's hospitality make you feel right at home. This is a great place for families with children, as there are sheep, geese, goats, and other farm animals to entertain them. Jerry will show you his video of Mount Desert Island and help you with your sightseeing plans at Acadia National Park. There are ten rooms with accommodations for about thirty people. Two rooms have private baths. Guests are permitted to use the kitchen facilities.

Average rates: Double, $40–$75; single, $30. Includes continental-plus breakfast. *Credit cards:* None; personal checks accepted. *Open:* May 1 to February 28. *Owners:* Barbara, Jerry, and Sam Keene. *Directions:* Continue on Route 3 once on Mount Desert Island as if going to Bar Harbor and the ferry terminal. About 3 to 4 miles down Route 3 you will come to the Hulls Cove hamlet. Turn right onto Crooked Road, just before the Chart Room Restaurant. The inn is about 100 yards up Crooked Road on the right. The sign is lighted at night, but we had trouble locating Crooked Road off Route 3. You might want to call for detailed directions once on the island. *Children:* Yes. *Pets:* No. *Smoking:* No.

THE MAPLES INN
16 Roberts Avenue
Bar Harbor, Maine 04609
(207) 288-3443

This bed & breakfast has six beautiful rooms named after trees and shrubs—such as the "White Birch Suite"—and is located on a quiet, tree-lined side street within walking distance of shops and restaurants. Acadia National Park is five minutes away. All rooms include a private shower bath and a fluffy down comforter. Some rooms have four-poster and brass beds and an extra sitting room. A library with an old-fashioned rocker is available for those who like to read on vacation. A hearty breakfast is served as are afternoon refreshments.

Average rates: Double, $80–$115. *Credit cards:* MasterCard and

Visa. Personal and traveler's checks accepted. *Open:* All year. *Owner:* Susan Sinclair. *Directions:* Take Route 3 into Bar Harbor. Take first left onto West Street, take next left onto Cottage, and then fourth right onto Roberts. It is a green house on the left. *Children:* Twelve and older. *Pets:* No. *Smoking:* No.

LONDONDERRY INN
Star Route 80, Box 3
Belfast, Maine 04915
(207) 338-3988

This 1803 restored farmhouse and guest house sits on fifty-one acres of private woods and fields where guests can wander or cross-country ski to their hearts' content. The four spacious guest rooms, furnished with period country pieces, are charming. A full breakfast of fruit bowl, fresh muffins and breads, granola and yogurt parfaits, eggs, meats, and beverages is served in the large country kitchen. You can relax and chat in the living rooms, play the piano in the library, or enjoy the wonderful sunporch. Antiquing, swimming, windjammer cruises, and summer theater are nearby.

Average rates: Double, $45–$50 plus tax; single, $42 plus tax; additional person in room, $10. *Credit cards:* None. *Open:* All year. *Owner:* Suzanne Smedley. *Directions:* Heading east from Augusta on Route 3, it is 1 mile from Belfast on the left. *Children:* Over twelve. *Pets:* No. *Smoking:* Restricted.

THE CHAPMAN INN
P.O. Box 206
Bethel, Maine 04217
(207) 824-2657

This old building was built by a ship captain, although it's hard to imagine one living so far from the sea! It has been a store, a tavern, and a boarding house. There are bedrooms with shared baths, a three-bed unit with a kitchenette, and a ski dorm in the main house. Other double rooms with shared baths are available in the annex across the street. There is a sauna, a billiard room, and a game room for guests. The ambience is plain and farmhouselike but comfortable and clean. We enjoyed our stay and walked down the hill to Michael's at L'Auberge for dinner. The surrounding mountains are beautiful year-round and present a splendid contrast to the Maine coast. The inn management is changing, so the breakfast menu might be different when you visit, but when we were there we had cream cheese-filled French toast with strawberry sauce, which was delicious. In the summer and fall guests can use a private beach with a canoe, picnic table, and beach chairs located on Songo Pond. If you are interested in downhill or cross-country skiing, Mount Abrams and Sunday River ski areas and many touring centers are only ten minutes away.

Average rates: Double, $55–$75; two-day minimum in ski season. Inquire about ski packages and group rates. Dorm, $25 per person, including full breakfast. *Credit cards:* MasterCard, Visa, and American Express. *Open:* All year. *Owners:* Douglas and Robin Zinchuk. *Directions:* Get off Maine Turnpike at exit 11 and follow Route 26 to Bethel. Take Route 5 to Main Street. The inn is on the north end of the common at the corner of Mill Hill and Main Street. *Children:* Yes. *Pets:* No. *Smoking:* Restricted.

KENNISTON HILL INN
Route 27, P.O. Box 125
Boothbay, Maine 04537
(207) 633-2159; (800) 992-2915

This two-hundred-year-old colonial farmhouse has been tastefully decorated in period furniture that gives it an authentic early American charm. As you enter the living room, you will see a large, open-hearth fireplace with cranes and baking ovens. The inn has ten beautiful rooms, four with fireplaces and all with private baths, pretty wallpaper, and quilted bedspreads. The porch, living room, and the patio with an umbrella table set will give you many places to relax and chat with your hosts and other guests.

A full country breakfast is included in the room rent and served in the dining room, which has a fireplace. You will be surprised by the creative dishes on the menu. A typical breakfast might include ham and Swiss cheese in puff pastry or a three-cheese and bacon pie.

231

Average rates: $65–$95, double occupancy. *Credit cards:* MasterCard and Visa. *Open:* Year-round. *Owners:* David and Susan Straight. *Directions:* Going east on Route 1, take a right on Route 27 after Wiscasset. Go south on Route 27 for 10 miles. The Kenniston Hill Inn is at a large bend in the road on your left, set back under large trees. It's a white colonial building with an American flag in front. *Children:* Fourteen and over. *Pets:* No. *Smoking:* No.

WELCH HOUSE
36 McKown Street
Boothbay Harbor, Maine 04538
(207) 633-3431

This newly refurbished inn on top of McKown Hill overlooks the beautiful harbor with a grand view from its breakfast or sun room and its observation deck on the second floor. People who have been here in the past are in for a pleasant surprise: Rooms are now furnished with a mix of new and antique furniture and all have private baths. A continental-plus breakfast is included within the reasonable rate. Martha makes homemade granola and a fresh fruit platter every morning. David is particularly proud of his landscaping—he's put in a fountain and tiled fish pool next to the huge chestnut tree in front. You can walk to the business district to visit its shops, galleries, restaurants, harbor cruise boats, and dinner theater.

Average rates: $55–$90. *Credit cards:* MasterCard and Visa; personal checks accepted. *Open:* Mid-April to Mid-October. *Owners:* David and Martha Mason. *Directions:* Follow Route 27 south from Route 1 to Boothbay Harbor. Just beyond the brick post office, take the first right onto Howard Street. At the yield sign take a left across the road up the hill. The house is just over the crest of McKown Hill. *Children:* Eight and over. *Pets:* No. *Smoking:* Restricted.

Also recommended:

In Boothbay Harbor, the **Lion's Den Bed & Breakfast** offers reasonable in-season rates and a full breakfast. There's ample parking and it's a short walk to shops and restaurants. This B&B, open year-round, is located at 106 Townsend Avenue; call (207) 633-7367. **The Inn at Bath,** 969 Washington Street in Bath, can be reached at (207) 443-4294. This 1830 Greek Revival house in the historic district has five guest rooms ranging in price from $45 to $85; a suite for a family costs $150. A full breakfast is served.

THE NOBLE HOUSE
37 Highland Road
Bridgton, Maine 04009
(207) 647-3733

If you are looking for a friendly couple and a Victorian mansion, then this is the place for you. It's decorated in a classic Californian style with bold yet very tastefully coordinated colors. There's a crystal clear lake and boathouse across the street. The Starets family moved from the San Diego area to do what they had dreamed about for many years: run a bed & breakfast in New England. Dick flies for Pacific Southwest Airlines, and Jane manages the home and takes care of the four kids.

When you enter the home you immediately have a feeling of quiet, orderly elegance. The dining room where you take the complimentary, gigantic, gourmet, full breakfast is set with china dishes, spread fan napkins in the crystal, and silk flowers, all in a blue-green theme. It looks like something out of *House Beautiful.* There's a grand piano and a pump organ in the living room. There are seven bedrooms, beautifully decorated with quilts, and one has a four-poster bed. You will feel very posh and well cared for here. As Dick says, "We like to get to know the people who stay here, visit with them, and make them feel at home. We even invite them to the neighborhood barbecue." The extras are the nearby golf course, the dock at the boathouse for swimming and boating, horseshoes, croquet by the lake, three whirlpool baths, and a hammock for a real old-fashioned New England afternoon nap. There are nine guest rooms; six with private and three with shared baths.

Average rates: Double: in season (Memorial Day to October 15), $68–$110; off-season, $70. *Credit cards:* MasterCard, Visa, and

American Express. *Open:* Year-round. *Owners:* The Starets family
(Dick and Jane). *Directions:* Take exit 8 off I-95 and go west on
Route 302 to Bridgton. In Bridgton, take a left at the traffic light
(you are still on 302). After the Dairy Treat, take the first right;
then go right again. This is Highland Road. The Noble House is
a big yellow house about ¼ mile up on your right. It is about one
hour from Portland. *Children:* Yes. *Pets:* No. *Smoking:* Restricted.

DOVE BED AND BREAKFAST
16 Douglas Street
Brunswick, Maine 04011
(207) 729-6827

You'll enjoy the quiet and coolness of this dignified Dutch
colonial house only a mile from Bowdoin College. The inside is
homey, with pleasant floral wallpapers in the guest rooms, all
with shared baths. You may use the large living room and the
piano. Your complimentary continental breakfast of fresh fruit,
five kinds of muffins, cereal, and coffee or juice is served in the
colonial dining room with Shaker-style chairs and walls bedecked
with rows of fruit and flowers. Relax on the cool deck or try the
badminton on the lawn under the tall oaks and white pines.
Thomas Point Beach is only 4 miles away, and it is also quite
close to Freeport, Portland, all the peninsulas, the Bath
Performing Arts Center, and Maine State Music Theater.

Average rates: Double, $49; single, $45; extra adult, $10; and a
small amount extra for children. *Credit cards:* None. *Open:* All
year. *Owner:* Diana Dove. *Directions:* Take Route 1 to Brunswick.
Where Route 1 turns left at Cumberland Farms, go straight
ahead. Take a right on Maine Street, and stay on Maine to
Bowdoin College. About four streets down on your right, take a
right at Columbia Avenue. Go 2 blocks to Douglas Street, and the
Dove will be on the corner. *Children:* Yes. *Pets:* No. *Smoking:* No.

BIRCHWOOD MOTEL
Route 1
Camden, Maine 04843
(207) 236-4204

This attractive motel stretches out on a hill north of Camden and has a view of the ocean. Its natural shingles and long white porch with red geraniums make it appealing and homey. The sixteen rooms are large and paneled, with maple furniture, large bathrooms, and new color televisions. They are spotless. Mr. Fitzpatrick keeps one refrigerator in the office for guests to use; he is a friendly man with a subtle Irish sense of humor. Camden State Park is right next door, and you may picnic under the trees in a wonderful section across from the park.

Average rates: Double in season; $40–$60; slightly less in spring and fall. *Credit cards:* MasterCard, Visa, Discover, and American Express. *Open:* May 1 to November 1. *Owner:* John Fitzpatrick. *Directions:* Go 3 miles north of Camden center on Route 1 and the motel will be on your left, just after the entrance to the park. *Children:* Yes. *Pets:* No. *Smoking:* Yes.

Also recommended:

The **Sunrise Motor Court** in Camden was mentioned to us by the Chamber of Commerce as a place where folks have been very satisfied. The neat little gray cottages with a harbor view are $42–$65 per couple. Complimentary baked goods and coffee are served for breakfast. Call Ray and Jean Lewis at (207) 236-3191.

THE ELMS
84 Elm Street (Route 1)
Camden, Maine 04843
(207) 236-6250

Candles lit at each window bid you welcome to this 1806 colonial built by Captain Calvin Curtis. Three guest rooms with private baths and three with shared baths are available. An elegant colonial decor is maintained in this gracious home with beautiful dining room where a full breakfast is served before the fireplace. Stratas and fajitas are a few of the creative egg dishes served with fresh-baked blueberry muffins and breads. You are within walking distance of the harbor where you can watch the windjammers and take harbor cruises. Ask for rooms away from the street side if you like it quiet.

Average rates: $64–$85 in season; $50–$60 in winter. *Credit cards:* MasterCard and Visa. *Open:* All year. *Owner:* Joan James. *Directions:* Take Route 1 north through Bath to Route 90. Turn left on 90; go to Route 1. At Route 1 turn left and proceed for approximately 1 mile. The Elms is on the right. *Children:* Twelve and over. *Pets:* No. *Smoking:* No.

SWAN HOUSE
49 Mountain Street
Camden, Maine 04843
(207) 236-8275

Perched at the foot of Mount Battie, the Swan House is a nice off-the-beaten-path location for a restful stay in the Camden area. There are six guest rooms, all with private baths. A pretty sun porch off the living room in the main house offers a pleasant outdoors feeling as you enjoy your full breakfast. The rooms are all named after swans. The Swan Lake Loft in the Cygnet Annex is especially pretty. You can also relax in the shaded gazebo. Antiques and choice prints give this place an old-fashioned country feeling. It's nicely decorated but not overdone. The resident manager can direct you to the best restaurants.

Average rates: Double, $75–$100; extra person, $15. *Credit cards:* MasterCard and Visa. *Open:* May to November. *Manager:* Chrysanthe Soukas. *Directions:* When entering Camden from the south on Route 1, continue to the junction of Routes 1 and 52 (Mountain Street) and turn left onto 52. Drive 3 blocks (½ mile) up the hill. The inn is on the hill on your right. The driveway is past the sign. *Children:* Over eight. *Pets:* No. *Smoking:* No.

CAPE NEDDICK HOUSE BED & BREAKFAST
1300 Route 1, P.O. Box 70
Cape Neddick (York), Maine 03902
(207) 363-2500

This one-hundred-year-old home, where John's father was born and raised, is a family-run guest house just as it was years ago. Dianne's favorite task is cooking the complimentary full breakfasts of homemade popovers, apple fritters, and other goodies, served with wild raspberry jam. They have on the premises a gift and craft shop in their little antique post office. The six guest rooms are graced with Victorian high-backed walnut and oak beds, marble-topped commodes and dressers, pitchers and bowls, Dianne's lovely homemade quilts, and hooked rugs. There are three modern baths, which makes one shared by every two rooms.

Average rates: In season, $70; off-season, $55–$60. *Credit cards:* None. *Open:* Year-round. *Owners:* Dianne and John Goodwin. *Directions:* From I-95, take the York–Ogunquit exit, go north on Route 1 for 4 miles, and you'll see the house on the left at the corner of Route 1 and River Road. *Children:* Over five. *Pets:* No. *Smoking:* Restricted.

THE BARNSWALLOW
Bristol Road, HC 61–Box 135
Damariscotta, Maine 04543
(207) 563-8568

The Sherrills enjoy sharing their 1830 cape with you. They looked for two years to find the right home in which to open a B&B. The two front parlors are beautifully decorated and both have fireplaces. Fran especially noted the hand stenciling, the lovely prints, and the bright and cheery feeling of this home. The three guest rooms have modern, private baths. You can choose double, queen-sized or twin beds. A special continental breakfast is served in the large country kitchen.

Average rates: Double, $55–$70; single, $5 less. *Credit cards:* None;

personal checks accepted. *Open:* All year. *Owners:* Rachael and Chuck Sherrill. *Directions:* From coastal Route 1, exit on Business Route 1 in Newcastle. Go down Main Street to Route 129/130 by the Baptist Church. Turn right. Barnswallow is 1.6 miles south of town on the left. *Children:* Over twelve. *Pets:* No. *Smoking:* Restricted.

OAK GABLES B&B
Pleasant Street
Damariscotta, Maine 04543
(207) 563-1476

Oak Gables has thirteen acres of fields and orchards bordering the Damariscotta River. As you wind your way up to this 1850 farmhouse, tall, stately white pines and oaks make it stand out as if it were a manor house on the hill. We found this bed & breakfast on a hot day in July, and as soon as we carried in our bags, we made a beeline to the large pool. What a relief! The bedrooms have wide pine floors and are nicely decorated in subtle greens, pinks, and blues. There are twin and double beds. All guest rooms share baths. One suite with a private bath has its own entry and porch. The huge living room has a television corner. The slate fireplace, pegged pine floors, and expansive windows with river views lend a warm and pastoral atmosphere. A deluxe continental breakfast is served in the dining room, which has unusual floor-to-ceiling windows, bringing the outside in. There is a boathouse on the river with a Ping-Pong table and lounge chairs. An immaculate cottage and apartments outside the main building are available on a weekly basis.

Average rates: Double, $60–$75, additional person $10. *Credit cards:* None. *Open:* All year. *Owner:* Martha Scudder. *Directions:* Take Business Route 1 into Damariscotta. Turn left at the Information Bureau. Go 1 block, take the one-way street to the stop sign, and go left on Pleasant Street. Pass through the stone gates and you are there. *Children:* Yes. *Pets:* No. *Smoking:* No.

CAPTAIN JOSIAH A. MITCHELL HOUSE
188 Main Street
Freeport, Maine 04032
(207) 865-3289

This sea captain's home, built in 1789, has a Victorian decor with oriental rugs, canopy and four-poster beds, and wicker furniture. The back veranda has tables for lounging in the afternoon shade. A recent remodeling of the east wing added new rooms with ornate and colorful quilts, rugs, and curtains to make a total of seven guest rooms, each with full or half baths, some with private entrances. The Abby Mae room is decorated in pink and roses. Rooms on the lower floor are cooler in the summer. A full breakfast is served in the large kitchen or on the porch. Golfing, hiking, swimming in Winslow Bay, and outlet shopping are available nearby. The L.L. Bean outlet is within walking distance.

Average rates: $75–$80 in season; less off-season. *Credit cards:* MasterCard and Visa (extra charge to use card). *Open:* All year. *Owners:* Alan and Loretta Bradley. *Directions:* Exit off I-95 to Freeport. Travel east on Route 1, or Main Street in Freeport, past L.L. Bean, and then pass twenty more houses on the right. It's a white clapboard house. *Children:* All ages, crib available. *Pets:* No. *Smoking:* No.

BUFFLEHEAD COVE B&B
Box 499, Route 35
Kennebunkport, Maine 04046
(207) 967-3879

This bed & breakfast is a wonderful surprise. You drive down a dirt road and meander till you see the sign; then you see the most inviting scene. Large trees grace the property surrounding the big gray house with a great porch overlooking the river. Once inside, you'll see that Harriet has made the inn a vision of comfort and beauty. The spacious common room with the fireplace as a focus is bedecked with giant bright flowers. The five guest rooms have flowers, dainty laces, and lovely stenciling, some matching the bedspreads or other floral articles in the rooms.

Window seats and sweetly decorated desks are in every corner. Extra puffy pillows on every bed and soft, pale, peachy orange colors are very enticing. A full, hearty breakfast of fresh fruit, homemade breads, juice, and coffee is served. The main course varies from asparagus strata or eggs Benedict to cranberry pancakes with orange sauce.

Average rates: Double, $75–$120; less in winter. *Credit cards:* All major. *Open:* All year. *Owners:* Harriet and Jim Gott. *Directions:* From I-95, take the Kennebunkport exit. Turn left onto Route 35, continue through town, and, at the lights, bear right toward Kennebunkport. Stay on 35 till you reach Goldberg Realty Office on the right. Just after that, look for a small sign on the left to Bufflehead Cove, a dirt road; take that to the inn. *Children:* Yes. *Pets:* No. *Smoking:* Restricted to downstairs.

LAKE BROOK GUEST HOUSE
R.R. 3, Box 218
Western Avenue
Kennebunkport, Maine 04046
(207) 967-4069

A splash of pink flowers is the first thing you notice as you arrive at this cozy bed & breakfast, and they'll follow you right into the house as fresh-cut flowers in colonial guest rooms with soft, warm colors and fluffy rugs. Flowers bedeck the dining room, too, where you'll sample some of Carolyn's cheese strata or baked French toast. Try bird watching over the tidal brook out back from her wraparound porch, or bike (you can borrow one from Carolyn) to town or the beach. Scratch Cali, the cat, under the chin. There are four rooms; three have private baths. Children are welcome, but you must provide your own porta-crib and feeding chair.

Average rates: Double: in season, $60–$80; off-season, $50–$70. Single, $40–$60. *Credit cards:* None. *Open:* Year-round. *Owner:* Carolyn McAdams. *Directions:* From Route 95, take exit 3 to Kennebunk. Go left onto Route 35 through downtown Kennebunk. Stay on Route 35 and bear right at the town hall.

Continue on Route 35 and turn right at the next right, 9-35. Go ¼ mile on 9-35. Lake Brook is across from the Hennessey House restaurant. *Children:* Yes. *Pets:* No. *Smoking:* Restricted.

THE WELBY INN
Ocean Avenue, P.O. Box 774
Kennebunkport, Maine 04046
(207) 967-4655

This inn, although a bit on the high side for our budget, has many visual and comfort treats. Betsy made the beautifully decorated tile buffet shelf in the attractive dining room. She has decorated all her baths with some of these hand-painted, kiln-fired tiles depicting country scenes or with floral designs. She also sells the tiles in a tiny adjoining shop, along with her original watercolors and notecards. As you enter the cypress-paneled living room, you'll note the day's delectable breakfast menu on a blackboard propped near some flowers on the grand piano. The seven rooms are lovely with flowered papers. A continental breakfast in bed is available on request. There is a guest pantry with a sink and refrigerator off the dining room. The inn is only a short walk to Dock Square, shops, galleries, and the beach.

Average rates: Double: in season, $80–$90; off-season, $55–$75. *Credit cards:* American Express, MasterCard, and Visa. *Open:* April through December. *Owners:* David and Betsy Rogers-Knox. *Directions:* From I-95, take exit 3, turn left onto Route 35, and follow the signs through Kennebunk to Kennebunkport. Take a left at the traffic light, go over the drawbridge, and take the first right onto Ocean Avenue. The inn is ½ mile down on the left. *Children:* Yes, over eight. *Pets:* No. *Smoking:* No.

Also recommended:

The **Green Heron,** in Kennebunkport, is a bed & breakfast with the lowest rates in town according to owner and host Wallace Reid. His wife, Virginia, has the reputation of putting on the best breakfast north of Boston for a selected few who are allowed to come "off the street." We couldn't see a room because it was full, but we wanted to alert you to this real gem of a place.

It gets its name from the birds you can see out of the dining room windows, foraging about the edge of a nearby saltwater pond. The address is Drawer 151, Ocean Drive, Kennebunkport, Maine 04046. Reservations for breakfast, at least a day in advance, are absolutely necessary! Call (207) 967-3315.

Another good buy, in the nearby town of Kennebunk, is the dignified **Kennebunk Inn** at 45 Main Street. We stayed there with our teenage daughter in a lovely colonial room with a high bed for a very fair price. Doubles are reasonably priced and the LeBlancs are very cordial and helpful.

AUGUSTUS BOVE HOUSE
R.R. 1, Box 501
Naples, Maine 04055
(207) 693-6365

Known as the Hotel Naples in the horse and buggy days, this Victorian B&B has been restored and beautifully decorated by Arlene Stetson in colorful flowered wallpaper and coordinated rugs and drapes. Long Lake and Brandy Pond are within view, making this a very picturesque lake setting. Each of the twelve rooms is different. Some have private and some have shared baths, and there are king-sized, queen-sized, full, and twin beds. A full breakfast is served. When we were there, it was orange juice, fresh fruit cup, muffins, raspberry twists, and French toast. There are many activities to engage in, too numerous to list, but they include water sports, parasailing, horseback riding, antiquing, golfing, and boat cruises aboard the *Songo Queen*. In the winter ski nearby at Pleasant Mountain. Inquire about the winter ski specials.

Average rates: Double: spring through fall, $59–$79; winter, $49–$59. Special two-night package, $125. *Credit cards:* MasterCard, Visa, and Discover; personal checks accepted. *Open:* All year. *Owners:* David and Arlene Stetson. *Directions:* Take exit 8 from Maine Turnpike (Route 495) to Route 302. Follow 302 to junction of Routes 302 and 114. The B&B is on your left. *Children:* Yes. *Pets:* By prior arrangement. *Smoking:* Limited.

THE CAPTAIN'S HOUSE, B&B
River Road, P.O. Box 242
Newcastle, Maine 04553
(207) 563-1482

When you enter the Sullivans' house, you are impressed with the wide hall and antique center stairway and the warm spirit of welcome that prevails. Susan has made the handsome balloon curtains in the country-style rooms. All guest rooms are spacious and nicely furnished with old white-painted metal and antique beds and bureaus. All guest rooms have shared baths. Two have fireplaces, as does the dining room, where a truly hearty breakfast is served. Joe, a cook at a local restaurant, loves to rustle up blueberry buttermilk pancakes, French toast, or cheese omelets, along with bacon and sausage—your choice. In summer, this family with two young children shares the television room with guests. In winter, they open up a large living room with a fireplace. In any season, you'll be able to sit on the front porch swing and gaze at the Damariscotta River.

Average rates: Double, $50–$60. *Credit cards:* None. *Open:* All year. *Owners:* Susan Rizzo and Joe Sullivan. *Directions:* From Route 1, take exit to Damariscotta; then take first right onto River Road. The house is the second one on the right. *Children:* Yes. *Pets:* No. *Smoking:* Restricted.

GOSNOLD ARMS
Box HC 61, P.O. Box 161
New Harbor, Maine 04554
(207) 677-3727

This lovely saltwater farmhouse and cottages are off the beaten track and great for those who want a serene vacation by the sea. There are views of the harbor, boats, and a chance to fish at a nearby beach. One of the finest area restaurants is on the premises. The lobsters you eat there are caught fresh every day and left in a bag in the water at the end of the dock.

We think Gosnold Arms is an excellent bargain. Some rooms are old-fashioned with painted metal beds, and some are like modern motel rooms. All are color-coordinated, and some of the cottages have extra beds and extra rooms—good for families. Breakfast is included in the room rate. This inn has more than ten rooms, all with private baths. There is a dock with rowboats, and you can play badminton and croquet. You also can go fishing on Hardy's party boat across the street.

Average rates: Double, $89–$115; single, $65–$75; off-season, 15 percent discount. *Credit cards:* MasterCard and Visa. *Open:* Mid-May to November 1. *Owners:* William and Perry Phinney. *Directions:* From Route 1, take Route 130 south through Damariscotta and Bristol and down to New Harbor. Go left on Route 32, and the inn is a block up on the left from the fishing docks. *Children:* Yes. *Pets:* No. *Smoking:* Restricted.

LAKESIDE ANTIQUES BED AND BREAKFAST
Route 114
North Sebago, Maine 04029
(207) 787-2949

The highlight of this bed & breakfast is the charm of Vivian Kenney and her sincere interest in her guests. The rooms are graciously decorated with soft colors and have very comfortable beds. You'll have a choice of king, queen, double, or twin beds. You'll enjoy all the homey touches, like tea and cookies when you arrive or at bedtime, candy in your room, limited kitchen privileges, and use of her gas grill, beach chairs, and fishing poles. You can also use her cozy den with a television at night. She serves a complimentary, wonderful full breakfast, including fresh fruit or juice, eggs or French toast, coffee or tea, and often some little added surprise. It is served in her handsome dining room on a pretty service with cranberry cloth napkins and table mats. (An excellent place for other meals is the **Keg Restaurant,** recommended by Vivian and located on Route 114 near the center of East Sebago.) There are wood stoves in both the kitchen and the den, but she has oil heat also. Take a swim right across the street at Nason's Beach on beautiful Lake Sebago or hike on a couple of woodsy trails that Vivian will tell you about. Her well-behaved, apricot miniature poodle will greet you, and you might enjoy a browse through her very orderly antique shop.

Average rates: Double, $40; all rooms share a bath. Children are $10 extra. *Credit cards:* None. *Open:* June 1 to October 15. *Owner:* Vivian Kenney. *Directions:* From I-95, take exit 7. Go north on Route 114 for about 28 miles. First you'll come to East Sebago, and about 2 miles north of that, look for Nason's Beach on the right. The bed & breakfast is the red house about a block farther on the left, across from the Nason's Beach trailer park. *Children:* Yes, over five. *Pets:* No. *Smoking:* On porch only.

THE INN AT TALL CHIMNEYS
94 Main Street, Box 2286
Ogunquit, Maine 03907
(207) 646-8974

The owner of this charming house grew up in New Hampshire and spoke enthusiastically about the new kitchen for guests with a refrigerator, microwave, and gas stove. He has also added two new sitting rooms in Oriental decor. His complimentary continental breakfast of fresh fruit and a variety of coffee cakes, muffins, or doughnuts is served on the deck. All eight rooms have antique furniture, mellow colors, and coordinated wall prints. Some rooms are small, but each has a chair for reading; some have little balconies. Four of the rooms have private baths. You'll enjoy sitting and chatting under the tall trees in the yard overlooking the gardens. A hot tub is also available.

Average rates: Double: Summer, $57–$75; fall, $43–$50. *Credit cards:* MasterCard and Visa; personal checks for reservations. *Open:* April to November. *Owner:* Bob Tosi. *Directions:* From I-95, take exit 1 to York and Ogunquit. Go left onto Route 1 and proceed for about 9½ miles. The inn is on the right just past the information center. *Children:* Yes. *Pets:* No. *Smoking:* Yes.

LITTLE RIVER INN
BED AND BREAKFAST AND GALLERY
Route 130
Pemaquid Falls, Maine 04558
(207) 677-3678

You'll like the pastoral setting and this tastefully decorated 1840s farmhouse. The rooms are sweet and cozy; some of the new rooms are rustic with skylights over the art gallery. One room has a fireplace and extra beds for a family. Some have shared baths, and some have private ones. Kristina's delicious banquet breakfast is special and is included in the room rent. The property backs up to the Pemaquid River. The Pemaquid Lighthouse, archaeological digs, antique shops, fishing, and swimming are nearby. There are eight guest rooms.

Average rates: Double, $40–$60; $5 less for single; extra person over twelve, $10; children a small amount extra. *Credit cards:* MasterCard and Visa. *Open:* All year. *Owner:* Kristina Khan. *Directions:* Take Route 1 to Damariscotta. From Main Street, turn onto Route 130 south. The inn is 9½ miles south on the left side. *Children:* Yes. *Pets:* No. *Smoking:* No.

INN ON CARLETON
46 Carleton Street
Portland, Maine 04102
(207) 775-1910

This B&B is a restored Victorian townhouse with a mansard roof in the West End Promenade District; not too far from the Museum of Art, the Performing Arts Center, and the Cumberland Civic Center. There are seven rooms appointed with period furniture, some with clawfoot tubs, marble mantels, and wide pine floors, and some with fireplaces. A continental-plus breakfast is served at a dining room table in the lovely parlor. This is a nice stepping-off place from which to explore the Old Port Historic District and other Portland features. There are three rooms with private bath, four with shared.

Average rates: Double: $75–$95 in season; $60–$80 off-season. *Credit cards:* MasterCard, Visa, and Discover; personal checks accepted. *Open:* All year. *Owner:* Susan Holland. *Directions:* From Route 295 take exit 5A for Congress Street. Follow Congress through three lights. Turn right on Neal Street. Go 2 blocks and turn left on West Street. Go 1 block and turn left on Carleton. It is the second door on the left. *Children:* Yes. *Pets:* No. *Smoking:* No.

THE CARRIAGE HOUSE
Route 1, Box 238
Searsport, Maine 04974
(207) 548-2289

This enormous yellow Victorian house was built in 1874 and once belonged to Captain John McGilvery. For those who love antique four-poster beds, marble fireplaces, bay windows, and porches, this is a great place to stay. Take pleasure in the soothing view of Penobscot Bay across the street. Two of the guest rooms have working fireplaces, and many have lace curtains. The hosts serve a yummy continental breakfast (included in the room rate) in the big, warm, charming kitchen, with beams and a wood stove. The well-known artist Waldo Pierce lived here, and the owners think there may be a painting of his under the hall wallpaper!

Guests can play croquet, badminton, or horseshoes on the lawn. There are many indoor games, such as cribbage and Trivial Pursuit, for rainy days, and children are very welcome. A crib and a cradle are available, and babies stay for free!

Searsport is the antique capital of Maine, and it is less than an hour to Bar Harbor or Camden from here.

Jordan's Restaurant, in Searsport on the waterside, is said to be the most reasonable restaurant in the area.

Average rates: Double, $65; extra child or adult, $10. *Credit cards:* MasterCard and Visa. *Open:* All year. *Owners:* Alden and Catherine Bradbury. *Directions:* Take Route 1 east from Searsport. The inn is less than ½ mile east on the left side. *Children:* Yes. *Pets:* No. *Smoking:* Restricted.

THE ISLAND HOUSE
Clark Point Road, Box 1066
Southwest Harbor, Maine 04679
(207) 244-5180

This lovely house, built in 1866, was the first summer hotel on Mount Desert Island. It has many unusual features, such as beautiful high wainscoting made of dark, satiny wood in the dining room, curly maple banisters, and wide-board floors. A double slide-out door between the two living rooms can be shut for privacy. All four rooms are handsomely decorated with simple beauty. One is powder blue and has a fireplace, two have double beds, and two have twins. Ann Gill will share her recipes with you, if you contribute one of your own favorites to her Island House Cookbook. She changes her breakfast menu (included in the room cost) every day; typical fare might be four or five different muffins or coffee cakes, eggs Florentine, or a casserole. She also is quite musical, has a piano, and encourages her guests to bring an instrument and join in. There is a large lawn with swings and a wonderful side porch for lounging. You can walk to the Mount Desert Oceanarium, lobster wharves, and to town very easily.

Average rates: Double, $50–$55; single, $40–$45. Loft efficiency apartment for two, $95. Small amount for extra person. *Credit cards:* None. *Open:* One room all year; four rooms from mid-April through October. *Owners:* The Gills. *Directions:* From Route 1, go south on Route 3 and turn onto Route 102 south to Southwest Harbor. Turn left at the blinker on Main Street, and then onto Clark Point Road. The Island House is ½ mile down this road on the left. Mrs. Gill cautions you to bear right at the fork on Clark Point Road. *Children:* Yes. *Pets:* No. *Smoking:* No.

PENURY HALL BED AND BREAKFAST
Main Street, Box 68
Southwest Harbor, Maine 04679
(207) 244-7102

Located right in the center of town, this bed & breakfast has much to offer. They serve a complimentary, wonderful full country breakfast (date-walnut French toast or eggs Benedict) in the soothing light-green dining room overlooking the garden. The rooms are bright and have antiques mixed with modern pieces; all have original paintings on the walls. There are three guest rooms, two with double beds and one with twins, all with shared baths. You can people-watch from the front porch, swim at Echo Lake, visit Acadia National Park, or rent a sailboat, canoe, or Windsurfer at low prices. A sauna can be used for a very small amount, too. We were told by a ranger, who led walks for bird-watchers in Acadia National Park, that the marshes of Southwest Harbor are his favorite place for bird watching.

Average rates: In season: double, $55; single, $45. October to June, rates are lower. *Credit cards:* None. *Open:* All year. *Owners:* Gretchen and Toby Strong. *Directions:* From Route 1, take Route 102 to Southwest Harbor. Take a left at the blinker onto Main Street, and Penury Hall is about 100 yards down on the right, a gray and white house with a red door. *Children:* No. *Pets:* No. *Smoking:* Restricted.

CAP'N FROST BED AND BREAKFAST
241 West Main Street
Thomaston, Maine 04861
(207) 354-8217

This is a very cute Cape Cod home with a touch of England in the decor. The dining room is like a pub or taproom, with a serving bar and a long table with Windsor chairs, done in white with dark green trim. One living room has a fireplace; the other, more like a library, has a wood stove backed by blue and white tiles hand-painted by the owners. In fact, you will be amazed by the craft work done by Harold and Arlene. Make it a point to stop here, as this is one of the best bargains on the coast. You get a full breakfast, a choice of hotcakes, bacon and eggs with a muffin, jams and cereals, juice, fruit—the works—at an exceptionally reasonable rate. There are three rooms, one with private bath and private entrance. There is a porch at the rear and a sundeck. The Frosts will make you feel you're in jolly old England.

Average rates: Double, $40 and $45. *Credit cards:* MasterCard and

Visa; personal checks accepted. *Open:* March to November (but call ahead in the off-season to be sure). *Owners:* Arlene and Harold Frost. *Directions:* Traveling east (north) on Route 1, it is 1 mile past the Thomaston line and the iron bridge, or ¼ mile beyond the Route 131 intersection, on the left. It's a white Cape Cod house. Or, traveling west, it is 1 mile from the center of the village, two places after the convenience store. *Children:* Yes. *Pets:* No. *Smoking:* Restricted.

MIDDAUGH BED AND BREAKFAST
36 Elm Street
Topsham, Maine 04086
(207) 725-2562

This house was built in 1832 by a merchant and is recorded on the National Registry of Historic Places. We were impressed by the elegance of the living room, library, sitting room, large country kitchen, and the sun porch off the kitchen, where a full breakfast is served. It is included in the room rate. There is one bedroom with a queen-sized bed and private bath, and one room with a medium-sized bed with a shared bath—the blueberry room. Everything is spic-and-span clean and decorated in a colonial style with a touch of modern. Note the homemade, hand-printed drapes. The side lawn is shaded and has white metal furniture for lounging. You will enjoy the quiet splendor of Elm Street in Topsham with its many colonial mansions and homes. Call ahead for availability and reservations. A crib is available.

Average rates: $50 per room; extra person, $5–$10 depending on age; special rates for extended stays. *Credit cards:* None. *Open:* Year-round. *Owners:* Dewey and Mary Kay Nelson. *Directions:* From Route 1 in Brunswick, turn left onto Route 201, and go over the bridge into Topsham. You'll be on Main Street. Go to the traffic light, turn right onto Elm Street, and the inn is about ½ mile up on your right. *Children:* Yes. *Pets:* No. *Smoking:* No.

THE WALKER–WILSON HOUSE
2 Melcher Place
Topsham, Maine 04086
(207) 729-0715

This Federalist colonial built in 1803 by Sam Melcher for Gideon Walker has been restored to original period decor by Annie and Skip O'Rourke. The four rooms have colonial colors with antique beds and beautiful flowered wallpaper. We noted the original hand-carved moldings and other woodwork. Fireplaces abound. The dining room is impressive with its pretty dishes and glassware. You'd think you were in Williamsburg. Fresh-ground coffee greets you in the morning along with soufflés, muffins, and all you would expect in a complete country inn breakfast. This bed & breakfast inn drew rave notices from guests who also stayed at our B&B in York.

Average rates: Double: $75 in season; $65 off-season. Additional person, $15. *Credit cards:* Visa and MasterCard; personal checks accepted. *Open:* Year-round. *Owners:* Annie and Skip O'Rourke. *Directions:* Take exit 24 off I-95 and go south toward Topsham for 1.3 miles. It's on the left, but faces Melcher and is set high up on a hill on a downgrade. *Children:* Yes; high chair available. *Pets:* No. *Smoking:* Restricted.

BROAD BAY INN AND GALLERY
Main Street, P.O. Box 607
Waldoboro, Maine 04572
(207) 832-6668

Libby is an energetic innkeeper. She offers art workshops with international artists and candlelight gourmet dinners on Friday and Saturday (with advance reservations). The lovely Victorian home is a feast for the eyes both inside and out. A deck overlooks a garden, and there is a wonderful art gallery in the barn with new shows every three weeks in the summer. One of the highlights of the house is the gracious dining room, where breakfast is served on embroidered linen and English china. Fruited ambrosia, eggs Benedict, baked apples, quiches, and omelets are featured. One room has a crocheted fishnet canopy bed and pineapple bedspread and a lovely piece of furniture called Sarah's Armoire; another room has oak antiques and shuttered windows. Another, called Treetops, is suitable for teenagers with its treetop view, country furnishings, and steep stairway. White terrycloth robes are provided for all guests. All baths are shared or semi-private.

Average rates: Double: $45–$70 in summer; $35–$60 in winter. *Credit cards:* MasterCard and Visa. *Open:* All year. *Owner:* Libby Hopkins. *Directions:* From Route 1 south, take the next right after the "Welcome to Waldoboro" sign; this will be old Route 1 or Main Street. Go through the intersection and up the hill on the left. *Children:* Yes, twelve and over. *Pets:* No. *Smoking:* Restricted.

TIDE WATCH INN
55 Pine Street, P.O. Box 94
Waldoboro, Maine 04572
(207) 832-4987

This cozy, comfortable B&B is run by a lovely couple who will make you feel at home right away. It is across the street from the town landing, where you can watch clammers take off in their outboards just before low tide. Both Fran and Andrew Wyeth have painted the scene across the river. Mel makes an extra-full breakfast that features animals made out of fruit. He's a semi-retired chef from the Red Coach Grill. There are private and shared bath doubles, neat and clean, some with water views. This is a good jumping-off spot for side trips to Wyeth's farm in Cushing or a visit to the country fair in Union, shopping trips for sauerkraut at Goodwin's, a ride to Pemaquid Light, and all those other great treats in the Maine midcoast region.

Average rates: Double, $50–$60; single, $40–$50. *Credit cards:* None; personal checks accepted. *Open:* Year-round. *Owners:* Kathy and Mel Hanson. *Directions:* In Waldoboro turn right off Route 1 onto Route 32 at the yellow blinking light. Take the first left; then, at the bottom of the second hill before the bridge, turn right on Pine Street. The inn is the third house on the right. *Children:* Yes. *Pets:* No. *Smoking:* First floor only.

WELLS INN
Route 1 and Lower Landing Road
P.O. Box 63
Wells, Maine 04090
(207) 646-3488

This lovely 1820s guest house with a huge porch is quite a find in an area of high prices. This reasonable inn has been in operation for many years by the Mastellers who brought up their five children here. The eight rooms are attractive and clean. The high spool beds are comfortable with puffy feather pillows. The smaller rooms cost less, but the larger rooms have two double beds. You can stay in these with children for a very good price! We stayed in a room with pink curtains and bedspreads and lovely old-fashioned floral wallpaper. We each sat in a padded, antique hightop rocker and watched television. The innkeeper was very pleasant and found Fran a Dacron pillow because of her allergies. Complimentary coffee but no breakfast is served here, but there are good places nearby, on Route 1, such as Congdon's, the Maine Diner, or Munroe's Anchor Restaurant on Miles Road.

Average rates: Double with shared bath, $25–$35; double with private bath, $40–$55; extra person $5. Reduced rates in fall and spring. *Credit cards:* MasterCard, Visa, and American Express. *Open:* May to mid-October. *Owners:* Gene and Nancy Masteller. *Directions:* Take exit 2 from I-95 to Route 1. Turn left and the inn is about a block away on the right. *Children:* Yes. *Pets:* No. *Smoking:* Yes.

THE HAVEN
Church Street, Box 2270
Wells Beach, Maine 04090
(207) 646-4194

This is a sanctuary for those who like to be close to the beach and have modern conveniences and elegant accommodations. The building is a converted Catholic church with, of course, cathedral ceilings. Bright colored pillows in the wicker furniture in the lobby and white walls enhance the relaxing mood. The rooms are off the main hall, except for a pair at the rear, upstairs from the dining and living room area. Both private and shared baths are available, and there are two suites. Rooms are decorated in modern style with bright colors. A continental breakfast is served at separate tables. The deck at the rear of the building has an umbrella table and lounge chairs and provides a beautiful view of the marsh and bird sanctuary. This is the home of the owners.

Average rates: In-season: $68–$72; suite, $120. Off-season, $38–$95. Extra person, $10. *Credit cards:* MasterCard, Visa, and American Express. *Open:* April to October 15. *Owners:* Rick and Donna LaRose. *Directions:* From I-95 take exit 2 to Wells. Turn right on Route 1. Turn left at next set of lights on Mile Road. Turn right on Church Street, the second street after Billy's Chowder House. The Haven is down about 2 blocks on the right. *Children:* Yes. *Pets:* No. *Smoking:* Restricted.

THE SCOTLAND BRIDGE INN
Scotland Bridge Road and Route 91
P.O. Box 521
York, Maine 03909
(207) 363-4432

This delightful bed & breakfast is in a quiet setting in the country outside of York Village and is ideally situated for the weary traveler who wants to get away from the highway noise. You will find a nineteenth-century home that has been elegantly decorated by your host, Sylvia Batchelder. Three rooms have shared baths. One two-room suite has a private bath. All the rooms are done in antiques, although the beautiful living room and dining room are in a more traditional decor. Your host makes you feel right in New England by the use of four-poster and canopy beds. The complimentary full breakfast consists of a sumptuous offering of fresh fruit, cheese, sweet breads, strudel, and coffee or tea. It is served in the large dining room. The complimentary tea or cold drinks are served at four o'clock in the afternoon and may be enjoyed on the large front porch before you go out for dinner. This farmhouse inn is a neat way to start your Maine vacation.

Average rates: Double, $65–$85. *Credit cards:* MasterCard and Visa. *Open:* Year-round. *Owner:* Sylvia S. Batchelder. *Directions:* From the York exit off I-95, turn right on Route 1 at the blinking yellow light. Go about 1 mile and take a right at Starkey Ford onto Route 91. Wind your way down this road 2.2 miles. The inn is on the left at the intersection of Scotland Bridge Road and Route 91. *Children:* Yes. *Pets:* No. *Smoking:* Restricted.

THE WILD ROSE OF YORK BED & BREAKFAST
78 Long Sands Road
York, Maine 03909
(207) 363-2532

We got so excited writing this book that we started our own bed & breakfast in our lovely 1814 captain's house, just 1 mile from several beaches. Frank was a professor of biology. Fran, a watercolor painter, features art workshops and has a small gallery. We serve our full breakfast—melons or berries and Fran's famous filled crepes or Belgian waffles with nuts—either on the beautiful large porch or in the green and white colonial dining room. Enjoy our cozy bedrooms with antique beds, puffy quilts, and fireplaces; all rooms have private baths. Bring your musical instruments and sing with us in the comfy large living room with an oversized fireplace and a piano. In summer, an old-fashioned trolley will run you to the beaches, historic houses, or Nubble Point Lighthouse. Antique shops and factory outlet stores are very close by, and it's only fifteen minutes to Old Portsmouth where there are free summer concerts, the Strawbery Banke, and eighty or more good restaurants. During the winter there is sliding on our front hill and great cross-country skiing on a golf course and in nearby woods.

Average rates: Double: $65 in summer; $50–$55 in winter. Extra adult, $20. Children, $5–$10. With seven-day stay, one day free. High chair is available. *Credit cards:* None. *Open:* Year-round. *Owners:* Fran and Frank Sullivan and family. *Directions:* From Route 95, take exit to York. Turn right onto Route 1 at end of exit. Do not go toward Ogunquit. Go south 1 block and take a left at the stoplight onto York Street. Go about 1 mile to a Civil

War monument. Bear left onto Long Sands Road. Go 1 block, pass York Heights Road, and the second house on the left is ours. In icy weather, turn left onto York Heights Road and enter at the back driveway from Fernald Street. *Children:* Yes. *Pets:* No. *Smoking:* No.

INN AT HARMON PARK
York Street, P.O. Box 495
York Harbor, Maine 03911
(207) 363-2031

This beautiful Victorian inn, built in the 1800s, has a very welcoming entryway with a handsome stairway. This house has a lovely country decor with wicker and oak in each room. You will have a full breakfast on a sweet side porch with separate tables—everything is green and white, and the porch overlooks the garden, where fresh flowers are grown for all the rooms. There is a comfortable common room to sit in and a very large wicker-furnished porch. It is a short walk to York Harbor Beach and a trolley ride away from Nubble Lighthouse.

Average rates: In season: double with private bath, $69; double with shared bath, $59. Off-season (after Labor Day): double with private bath, $60; double with shared bath, $50. *Credit cards:* None; personal checks accepted. *Open:* All year. *Owners:* The Antal family. *Directions:* From I-95 York exit, go right onto Route 1 to the next set of lights. Take Route 1A (York Street) through York village, into York Harbor. The inn is located on the corner just past St. George's Church on the right. *Children:* Yes, all ages. *Pets:* No. *Smoking:* No.

WHERE TO EAT

KENNEBUNK FAMILY RESTAURANT
Post Road, Route 1
Arundel, Maine 04046
(207) 985-6672

If you want to know where the locals go to get away from the tourists and high prices, this is the place. It is plain, but plenty of good home cooking by owner-chef Dan Dedrick keeps you coming back. It used to be downtown, but the same menu, with diner-like food, is available at the new location. There are twenty tables—not fancy, but neat and clean. Breakfast is served all day. Dan features hot dinners with potato and vegetable, chowders, children's specials, subs, and hamburgers. It's a great place for the whole family and easy on the pocketbook. There's plenty of parking.

Average prices: Breakfast, $3–$5 (full and complete); children's specials, over $2; hamburgers and subs, under $3; dinner, $5–$8. Ice cream and frappés at very reasonable prices. *Credit cards:* None. *Hours:* Monday through Saturday, 6 A.M. to 9 P.M.; Sunday, 6 A.M. to 2 P.M. *Owner:* Dan Dedrick. *Directions:* Take exit 3 to Kennebunk off I-95. Turn left onto Route 35 toward Kennebunk. Continue on to Route 1 intersection and traffic light. Turn left and go north on Route 1 about 1½ miles. The restaurant is on the left.

JORDAN'S RESTAURANT
80 Cottage Street
Bar Harbor, Maine 04609
(207) 288-3586

This is where the locals have breakfast and where you hear what's going on. The prices are good for Bar Harbor. Their reputation has been made on their blueberry muffins, pancakes, and homemade soup. Breakfast is served all day. There is plenty of room at the counter, booths, or tables, and in a new addition at the back with more tables. Jordan's is neat and clean with knotty pine walls. You can have a sandwich here for lunch or a noontime dinner (they close at 2 P.M.). If you have to get out for an early fishing expedition or a sunrise bird-watching hike at Acadia National Park, this would be the place for breakfast. They start serving at 5 A.M.

Average prices: Full breakfast, about $5; omelets range up to $4; blueberry pancakes, $3. Lunch sandwiches, mostly $2–$3. Dinners all under $7, for ham, fried haddock, steak sandwich, scallops, and more. *Credit cards:* None. *Hours:* Monday through Saturday from 5 A.M. to 2 P.M.; Sunday from 6 A.M. so the cook can sleep late. *Owner:* David Paine. *Directions:* Take Route 3 to Bar Harbor. This becomes Eden Street. Take a left onto Cottage Street. It is halfway down Cottage Street on the right just after the supermarket. There are big glass windows in the front.

"124 COTTAGE STREET"
124 Cottage Street
Bar Harbor, Maine 04609
(207) 288-4383

This is the place people rave about in Bar Harbor. If you aren't stuffed when you leave, it's your own fault. One chef's job is to manage the over-fifty-five-item salad bar. There is a bread buffet of five or six choices with homemade jams. There is a wide variety of items from pastas to seafoods and Cajun delights. Two new items are drawing rave reviews: bouillabaisse and cold shell platter. Both Bruce and Pat LaMotte love to cook, and they have been able to offer an appealing menu to the locals and summer visitors alike. The porch dining, the interior oak tables, and the new addition at the rear with sliding doors to the garden offer a relaxed and pleasant dining experience. This is our outstanding choice for restaurants in the middle-priced range in Bar Harbor. There are 110 tables, and high chairs are available.

Average prices: Dinner only. Items from $10 to $19; average entree, $14. Salad bar only, $8 (a meal in itself). *Credit cards:* MasterCard and Visa. *Hours:* 5–11 P.M. every day. *Owners:* Pat and Bruce LaMotte. *Directions:* Coming into Bar Harbor on Route 3 (Eden Street), pass West Street on the left, then turn left on

Cottage. It is about 100 yards down on your right and looks like a converted home with porch. A large sign is in front.

Also recommended:

George's is the reasonable gourmet restaurant in Bar Harbor, at 7 Stephens Lane, just off Main Street behind the First National Bank. Reservations are requested. Telephone (207) 288-4505. The **Acadia Restaurant and Sandwich Shop** on Main Street is a good savings and a fine place for children. People rave about their chowder. Fran had an inexpensive but tasty, large hamburger. It is cool and comfy and has courteous waitresses. **Maggie's Classic Scales,** at 6 Summer Street, features pasta and fish dishes. Telephone (207) 288-9007.

GEARY'S BASS HARBOR RESTAURANT
Route 102A
Bass Harbor, Maine 04563
(207) 244-7855

The Geary family has taken over La Mae's Restaurant and continues the tradition of wholesome, good Down East cooking and hospitality. Daughter Margaret, a graduate of the Culinary Institute of America, is head chef. Lunches are a variety of sandwiches and mini-dinners such as haddock and other seafoods. The dinner menu provides you with broiled or deep-fried seafood or New York sirloin. Friday and Saturday in summer prime rib is available. Daily specials are featured when Margaret can show her skill at gourmet dishes like chicken picatta. This folksy little restaurant is good for the whole family.

Average prices: Lunch; $3–$7; sandwiches are less. Dinner, $7–$14. *Credit cards:* MasterCard and Visa. *Hours:* May to October, 11:30 A.M. to 9:30 P.M. daily. Closed Mondays in shoulder season (spring and fall). *Owners:* Ann and James Geary. *Directions:* From the center of Southwest Harbor, continue south on Route 102 and 102A and Bass Harbor. You'll find the restaurant on the left, almost across from Tremont's Firehouse.

Also recommended:

Kristina's Bakery, at 160 Center Street in Bath, has a deck for use in the summer. It's an excellent eatery for breakfast, lunch, or dinner—large, sprawling place with interesting rooms all over. Creative soups, salads, sandwiches, and entrees are served at reasonable prices. Get off Route 1 and ask directions. Everybody knows this place. Telephone (207) 442-8577.

THE EBB TIDE RESTAURANT
Commercial Street
Boothbay Harbor, Maine 04538
(207) 633-5962

Recommended to us by two innkeepers, the Ebb Tide is small and homey and has knotty pine booths and pretty colonial paper with a pineapple design. They serve all three meals and feature a very unusual "seafood lover's delight," which consists of all fish or shellfish (clams, shrimp, scallops) and no trimmings at a very decent price. In fact, all their prices are excellent, and they have "week-edge" specials on Friday and Monday nights. After Labor Day, there are nightly and daily specials at lunch and dinner. They have a super baker. The generous servings of peach short-cake and apple coffee cake we had were delicious. Children's portions are also available.

Average prices: Full breakfast, $3–$6; lunch, $3–$10; dinner, $6–$13. *Credit cards:* None. *Hours:* Every day. In spring, summer, and fall 6:30 A.M.–9 P.M.; in the winter, 7 A.M.–7:30 P.M. *Owners:* Peter and Nancy Gilchrist. *Directions:* From Route 1, take Route 27 south to Boothbay Harbor. Go right on Commercial Street along the water. The restaurant is on your right.

Also recommended:

In Boothbay, a restaurant where we have eaten that should be tried for its good-sized portions is **McSeagull's Restaurant** on the wharf. It's cozy and friendly, and the townsfolk like to eat there.

THE GREAT IMPASTA
42 Main Street
Brunswick, Maine 04011
(207) 729-5858

The customers waiting on the sidewalk give you a clue that this is a popular place. In the summer when we were there, we waited for a table longer than we like. The creative Italian food was excellent. There are "Pastabilities" and Italian dishes of seafood, chicken, and veal. You will have a time trying to decide. Most dishes are accompanied by an antipasto salad and a braided bread dipped in butter and garlic. Many vintage wines are available by the glass, and a special ground coffee is featured each day. There is a second Impasta at Bailey's Island, which might be less crowded. The air conditioner didn't work when we were there, but we enjoyed ourselves. A wide variety of dishes is offered for lunch as well. There is even a tea menu featuring scones. Bring the bambinos—there is something for them, too. Non-smoking tables are available.

Average prices: Lunch: pasta, $4–$5; sandwiches, $3–$5. Dinner, $8–$12. Tea, $2–$4. *Credit cards:* All major; personal checks accepted. *Hours:* Every day, all year. Lunch: Monday–Saturday, 11:30 A.M.–4:30 P.M. Dinner: Monday–Thursday, 4:30–9 P.M.; Saturday and Sunday open until 10 P.M. *Owner and Chef:* Alisa Baker Kaffin. *Directions:* Take I-95 to Route 1 to Brunswick. Go through Brunswick until the turnoff for Topsham, but go right up ramp to Brunswick's Main Street. Turn right, and Great Impasta is immediately on right. You can park on the side or in back.

VILLAGE RESTAURANT
7 Main Street
Camden, Maine 04843
(207) 236-3232

This is a favorite of local folk, set right in the center of many high-priced restaurants. The rear tables overlook the harbor, which is world famous for the tall ships moored there on weekends. You can feast on delicious fresh seafood and excellent chowders prepared for both lunch and dinner. Appetizers featured include the Farmer's Basket (fried zucchini, green pepper, and onion rings) and clam or scallop stew—yum. Sandwiches and salad plates are available. You can also order special dinners for children under twelve. Ask your waitress for the freshly baked pies and pudding dessert offerings.

Average prices: Lunch, $6–$8; sandwiches, $4–$8; dinner, $9–$16. *Credit cards:* MasterCard and Visa ($20 minimum). *Hours:* 11 A.M. to 9 P.M. daily in summer; closes at 8 P.M. and closed Tuesdays off season. *Owner:* Paul Prescott. *Directions:* Heading north into Camden on Route 1 (Main Street), proceed through the big intersection at the bottom of the hill. The Village Restaurant is the second or third building on the right after the light.

BACKSTREET LANDING
Elm Street Plaza, Box 326
Damariscotta, Maine 04543
(207) 563-5666

This is the restaurant that most bed & breakfasts recommend in the Pemaquid region. It has an upscale and beautiful modern decor with screened-in porch dining in the warmer months. Those of us watching our cholesterol love the menu. Heart symbols identify items that are more healthful. We both love their fish dishes and homemade salad dressings. You will find tasty homemade soups, chowders, and cioppino as starters or filling lunch meals. Some other creative specialties are Greek shrimp; a medley of pasta dishes; stir-fried vegetables with beef, shrimp, or chicken; and scrumptious homemade desserts. The setting by the Damariscotta River makes this a relaxing place to have a drink and dinner—a far cry from the bustle of the cities to the south. A nonsmoking area is provided, and there is a room for special functions that seats forty.

Average prices: Lunch, $4–$7; dinner, $6–$15. *Credit cards:* MasterCard, Visa, and American Express; personal checks accepted. *Hours:* 11:30 A.M. to 11 P.M. Monday through Saturday. Open for Sunday dinner November–April; closed Sunday the rest of the year. *Owner:* Marcia Davison. *Directions:* Take Route 1 to Damariscotta. Get off on Business Route 1 and turn in by Remy's Department Store. Continue to the right behind Western Auto Store. It's on the tidal river bank.

SCHOONER LANDING
Main Street
Damariscotta, Maine 04543
(207) 563-3388

This restaurant is on the pier at the town wharf with a nice view of the Damariscotta River and boat moorings. When we were there, Frank had a very tasty chicken salad and a beer on the outside porch. It was very hot that July. At that time they didn't have air conditioning, but this was during a heat wave, and usually the breeze off the water should be enough to keep you cool. The new owners offer varied menus for both lunch and dinner: seafood, pita pouches, hot sandwiches, club sandwiches, and a host of appetizers for lunch and fish and shellfish, beef, veal, lamb, many chicken dishes, and duck for dinner. There's a full bar. The service is good, and the pretty blue and gray decor accents the nautical ambience.

Average prices: Lunch, $6–$9. Dinner entrees, $13–$18; thirteen items at $13. *Credit cards:* MasterCard and Visa. *Hours:* Lunch, 11 A.M.–4 P.M. Dinner, 5–10 P.M. *Owners:* Kathy and Randy Dunican. *Directions:* In Newcastle exit Route 1 onto business Route 1 through Damariscotta. After your cross the bridge between Newcastle and Damariscotta, turn right down the driveway to the wharf.

PINE GROVE RESTAURANT
Routes 1 and 1A
Damariscotta, Maine 04543
(207) 563-3765

This is definitely the most popular family restaurant in the area for meals. We have been visiting it for over ten years and it has been changed and redecorated a number of times, but it always has good meals. It is pine-paneled and has tables, booths, and some separations to cut down on noise and provide more privacy. The soft new rug is a great addition, and the salad bar is the area's finest. Bob must be a good manager, as the waitresses seem relaxed and good-natured. They offer a good variety of entrees for excellent prices and have children's portions. Their rolls, pies, and muffins are all homebaked.

Average prices: Lunch: many sandwiches in the $2 to $4 range; hamburger over $2; lunch specials between $3 and $6. For dinner, you can get lasagna with garlic bread, a small salad, and a beverage for under $7. Pan-fried haddock and sole thermidor are under $8; barbequed chicken is $8; small sirloin steak is over $8. Best bargain of all at the time we were there was twin boiled lobsters! Light-appetite meals run about $4 to $6. *Credit cards:* MasterCard and Visa. *Hours:* Every day, 7 A.M. to 8 P.M. *Owners:* William and Robert Beale. *Directions:* Going north, it is on Route 1 about 1 mile from the first Damariscotta turnoff from Route 1 on the right.

Also recommended:

Near Damariscotta in Waldoboro is the legendary **Moody's Diner** on Route 1. It is a mainstay for the natives of this area. We have tried breakfast, lunch, and dinner here and have been quite satisfied. It is open all year from very early morning to late at night.

We'll let you in on our secret for yummy snacks or even a meal. At the **Texaco station** on Route 1 in Waldoboro, you can pick up delicious fried chicken by the piece for under $2!

Reunion Station, a family dining restaurant on Route 1 in Damariscotta, draws lots of hungry passengers to their freight cars with great sandwiches, salads, and lunch and dinner specials. Prices are very reasonable. Going north on Route 1, it's the first place on the left after the Pine Grove Restaurant.

FRIAR'S FISH
Eliot Commons, Route 235
Eliot, Maine 03903
(207) 439-0808

This is a new addition to our list of best buys in New England. A fabulous salad bar and inexpensive seafood, all fresh and served in portions of various sizes, keep the locals coming back to this restaurant. You will be amazed at the prices for what you get. We like the mini-dinners, which are enough for our appetites. If you order a regular meal, you get the long salad bar that includes baked beans, tapioca pudding, and a loaf of different breads to slice—it is hard to fit in the regular meal. We like to go back and get the tapioca pudding or fruit for a dessert. Sometimes we just get the salad bar and chowder for an inexpensive lunch.

Average prices: Lunch and dinner, $5–$14; most full meal items, about $9; sandwiches and clubs $2–$7. *Credit cards:* MasterCard and Visa; no personal checks accepted. *Hours:* 11 A.M. to 9 P.M. in summer; closes 8 P.M. in winter. *Owner:* Steve Spinney. *Directions:* From I-95 exit onto Route 236, and go west on 236 from the Kittery rotary to Eliot. The restaurant is about 2 or 3 miles up, on the left in a strip mall.

JAMESON TAVERN
115 Main Street
Freeport, Maine 04032
(207) 865-4196

You are greeted by a patio with umbrellas where you can dine outdoors, or you can go to the left into the taproom, or if you want to dine more formally, turn right into a Sturbridgelike cluster of rooms for a candlelight, flowers, and tablecloth setting. The taproom and patio have lighter fare—sandwiches, quiches, melts, a variety of salads, and burgers and such. The dining room has reasonably priced entrees ranging from scallopine of veal marsala to chicken amaretto to creative seafood dishes to Cajun sautéed scallops and sausage. Leave time to consider this menu; it has twenty-six tempting items. The tavern was originally the home of

Dr. John Angier Hyde. Captain Samuel Jameson bought it and his widow ran it as a tavern between 1801 and 1828. Freeport served as a strategic stagecoach town then between Portland and cities to the north and "down east." Papers were signed here granting Maine separation from Massachusetts. Ask for the history from your waiter or waitress. Rooms are accessible to the disabled. No cigar or pipe smoking is allowed.

Average prices: Taproom and patio (in summer), $5–$9; dinner entrees, $12–$19. *Credit cards:* All major credit cards. *Hours:* Taproom: 11:30 A.M.–midnight; dining room: lunch, 11:30 A.M.–2:30 P.M.; dinner, 5–10 P.M. *Owner:* Edward McBride. *Directions:* Coming from Portland on I-95, follow signs into Freeport. Drive down Main Street, Route 1, past L.L. Bean on the left. The restaurant is next door.

THE TOWN LINE RESTAURANT
Route 1, RR 1, Box 630
Kittery, Maine 03904
(207) 439-3401

This place has had a revival over the last six years because of the patience and attention to detail of its new owner. There are daily specials of roast turkey, roast pork, American chop suey, Shepherd's pie—diner fare with some different wrinkles such as real mashed potatoes and super homemade pies made by one of the waitresses. We liked the staff's friendly attitude and the relaxed atmosphere. The breakfast menu is comprehensive, listing low cholesterol items as well as dishes such as griddle cakes, omelets, and even eggs and baked beans and/or kielbasa. The Line House Platter of clams, scallops, haddock, and native shrimp is enough for two and can be split. If you're in the vicinity of the Kittery outlet stores, a drive north to this restaurant will be rewarding. Whether you get a sandwich or a full dinner, you'll be satisfied.

Average prices: Breakfast, $3–$5; lunch and dinner, $4–$11 (dinner specials at $5); sandwiches, $2–$5, except for clam and lobster rolls. *Credit cards:* None. *Hours:* Seven days a week. In season,

7 A.M. to 9 P.M.; off-season, closes at 8 P.M. *Owner:* Steve Guidice. *Directions:* From I-95 take Route 1 south from York or north from Kittery. If traveling north, look on the left about 2 miles after Maine Outlet for a gray building with blue trim.

THE LOBSTER POUND RESTAURANT
Route 1
Lincolnville, Maine 04849
(207) 789-5550

An old downeaster once said, "If you want to find out where the best place to eat is, just follow the crowd." How right he was! This restaurant has a huge following, but don't be turned off by the many cars in the parking lot, because there is plenty of room inside and on the new deck. We found this was an especially good bargain because it is just up the road from Camden, where prices are high. Breakfast is available here at a fairly reasonable price. The real bargain, however, is the fish and seafood. Dishes on the lunch menu are served until 5 P.M. Although the portions are smaller, they are adequate for most appetites. The service is fast and courteous. This is a family operation run for many years by the McLaughlin brothers and their wives and children. The takeout below this restaurant has excellent haddock chowder if you're in a hurry and want something special.

Average prices: Lunch of fried fish, clams, shrimp, or chicken with cole slaw and french fries—all under $10. Complete dinner with salad, potato, and beverage from under $11 to $16. *Credit cards:* All major credit cards. *Hours:* Every day from the first Sunday in May to October 20. Breakfast: July 4 to Labor Day, 7 to 11 A.M. Spring and fall, 11:30 A.M. to 8 P.M. Midsummer, 11:30 A.M. to 9 P.M. *Owner:* Richard McLaughlin. *Directions:* Take Route 1 north from Camden about 9 miles. The Pound is on your right just after the road into Isleboro State Ferry Terminal.

Also recommended:

You will find the best kraut dogs in New England at **Scott's Place.** It is a yellow wooden takeout stand in the parking lot in the first shopping plaza on your left when you enter Camden from the south on Route 1 (Elm Street), across from the Elms

Bed & Breakfast. Hamburgers and lobster rolls are also available. This favorite in New England ranks alongside Flo's Hot Dogs in Cape Neddick, Maine.

GOSNOLD ARMS RESTAURANT
Box HC 61, P.O. Box 161
New Harbor, Maine 04554
(207) 677-3727

As part of a congenial inn, this restaurant takes up the whole downstairs of the farmhouse. Although it is bright, cheerful, and cool, most people prefer to sit on the long porch with its many windows facing out to the harbor. There are no reservations accepted here, so get here early for a seat with a view. The Phinneys run blackboard specials every night, and they are generous with hors d'oeuvres of Roquefort and cottage cheese with crackers. We tried the deep fried haddock and the seafood supreme, fish, shrimp, and scallops in a delicate cream sauce— very good. We enjoyed their deep-fried baked potato, too. All entrees include a house salad, vegetable or potato, and homemade breads. We were offered many cups of coffee, as we sat there noticing that many of the diners, obviously returnees, knew the Phinneys and each other. We liked the relaxed and cared-for feeling of this restaurant. High chairs are available for children; smoking is restricted.

Average prices: Dinner, $8–$15; blackboard specials are very reasonable. *Credit cards:* MasterCard and Visa. *Hours:* Mid-June to mid-September, 5:30 to 8 P.M. daily. *Owners:* Perry and William Phinney. *Directions:* From Route 1, take Route 130 south to New Harbor, then take Route 32 east. The inn is on the left about a block from the fishing dock.

SAMOSET RESTAURANT
Route 130
New Harbor, Maine 04554
(207) 677-2142

This is a favorite of the family when we stay at our camp in Nobleboro. It is good year-round, not just during tourist season.

You find many local families here, wedding receptions, and a restaurant that is a hub of Pemaquid life. The food is good too. Excellent prices, a nice atmosphere, and cheerful waitresses make it a good place to go for breakfast, lunch, or dinner. The Leemans have added a screened-in porch (the third addition, so they must be doing something right). Check out the twin lobster special that always seems to be on the blackboard. Lobsters and steamed clams are very reasonably priced. The chowder prices are a little high, but the servings are generous. There is a salad bar in the second dining room. To the right of the front door is a takeout where you can get sandwiches, ice cream, and things like that. A nonsmoking room is available.

Average prices: Full breakfast, under $5; continental, under $2. Dinners range from $5 to $13. Daily special is baked beans and hot dogs, under $5; Friday special is corned hake, under $8; Saturday night special is prime rib, $14; Sunday special is their fabulous roast turkey with all the trimmings for $7. *Credit cards:* MasterCard and Visa. *Hours:* Spring through fall, 6 A.M. to 8:30 P.M.; winter, closes 7:30 P.M. *Owners:* Paul Leeman, Sr. and Paul, Jr. *Directions:* Take Route 129 south from Damariscotta. To get to Route 129, drive off Route 1 into Damariscotta and go east through town, and 129 is to the right at the top of the hill. You branch onto Route 130 a few miles south of Damariscotta. Continue about 10 miles to New Harbor. Just as you enter New Harbor, the Samoset is on your right.

BARNHOUSE TAVERN
Junction of Routes 302, 115, and 35
North Windham, Maine 04062
(207) 892-2221

This new find was made on a dreary, rainy day in August. We needed something to buoy our spirits, and we were pleasantly surprised at how reasonable the prices were in such a fancy place. We took advantage of their Tuesday and Sunday specials for under $8, a choice of five great entrees that came with soup and a beverage. Senior citizens get an extra 20 percent off. Early-bird specials are offered Monday through Thursday. The interior is designed like a barn, with lots of beams and woodwork showing—this gives it a north woods feeling. A solarium sits on the south side off the main dining room and loft. The cocktail lounge is on the north end. King-size manhattans and martinis cost under $2. The tavern is recommended by locals.

Average prices: One menu all day. Lunch, $5–$8; dinner, $8–$17; most items, $12 and under. *Credit cards:* MasterCard, Visa, and American Express. *Hours:* 11:30 A.M. to 10 P.M. every day. *Owners:* Fran and Colleen Pelletier. *Directions:* At the intersection of 302 and 115, go west on 115. It is two doors along on your left.

Also recommended:

Sandy's Flight Deck, diagonally across from Augustus Bove House on Route 302 in Naples, features a lakeside view and fantastic fried clams and other light menu items that are reasonably priced. Watch seaplanes take off. The **Country Squire** is also in Naples on Route 302, before the causeway, on the right. **Blackhorse Tavern** in Bridgton is expensive but good. **The Cracked Platter** in Harrison is another excellent choice that has been recommended to us by many people.

EINSTEIN'S DELI RESTAURANT
2 Shore Road
Ogunquit, Maine 03907
(207) 646-5262

Einstein's is a favorite among both locals and tourists. We have tried lunch, dinner, and late night snacks here and been satisfied each time. The ambience lent by the people working here having a good time adds to your pleasure. There are large and small booths, tables, and a counter, and the food is very tasty and creative. We've especially enjoyed their mushroom burgers, blueberry blintzes with sour cream, and hot open turkey sandwich with gravy and french fries. Grilled kosher hot dogs with sauerkraut is a favorite of Frank's. The soups, pies, muffins, and danishes are made by their own baker. The turkey is fresh and roasted on the premises. There is a full bar in the cafe in the back room. One night a week is Mexican night when you can get a full meal very inexpensively!

Average prices: Typical full breakfast is about $5, but there are many assortments from under $2 to $5. Imagine orange almond French toast for under $3! Bagels are served with most breakfasts. Sandwiches and salads run from under $2 to $5. Dinners, served with rolls, salad, potato, rice, and vegetable, run about $7. *Credit cards:* None; personal checks accepted. *Hours:* Monday through Saturday, 6:30 A.M. to midnight; Sunday, 7 A.M. to 9 P.M. Full bar open to 1 A.M. *Owner:* Jim Trowbridge. *Directions:* From I-95, take exit 1 to the Yorks and Ogunquit. Proceed north on Route 1. Einstein's is about 10 miles north in the center of Ogunquit on the right.

Also recommended:

From Ogunquit, go south on Route 1 and just outside of town you'll see **Flo's Hot Dogs** on the left in Cape Neddick. It is legendary among area folks. You must try the great hot dogs with Flo's homemade relish.

MISS PORTLAND DINER
49 Marginal Way
Portland, Maine 04101
(207) 773-3246

This is a classic Worcester diner, and it has been kept in top shape. You will see the original tile in front of the stools, the marble counter, woodwork, the curved ceiling, just as it came to Portland in 1947. The present owners have kept up the folksy spirit and good food that are a tradition in our best diners. You will find tasty haddock sandwiches, excellent homemade soups, meatloaf, turkey, and chicken dinners all made from scratch. The dinner comes with a potato, a vegetable or cole slaw, rolls and butter, and dessert. If you get here early in the morning, you will find out what's happening in Portland. When we were there, it was like a scene out of the television show, "Alice."

Average prices: All dinner items are under $5, except steak. Bowl of soup, under $2; homemade pies, $2 plus change a slice. The dinner selections run from chicken parmesan with spaghetti to sirloin steak. Breakfast includes three eggs, home fries, and toast for about $2 or the complete breakfast with three eggs and all the extras for under $4. Sandwiches (23 selections) are in the $2–$3 range. *Credit cards:* None. *Hours:* Year-round. Weekdays, 5:30 A.M. to 2 P.M.; Saturday, 6 A.M. to 1 P.M.; Sunday, 6 A.M. to noon. *Owners:* Randall and Irene Chasse. *Directions:* From I-95 (Maine Turnpike) going north, exit at 6A to I-295. Then take exit 7 from I-295, and at the traffic light turn right onto Marginal Way. The diner is on the right. Or, going south on I-295, take exit 7. Go right at the first light to Marginal Way. The diner is on the left.

Also recommended:

In Portland is **Horsefeathers,** a branch of the restaurant of the same name in North Conway, New Hampshire.

Near Portland, we found a convenient place to stop for dinner, with very tasty food and budget prices, in Yarmouth, right off I-95. Take exit 16 toward Yarmouth, and the **Birchwood Restaurant** is ½ mile up on the right, beside Shannon's Motel. It's a good place to take children.

Cole Farms in Gray has got to be the cheapest place to eat in Maine besides Moody's Diner. It is worth a stop if you are headed up the Maine Turnpike above Portland and need a break. One mile north of Gray, take exit 11 onto the Portland-Lewiston Road for good chow. Call (207) 657-4714. At **DiMillo's Floating Restaurant,** on Long Wharf in Portland, you eat aboard a large old ferryboat. Pay reasonable prices for excellent seafood and a spectacular view of Casco Bay. The upper deck, outside on the stern, is worth a visit for lunch if the weather is good. Parking is free. Call (207) 772-2216.

South of Portland on Route 1 in Scarboro is a fantastic bargain in family fare. It has unbelievable prices, quality, and quantity. It's the **Dunstan School Restaurant.** Call (207) 883-5261.

MUSCONGUS BAY LOBSTER COMPANY
Round Pond, Maine 04564
(207) 529-5528

This place has to have the cheapest boiled or live lobsters on the Maine coast. You have to fight your way past the smell of the bait shack, but once on the dock you will have the lobster feast of your life. Clams and mussels are also available. Picnic tables allow you to have a meal right on the dock with your own fixings. We bring a cooler with salad, bread, lemon for butter, a nut cracker (in case you're dealing with hard shells), drinks, plastic plates, and lots of paper napkins. We also bring our lobster-starved friends here when they visit us from states outside of New England. Bob Remy has four large housekeeping cottages for two or more people if you would like to get into some serious lobster eating. If you'd like to write them, the mailing address is: Renbro, Inc., R.R. 1, Box 14, Damariscotta, Maine 04543.

Average prices: Variable according to the lobster harvest. Usually $3 to $4 per pound cooked; butter melted for 50 cents. *Credit cards:* MasterCard and Visa. *Hours:* Early spring to late fall. *Owner:* Bob Remy. *Directions:* Take Route 129 south from Damariscotta and turn left at Bristol (sign posted). Take this road a few miles to Route 32, and turn left. Round Pond is a small village. After passing the general store on left, take a right toward the water. Bear right at the gift store. Take the next right, before the Anchor Restaurant. Park in the dirt parking area. The lobster cook shack is on the dock around to your left.

JORDAN'S RESTAURANT
Route 1, P.O. Box 378
Searsport, Maine 04974
(207) 548-2555

This homey restaurant with a nautical theme is very popular among the local people, and we learned why. With such a friendly and respectful atmosphere, a business can't help but be successful. Of course the many and varied dinner offerings are great, too. Frank tried the baked stuffed scallops and Fran tried the deep-fried jumbo shrimp; both were excellent. The clam chowder (really like a clam stew) was so good that we went back a second time. Margarine is served for those watching cholesterol levels. There are smoking and nonsmoking areas, chairs and booths, and a children's menu. Senior citizens get a 25 percent discount on Tuesday. It is open for breakfast, lunch, and dinner, and the service is excellent. The restaurant can seat about 130 people.

Average prices: Lunch specials from about $4 to $8; dinner ranges from about $8 to $11, with specials daily. *Credit cards:* MasterCard, Visa, American Express, and Diner's Club. *Hours:* All year, seven days a week, 7 A.M. to 9 P.M. *Owner:* Paul Gervais. *Directions:* It is in the center of Searsport, on Route 1 (Main Street), on the right as you go east (or north).

JANET'S
Route 102
Southwest Harbor, Maine 04679
(207) 244-5131

This seems to be the universal favorite of the local population at Bar Harbor as well as the folks we talked to at Southwest Harbor. It is a family-type restaurant serving pizza to prime rib with down east hospitality. You have to give Janet's a four-star rating for trying to please all palates. You can order a deli sandwich like a Reuben, or a chef salad in two sizes, and if you're watching your weight, there is low-fat milk. You name it and Janet has it. We thoroughly enjoyed our dinner there and rate the place as one of the best buys on Mount Desert Island. We had the deep-fried Maine shrimp and the broiled haddock. Both were delicious and fresh and were accompanied by vegetable, choice of potato or rice pilaf, salad with homemade dressing, rolls, and butter. The service was cheerful and attentive. Breakfast is also popular here, as contractors and fishermen meet here for some early morning scuttlebutt and savor the hearty dishes emanating from the kitchen.

Average prices: Full and hearty breakfast, under $4. Lunch plate of seafood, average $5. Dinner, $5 and up. *Credit cards:* MasterCard and Visa. *Hours:* May to October, 7 A.M. to 2 P.M. and 4:30 to 9 P.M. *Owner:* Janet Hendriksen. *Directions:* Take Route 3 south to Mount Desert Island. After the causeway, take a right onto Route 102 as if going to Southwest Harbor. Janet's is 9.6 miles from this intersection on the left. *Note:* May change hands soon.

THE BULL AND CLAW HOUSE
Route 1 North, R.F.D. #2, Box 653
Wells, Maine 04090
(207) 646-8467

The most popular place to eat in Wells, this informal place seats 325 people, yet you'll get plenty of personal attention from the young waiters and waitresses. A bit like the York Steak House, you choose your entree from numerous illustrated menus on the walls and then proceed to the cashier, where you pick up a number and any added coffee, dessert, or soup. As you pass through the line, they offer you extra items; be sure to ask the price of these as they are not marked. It has nothing of the crowded confusion sometimes found at similar places. You'll eat at small tables or shiny picnic tables in a huge room with long windows and plenty of space! The picnic tables are fun if you like to talk to other tourists from all over the country. A nice touch is a chilled bottle of wine, served with dainty wine glasses, which reminds one of an English picnic. The prices are very reasonable (fish prices may fluctuate a bit depending on market prices). There are lower-cost meals for the light eaters ("light bits"), and even lower prices on the children's menu. Steak, lobster, and seafood are their mainstays, but they serve pork and chicken also. All these dinners include an all-you-can-eat fifty-item "salad boat" and roll, and all but lobster include a baked potato. You can have as many coffee refills as you'd like, and you must try the famous breakfast buffet with a choice of forty items! In the winter there are many full meal specials with an all-you-can-eat "salad boat."

Average prices: Breakfast buffet, $5; children 40"–56", $2.50; under 40", free. Lunch and dinner, $3–$10. The "light bites" run from $2 to $4 and include a side of vegetables. (Fran tried the scallop kebab and it was scrumptious for over $4.) One-quarter pound hamburger is under $3. The "salad boat" alone is $5 and makes a fine meal! *Credit cards:* MasterCard and Visa. *Hours:* All year, daily. Summer, 7 to 11 A.M. (July 1–Labor Day only) and 11:30 A.M. to 10 P.M. Winter, 11 A.M. to 9 P.M. (8 P.M. on snowy evenings). *Owner:* Daryl Tudisco. *Directions:* Take exit 2 off I-95, and go 3 miles to Route 1. Turn left and the restaurant is about 2 miles north on the left.

CONGDON'S RESTAURANT
Route 1
Wells, Maine 04090
(207) 646-4219

In 1945, Clint and Dot Congdon opened a restaurant in Kennebunk, and "Nana's" homemade doughnuts were the star attraction. The doughnuts are still the greatest in this new combination of doughnut shop and restaurant. At the many booths or tables, you'll enjoy a fine meal at breakfast, lunch, or dinner for very reasonable prices. Choose from ten varieties of fancy pancakes, twenty different types of sandwiches, or their great seafood dinners! Any time of day try the homemade ice-cream pie with a topping, the sundae, or a parfait. The decor is homey with knotty pine walls and handsome wallpapers, and the service is great.

Average prices: Over $1 to $5 ("lobsta" pancakes). Congdon's special is two eggs, bacon, sausage, or ham, homefries, toast, and a doughnut for $5. Sandwiches run from $1 to $5. Hamburgers are $3. Dinners are around $8, but can be bought for less on the à la carte menu. Dinner includes potato, cole slaw, and a homemade dinner roll. *Credit cards:* MasterCard and Visa. *Hours:* April to June, daily, 6:30 A.M. to 10 P.M. Winter, closed Tuesday. Rest of the year, daily, 6:30 A.M. to 2 P.M. *Owners:* Diane and Garry Leech. *Directions:* Take exit 2 from I-95 toward Wells on Route 109. At Route 1, turn right, and Congdon's is about 1 mile south on the right.

MONTSWEAG FARM RESTAURANT
Route 1, R.F.D. 3
Wiscasset, Maine 04578
(207) 443-6563

We're sure this is a winner, as we've been eating here for over ten years, and it is always brimming with people! There is an inviting new room with black tables and chairs and a colonial look, plus a patio with tables, so you can eat outside. The blackboard specials are seafood and steak, all for a good price.

Another new addition is a counter grill where you can see your steak broiled, or even give it a turn yourself if the chef isn't too busy. You can also get manicotti, salmon cakes, chicken cordon bleu, or teriyaki, steak, or lobster any style at this versatile place. All meals are served with a choice of potato, salad, rolls, and coffee or tea. Steaks include onion rings and vegetables. It is very accessible to Bath, Wiscasset, or Boothbay Harbor. Lunch is served until 3 P.M.

Average prices: Lunch: sandwiches, about $4; lobster roll, $7; and usually there is a dish of the day special. Dinners, under $9 to $12, including fried Maine shrimp and 8-ounce sirloin teriyaki steak. The children's menu has dinners from $5 to $8. *Credit cards:* MasterCard and Visa. *Open:* Every day, 11:30 A.M. to 8:30 P.M. (9 on Friday and Saturday) in the summer; 11:30 A.M. to 8 P.M. in the winter. *Owner:* Nicholas Sewall; manager: Howard Larrabee. *Directions:* Take Route 1 north to the Bath Bridge. Then continue north for 5 miles. The restaurant is on the left on the Woolrich/Wiscasset line.

UNCLE BROCK'S
Route 27
Wiscasset, Maine 04578
(207) 882-9398

The innkeepers at Elfinhill Bed & Breakfast put us on to this great eatery in Wiscasset just up Route 27. The owner has cooked on research vessels and in many regular restaurants and now runs an inconspicuous place with great food at fantastic prices. The inside of the gray building is clean and nicely decorated in plain modern. The service is good. You have steak and seafood with "lite" items after 5 P.M. Club sandwiches, burgers, and fish sandwiches with french fries and slaw are available for under $5. But the big hit is prime rib on Friday and Saturday for $12. Yum!

Average prices: Lunch: sandwiches average $2.50; clubs, $4–$5; bowl of chowder, $4; soup of the day, $3. Dinner: $10–$12; most items, $10; blackboard specials, about the same price range. *Credit cards:* MasterCard and Visa. *Hours:* Monday to Thursday,

11 A.M.–8 P.M.; Friday and Saturday, 11 A.M.–9 P.M.; Sunday, noon–8 P.M. *Owner:* Brock Stanton. *Directions:* Coming into Wiscasett eastbound on Route 1, turn left onto Route 27 north as if going to Augusta. Uncle Brock's is about ¾ mile farther on the right.

Also recommended:

Right after the Wicasset bridge on Route 1 north (on left side) there is a takeout fish place called the **Sea Basket Restaurant** that started as a truck and has worked into a splashy building. The fish and crab rolls are well prepared, very fresh, and affordable. We recommend it!

Another specialty you may want to try in Wiscasset is the scrumptious ice cream at **The Milk-Shed,** just 1 block over from Route 1 before the bridge. Look for the signs on the left.

In the center of Brunswick, on Main Street on the left as you're going south, is another quite catchy restaurant where you can eat at sidewalk tables under a red canopy, reminiscent of Paris. **The Omelette Shoppe** offers fifty different international and more common omelets (artichoke, broccoli, Mexican, and all kinds of cheese from $4 on up). Or try "bulkie burgers" with feta cheese, fries, and salad for $4. Very chic!

We have been stopping for coffee and a snack for many years at the **Miss Brunswick Diner,** on the right across from Cumberland Farms, just before Route 1 North takes a sharp left turn in Brunswick. Another good, reasonably priced place to eat, on the right as you enter the outskirts of town, is **MacLean's Restaurant,** good for seafood. Another dollar-saving antic we have tried is stopping at the **cafeteria at Bowdoin College,** where the food was quite savory after a day of cross-country skiing. We remember their good beef stew and apple pie!

BOS'N'S LANDING
Route 1, Box 234
York, Maine 03909
(207) 363-4116

This is an old standby that we send our guests to, and they never come home disappointed. You can also tell by the number of cars there that this place is popular. The number of older people waiting for a table tells you the price is right. Seafood, fresh roasted turkey and pot roast, club sandwiches, a variety of sandwiches, chowders, steaks and chickens—there's something for everybody. There is a menu for "little skippers" under twelve. Homemade custards and puddings and shortcakes round out your meal. A cocktail lounge is available to you while you wait for dinner. There is a takeout window, and picnic tables are set along the York River so you can eat outdoors.

Average prices: Breakfast, $5. Lunch and dinner average $11; prime rib (Friday–Sunday), $14; sandwiches average $3. Children's menu items, $6. *Credit cards:* None; personal checks accepted. *Hours:* Mid-March–mid-December, Thursday–Sunday, 8 A.M.–9 P.M. *Owners:* Arnold and Donna Stadig. *Directions:* From I-95 take Route 1 north from Kittery or south from York. Coming from York it is on the right after you cross York River bridge.

FAZIO'S
York Village Shopping Plaza
38 Woodbridge Road
York, Maine 03909
(207) 363-7019; (207) 363-1718 for take-out

Where does one go in Maine to get delicious, homemade pastas? To Fazio's in York, of course. Annette Fazio brought her New York touch to the seacoast area, started her first restaurant, and became an instant hit. Everything is made on the premises, so you're in for the freshest of Italian dining. The decor is neat and comfortable with red-checkered tablecloths, tables with captain chairs, and booths. Fran's favorite is the seafood ravioli prepared by Fazio's other chef and co-owner, Kevin Leahy. Frank likes the linguini with their special sauce, a vegetarian tomato-based creation that surprises one who is used to meat sauces. Frank has to watch his cholesterol, and eating here is a treat for him. Other specialties to consider are the seafood lasagna and the broccoli- and cheese-stuffed chicken. The service is very good. Wine and beer are available. Nonsmoking tables are available. There are high chairs for children. Menu items are very reasonably priced. Annette said she wanted people to feel that they can come back often and not be scared away by the cost. It seems she got her wish.

Annette's new location in York includes a cocktail lounge and a pizza area.

Average prices: Dinner entrees average $9. Children's menu available. Items available from antipasti to Italian desserts. Your total bill won't be much over $12. *Credit cards:* MasterCard, Visa, American Express, and Discover. *Hours:* Every day: In season, 5–10 P.M.; off-season, 5–9 P.M. *Owners:* Annette Fazio and Kevin Leahy. *Directions:* From I–95 take the York exit. Go south on Route 1 for 1 block. Go left at the traffic light onto Route 1A (York Street). Go 1 mile to the monument on the left. Turn left onto Long Sands Road and take the first right onto Woodbridge Road. The restaurant is just past Foster's Flowers on the left.

NORMA'S
226 York Street
York, Maine 03909
(207) 363-3233

This delightful breakfast and lunch spot is neat and clean with pink and black tables and napkins. It offers a generous and tasty breakfast for the fisherman, tourist, and local alike. Lunch specials are always posted on the white bulletin board. These are hot dishes—usually good soups or chowders and always scrumptious desserts. This place offers very reasonable prices with quick and cheerful waitresses who seem to fly around the counter and tables. Frank's favorite meal here is a burger with the soup of the day, and on occasion, the bread pudding. Norma's is a favorite of locals.

Average prices: Breakfast, $3–$5. Lunch: sandwiches, $1.50–$3; hot dishes, under $5. *Credit cards:* None; personal checks accepted. *Hours:* Monday through Saturday, 6 A.M. to 2 P.M.; Sunday till 1 P.M. *Owner:* Norma Clark. *Directions:* From Route 1 take York Street or Route 1A into York Village. When you get to the Civil War monument, you will see Norma's behind it. Park on street or in lot to the left.

Also recommended:

The Loaf and Ladle in the Meadowbrook Mall on Route 1 in York has some unique choices for lunch. Their soups and pasta salads are excellent and varied; they have interesting baked goods; they also have good quiches and very yummy fresh fruit salad. Their soups are creative; their sandwiches exceptional, and the pecan pie and fudge cakes are hard to pass up.

Another good place for lunch in York is the **Sesame Tree Natural Food Store.** Their pita pockets with salad and avocado and cheese and tahini sauce are very tasty. They make good split pea and lentil soup, all vegetarian. This store is at 23 Woodbridge Road, off Long Sands Road about a block past the post office on the opposite side.

The third gem of a place for light eating is **Anderson's Bakery,** where you can get delicious sandwiches on fresh-baked breads, rolls, muffins, and pastries. In the winter there are soups like corn chowder, chili, or fish chowder. Sandwiches are all under $2—a rare thing in this town. The locals clean out the hot dogs on bakery rolls by noon, so if you're a dog freak, come early. The baker also makes a great turkey pie, which you can buy frozen. Anderson's is at the York Shopping Plaza on Long Sands Road in the Village.

AND KEEP IN MIND:
THE MARITIME PROVINCES

Nova Scotia, New Brunswick, and Prince Edward Island seem to be natural extensions of Maine, so we decided to add a few places to stay when there, all of which have been recommended to us. There are many great historic places to visit, not to mention small fishing villages that take you back in time, old forts and coal mines, and thousands of miles of coastline. Some of the beaches are as warm as those in the Carolinas. One of our favorite features is the Highland Games, played just as you'd see them in Scotland with kilts and highland flings, tossing of the huge log or *caber,* throwing of heavy stones, and races.

The rates in the follow places to stay are quoted in Canadian dollars.

Nova Scotia & New Brunswick

Bay View Pines Country Inn, R.R. 2, Mahone Bay, Nova Scotia B0J-2E0. Call (902) 624-9970, Curt and Mary Norklun. This inn is on the Lighthouse Trail on the south shore. Rates are $56–$66 for a double and $81 for a suite with whirlpool. There are eight rooms, all with private baths and a view of the water. It is an old historic farm on twenty-one acres with a beach and boathouse, forty-five minutes from Halifax. A full country breakfast is $2 extra and features locally smoked bacon. Continental breakfast is free. Three meals a day are served to guests only.

Boscawen Inn, 150 Cumberland Street, Lunenburg, Nova Scotia B0J-2C0. Call (902) 634-3325, Ann and Michael O'Dowd. This 1888 Victorian inn is located on the south shore of the island, 60 miles west of Halifax. Lunenburg is the fishing capital of Canada. The inn is open from Easter to December 31. They serve three full meals to guests and to the public; specialties are fresh fish and scallops. This Queen Anne–style inn has seventeen rooms priced from $35 for a room with shared bath, $65 for private bath, and $80 for large suites. Many rooms face the water.

Bread and Roses Country Inn, 82 Victoria Street, Box 177, Annapolis Royal, Nova Scotia B0S-1A0. Call (902) 532-5727, Don and Jeannie Allen. This inn is on the Evangeline Trail, in the northwest. It is a half hour from Digby and two hours from Yarmouth. The town, Canada's birthplace in 1605, has many historic points of interest such as Fort Anne. It's on a river basin. There are nine rooms, all with private baths, in this fine Victorian 1882 house decorated with antiques. Room rates are $55 for a single, $70 for a double and $75 for two double beds. Breakfast is reasonably priced.

Owen House Bed and Breakfast, Campobello Island, New Brunswick, E06-3H0. Call (506) 752-2977. Innkeeper Joyce Morrell is a watercolor artist who has her own gallery. The 1835 house with nine rooms has five fireplaces. It is quiet and historic and boasts a gorgeous view of Passamaquoddy Bay. You'll see some of the original furniture and china in the house. Double rooms cost $55 to $65, plus tax, and include a full breakfast. This B&B is open Memorial Day to Columbus Day. Visit President Roosevelt's summer home on the island.

PRINCE EDWARD ISLAND

Smallman's Bed & Breakfast, O'Leary, R.R. 1, Prince Edward Island C0B-1V0. Call (902) 859-3469, Arnold and Eileen Smallman. Open all year. They have a picnic table, a sandbox and swings, and a racehorse track for jogging. The rates are $20–$35 for a double and $15 for a single. Breakfast is $2.50–$3.75 per person.

Blakeney's Bed & Breakfast, 15 McLean Avenue, Box 17, Kensington, Prince Edward Island C0B-1M0. Call (902) 836-3254, Velma Blakeney. Open all year. No smoking. It overlooks Malpeque Bay and is near north shore beaches and deep-sea fishing. It is also close to church and town. Double, $30 with continental breakfast.

Anchors Aweigh Bed & Breakfast, 45 Queen Elizabeth Drive, Charlottetown, Prince Edward Island C1A-3A8. Call (902) 892-4319, Mary Hopgood. Open year-round, it overlooks a river and is handy to the Summer Festival. It has three rooms; one is a loft bedroom. The rates are $30 for single and $35 for a double. Breakfast is $1.50–$3.50 (light or full).

Partridge's Bed & Breakfast, R.R. 2, Panmure Island, Montague, Prince Edward Island C0A-1R0. Call (902) 838-4687, Mrs. Gertrude Partridge. It is surrounded by gorgeous beaches. Rent bikes or canoes or dig clams. The Johanna & Peter Condon House has doubles for $50 per night or $300 per week for two people. The Griffen House has doubles for $40 per night or $200 per week for two. Full breakfast is included in the room rate.

About the Authors

Fran and Frank Sullivan operate their own bed & breakfast, the Wild Rose of York, in York, Maine. As veteran budget-minded travelers in the United States and abroad, they bring a perspective from both sides of the welcome sign to their research and writing of this guide.

Here are some other fine books on U.S. destinations. All Globe Pequot travel titles are published with the highest standards of accuracy and timeliness. Please check your local bookstore for other fine Globe Pequot Press titles, which include:

Daytrips, Getaway Weekends in New England, $13.95
Recommended Country Inns series, $12.95
   Mid-Atlantic • Midwest • New England
   South • Southwest • West Coast • Rocky Mountains
Traveling With Children and Enjoying It, $11.95
The Bed & Breakfast Traveller, $11.95
Bed & Breakfast in New England, $13.95
Treasury of Bed & Breakfast, $12.95
Guide to Nantucket, $11.95
Guide to Martha's Vineyard, $11.95
In and Out of Boston with (or without) Children, $14.95
Boston's Freedom Trail, $7.95
Blue Laws, Brahmins, and Breakdown Lanes, $9.95
Guide to the Jersey Shore, $11.95
Guide to Cape Cod, $10.95

To order any of these titles with MASTERCARD or VISA, call toll-free 1-800–243-0495; in Connecticut call 1-800-962-0973. Free shipping for orders of three or more books. Shipping charge of $3.00 per book for one or two books ordered. Connecticut residents add sales tax. Ask for your free catalogue of Globe Pequot's quality books on recreation, travel, nature, gardening, cooking, crafts, and more. Prices and availability subject to change.